Sea otter Glacier Bay /
Necky Amaruk Double 18 long & 20½ beam
supposedly can carry 5-7 days stuff
w/o trouble

P9-AFN-525

Sea Kayaking

John Dowd

A Manual for Long-Distance Touring

Garage Dimensions
21 ½' long
19' 1" wide

GREY*S*TONE BOOKS
Douglas & McIntyre
Vancouver/Toronto

University of Washington Press
Seattle

starboard - right side (facing fwd)
port - left side (facing fwd)

Greystone Books
A division of Douglas & McIntyre Ltd.
1615 Venables Street
Vancouver, British Columbia
V5L 2HI

Canadian Cataloguing in Publication Data
Dowd, John 1945–
  Sea kayaking

  Includes bibliographical reference and index.
  ISBN 1-55054-563-9
  1. Sea kayaking.   2. Sea kayaking—Safety measures.   3. Kayak touring.   I. Title.
GV788.5.D69 1997   797.1'224   C96-910850-8

Originated by Greystone Books and published simultaneously in the United States of America by the University of Washington Press, Seattle

Library of Congress Cataloging-in-Publication Data
Dowd, John.
    Sea kayaking: a manual for long-distance touring / John Dowd.—
  Rev. ed., 4th paperback ed.
      p.   cm.
  Includes bibliographical references (p.) and index.
  ISBN 0-295-97622-5
  1. Sea kayaking.   2. Sea kayaking—Safety measures.   I. Title.
  [GV788.5.D68 1997]   96-40297
  797.1'224—DC21   CIP

Front cover photograph by David Nunuk/First Light
Cover design by George Vaitkunas
Text design by Val Speidel
Printed and bound in Canada
Printed on acid-free paper ∞

To Paul Souter, who provided the plans for my first kayak

CONTENTS

ACKNOWLEDGEMENTS

My thanks to Matt Broze, Dan Lewis, John Dawson and Mercia Sixta for their immediate and helpful contributions to this edition. Thanks also to Robert Haskell, John Hallovan, Jeff Cooper, Penny Wells, Wayne Horodowich, Michael McNulty, Joanne Turner, Herbie Meyer, Lee Moyer, Stephen Sherrer, Dave Weir, Larry Roy, Tim Dyer, Peter Garlick, Tom Watson, Whitney Smith, Cathy Piffath, William Barron, Yukimi Okamoto and Lynn Morrison, who responded to my questionnaire about teaching. A special thanks to Robert Bringhurst, my first editor, whose influence is still keenly felt after three subsequent editions, and to Marilyn Sacks and Nancy Flight for their patient editorial massaging.

Finally, thank you to Beatrice "Hawkeye," my good wife, for her usual valuable input.

A sheltered cove on the B.C. coast.

Grant M. Thompson

INTRODUCTION

The fourth paperback edition of this book comes in response to a steady stream of changes that have occurred in what was in 1981 an "off the wall" activity for a few eccentric individuals. Now sea kayaking is a popular mainstream activity for outdoor enthusiasts and is among the fastest-growing water sports in North America.

During the first ten of those intervening sixteen years, I turned my passion of twenty years into my livelihood, and, I confess, my kayaking flame dimmed insofar as getting out in the boat was concerned. It did not dim in other ways, however, and the time out, combined with the exposure to different points of view, has helped me to clarify my thoughts about the world of kayaking. In 1990 I sold my business interests in kayaking and to a large extent dropped out of the world of paddling, which had so dominated my life. In the years that followed I paddled almost exclusively with my children and from them discovered the gentler side of kayaking, which, in my youth, I had mostly skipped in my zeal for paddling challenges.

It has been personally gratifying to watch sea kayaking go mainstream and to know that I have contributed to this trend. Yet at the same time, I can't help but regret the passing of a time of innocence, a time when the sight of a sea kayak on the roof of a passing car was excuse enough to pull over and chat.

For paddlers, it has been a period of much learning and refining, and the threads of knowledge and communicable experience have formed a rich tapestry. Books on the subject have proliferated—and improved.

Kayak instruction has become an industry unto itself, and this edition of *Sea Kayaking* has devoted a new section to this development.

I have never been entirely at ease with the notion of "doing a course" in sea kayaking, believing instead that the best way to learn is from the sea. That was my way, and it resulted in this book, but I realize that if everyone tried to do it the pool of knowledge would be shallow indeed, and an unacceptable number of empty kayaks would be washed ashore as paddlers learned for themselves the value of adequate buoyancy and backup systems. True, I was involved with the establishment of the Ecomarine Kayak School in Vancouver, British Columbia, but this was mostly at the level of developing curriculum, and I was dragged kicking and screaming into it by the vision of my partner, one of this world's natural teachers, Christine Robinson, and her principal instructor, Dan Lewis.

The section on kayak instruction is based on the results of a questionnaire I sent to dozens of active sea kayaking instructors. I did this in the hope of highlighting the diversity of ideas that I realized was out there. And diverse they are. The downside of such diversity, of course, is that there are good and bad ideas, safe and unsafe practices being taught, and how, you may ask, could I favour such a cauldron of ideas when something as silly as the "All-In Rescue" is still being taught? My hope lies not so much in the detail, or even the process, but in the kayaking culture that allows the process to exist at all. I believe strongly in the wisdom of an informed, intelligent paddling community, and I find it encouraging that almost all instructors and schools of kayaking draw on the lessons offered by all the competing bureaucracies, taking what they want from each, mixing it with what they picked up from this or that instructor exchange or symposium and then filtering it through their own personal experience. This is a richness to cherish.

I have also added a chapter on sea kayaking for people with disabilities, another area that has grown tremendously since the previous edition of this book. The information in this chapter is based on the work of Mercia Sixta, who has been passionately involved in teaching kayaking to people with disabilities in Vancouver. Finally, I have added information on low-impact environmental paddling. If we wish to preserve the places in the wilderness that we love, we must all take care to treat these places with respect.

Early editions of *Sea Kayaking* to date have sold over 40,000 copies, but this is hardly an adequate measure of existing interest in kayak touring. Whereas the only books available on the subject at the time of the first edition were Adney and Chapelle's *The Bark Canoes and Skin Boats of North America* and a few British canoeing manuals, today there are many, as well as numerous guides telling you where to paddle and others explaining how to camp, forage and cook when you get there, together with the definitive work on kayak navigation by David Burch, *Fundamentals of Kayak Navigation.* Also, there are now several specialty magazines and articles on kayak travel adventures appearing in the mainstream press almost weekly.

Much has been printed on the history of kayaking, thanks to the research of John Heath, David Zimmerly, George Dyson and Eugene Arima in North America, H.C. Petersen in Greenland and John Brand in England. It is clear from their research that the best traditional Native kayaks were extremely sophisticated, well-designed craft from which our modern-day builders have learned a great deal yet stand to learn much more. Once again I have resisted the temptation to dabble in the field of kayak history, which I consider to be beyond the scope of this book. We are heirs to a long and complex tradition, one without surviving masters—just students, evidence and memories.

There is now, as there was long ago, a kayak for almost every purpose—from the slender West Greenland–style boats, originally designed for hunting among ice floes, to the 6.5-metre (21-foot) touring double or triple that cruised the Pacific coast. Each has its own merits and limitations, and each its band of dedicated advocates. My personal preference for a touring single is a roomy, relatively stable craft around 60 centimetres (24 inches) in the beam. Although I would pick this for solo coastal cruising, it might not be my first choice for day paddling off Hawaii, and I would want yet another craft for cruising with young children. It is this very diversity of boat design that makes sea kayaking so overwhelming for the first-time paddler looking to choose the right boat, and it is one of the objectives of this book to help clarify the kinds of choices that should be made.

I have based this book mostly on my own experience, but occasionally it has been necessary for me to write beyond what I know firsthand to present a more balanced picture of sea kayaking when covering such topics as instruction, obscure methods of rolling, kayak surfing and kayaking in sea ice. I have gratefully called upon the expertise of others, among them John Heath, whose knowledge of traditional kayaking techniques was first highlighted in Adney and Chapelle's aforementioned classic.

Because the knowledge required for sea kayaking is so encompassing, I have also frequently chosen to omit the general in favour of the specific. For example, my chapter on first aid ignores such essentials as rescue breathing and the treatment of bleeding, since these are well covered in general publications on the subject. It focusses instead on kayak-related ailments. I trust the reader to already know the basics—for know them he or she must when embarking on a sea journey.

Navigation, camping and general survival are other areas in which I have assumed that the reader is not a novice. The information presented here is geared to kayaking situations and seen from the viewpoint of a kayaker, particularly those problems most likely to be encountered on long kayak journeys. If you need specialized survival information, books such as the SAS *Survival Handbook* do the subject justice.

I have attempted to make this fourth edition suitable for paddlers of all levels, though with an emphasis on the more ambitious paddler. For blow-by-blow basics, I recommend David Seidman's excellent book, *The Essential Sea Kayaker*, which covers in detail much that I take for granted. The need for useful answers to kayaking problems usually calls for illustrations that provide lessons that are valuable to both the beginner and the experienced paddler. In most instances I have elected to present advanced examples in preference to basic ones in the belief that beginners' lessons are contained within an advanced situation but not vice versa. This is not to imply that paddling storms or wild lee shores or undertaking 20-mile crossings is the norm; it is not. Indeed, I counsel strongly in favour of a measured approach to new kayaking experience. It is my hope that this book will provide a vision of what is possible to those who bring an adventurous spirit to their kayaking.

Grant M. Thompson

Above: **Laguna San Rafael, Chile.** Below: **Using a long-focus lens enables a kayaker to obtain good photographs without disturbing the sea lion colony.**

Coastal Baja.

CHAPTER ONE

EQUIPMENT

THE BOAT

Sea kayaks are distinguished from river kayaks by a multitude of features for which we have one word: *seaworthiness*. A sea boat may or may not roll easily, but it must slice through or ride over waves of all sizes, track dependably regardless of the direction of the sea, respond to the paddle in windy conditions, carry your gear and stand up to continuous punishment from wave action, weather, sand, rocky beaches, sea ice and sometimes very large, very inquisitive fish.

Nevertheless, there are many types of boat to choose from, and every dedicated kayaker is his or her own best authority on "the best kayak." You have to choose the right one for your use. There are countless manufacturers, most of them very small operations, and design is by no means stagnant. The choice at present, however, comes down to two readily available though arbitrarily designated types of boat:

1 Narrow or special-purpose kayaks—usually single seaters designed for speed or liveliness
2 General touring kayaks—singles or doubles designed for efficient load carrying and greater stability

Most sea kayaks have a sharp prow and an angular or even knifelike forefoot. Amidships, the hull is often rounded and flattened in cross section. Farther aft, the cross section resumes its rounded V shape, and the stern itself may be as sharp as the prow. As a rule, sea kayaks have little rocker (the curvature upward of the keel-line towards stem and stern as the boat is viewed in profile), and where it exists, it enhances the manoeuvrability of the craft. A deep, sharp stern allows the boat to track through the waves without yawing under the alternating thrust of the paddle. The rounded section amidships allows the boat to lean smoothly into breakers, and the partial flattening under the cockpit increases stability. A high prow is found in some designs, including many of the surviving or recorded Inuit and Aleut boats. Such a bow adds buoyancy forward and may help reduce weathercocking in some designs. It can be a useful feature in ice but is of questionable value in open water and today is probably included more for appearance than function. In some hulls you will also see chines. These are ridges, angular in cross section, running lengthwise along the hull between gunwale and keel. In fabric or skin-covered boats they are caused by the tension of the skin across a framing rib; a similar feature is sometimes moulded into fibreglass boats such as models where the chine aids turning when the boat is leaned to one side.

Slalom kayaks, designed for quick turns in rivers rather than tracking at sea, have much more rocker than a sea boat, and their hulls are generally flatter in cross section amidships and considerably rounder at bow and stern. They are also shorter. A river boat is often used for surf kayaking and when fitted with a skeg or rudder will sometimes serve for a short sea voyage, but the compromise is not finally a happy one. Away from white water, it is better to have a kayak true to the ancestry of the craft: a boat designed specifically for the sea.

Narrow or Special-Purpose Kayaks

Narrow touring kayaks are usually single seaters between 5 and 6 metres (17 and 19 feet) long with a 46- to 58-centimetre (18- to 23-inch) beam. They commonly have a rounded hull, hard chine or moderate V hull with very little rocker. Essentially they are coastal craft, and a paddler using them in wind or open water must be comfortable with the technique of rolling. These boats depend on the skill of the paddler for their seaworthiness. They are, in essence, tippy. (Tippiness, however, is a relative term. How tippy a boat is depends on the paddler's familiarity with that type of kayak as well as on the paddler's weight distribution: a broad-shouldered man will have many more problems with balance than a lightweight woman with solid legs and hips, since most of the woman's weight will be close to the centre of gravity.)

Cam Broze

Above: **This design by Matt and Cam Broze is swift and narrow but can carry a load.**

The West Greenland and Aleut kayaks were made from sealskin with a fragile wood and bone frame, but today the best boats in this style are fibreglass or Kevlar. Although these 50- to 56-centimetre (20- to 22-inch) beam kayaks have been used on some impressive coastal trips, most notably the circumnavigations of New Zealand, Britain, Australia and Japan by Paul Caffyn and the circumnavigation of the Hawaiian islands by Greg Blanchette, they are best suited for day tripping and lightweight excursions because of their small size and rather wet ride.

The great advantages of narrow touring kayaks are the ease with which they can be rolled and their speedier hulls. (They generally have a top speed of around 6½ knots.) The most obvious disadvantage is their limited stowage space, which makes them less suitable for journeys on which food and equipment must be carried in quantity.

Their most serious drawback, however, is that unloaded they are neither stable enough nor roomy enough to provide real relaxation or even to serve as a platform for photography. They are deadly if their occupant becomes exhausted or incapacitated at sea in severe conditions, unless rafting up is an option or external flotation is added.

At the fringe of what can be considered a sea kayak—and not part of the focus of this book—is a variety of specialty boats used exclusively

Joel Rogers

Folding kayaks have made a wide range of locales available to adventurous paddlers.

for ocean racing, surfing or both. Most distinctive among these is the surf ski, a long (6.5 metres, or 21 feet), narrow (48 centimetres, or 19 inches) kayak designed for sitting on rather than in. A foot-controlled rudder assists the paddler in following seas and cross winds, while a quick-release belt keeps the paddler in place during turbulence. Not surprisingly, surf skis are mostly used in the warm waters of Australia, South Africa and Hawaii. The most famous race for this class of kayak

Elan Sun Star

Ann E. Yow

Above: **Narrow sit-on kayaks or surf skis evolved for tropical use.**

Below: **Dyson's baidarka replicas cruise the Pacific coast.**

is the annual escorted downwind dash across Hawaii's Molokai channel, with an average speed that sometimes exceeds 8 knots. In the Pacific Northwest and the Great Lakes, a new breed of sit-in ocean-racing kayak has evolved to give an edge to competitors. This craft is best described as a cross between a downriver racing boat and a sea kayak.

Another wrinkle to kayak design for the sport of surfing has been the evolution of the wave ski. To call this planing, hulled, sit-on board a kayak is stretching the definition of the word, but some manufacturers show bikini-clad women paddling them with a beer cooler secured to the stern! In their element on the face of a 3.6-metre (12-foot) Hawaiian breaker, however, these stubby little craft are clearly the end product of a very specialized line of evolution, and they make surfing in a touring kayak resemble trying to ride a log to shore.

General Touring Kayaks

General touring single seaters are much more prevalent than their narrow counterparts. They are generally shorter—between approximately 4 and 5 metres (14 and 17 feet)—and feature a beam of about 58 to 69 centimetres (23 to 27 inches), yet some have a grand 80-centimetre (32-inch) beam and are so stable you can stand up in them. The greater stability of general touring boats enables you to rest and relax in them, though in extreme cases it tends to discourage the learning of dependable, more advanced paddling skills. These boats generally have a greater load-carrying capacity than the narrow singles and give a much drier ride. But because they are designed to be paddled loaded, their higher profile can make them vulnerable to wind when empty.

The beamier singles are usually not as fast, maybe a half-knot slower than their skinnier brethren, and are more difficult to roll, but they are far less likely to require rolling.

Having clearly defined two types of singles, narrow and general touring, I will now muddle the distinction by pointing out that there are a number of cross-over models of boats that could almost be placed in either category.

The immediate ancestor of the hardshell cruising kayak, single or double, is the collapsible kayak or foldboat—a design pioneered by the German tailor Hans Klepper around the turn of the century and itself based on original boats from the Canadian Arctic. The German models were originally manufactured for lakes and rivers. They have long since lost their pre-eminence in the field to hardshell kayaks of fibreglass and polyethylene, but because some of these collapsibles are suitable for use on the open sea and are convenient for travellers, they have continued to be popular in Europe and North America.

Unlike the Native peoples of Northern Canada and Greenland, who used single-seat kayaks for inshore hunting, the Aleuts of Alaska designed two-seat models for longer, more exposed voyages. These boats were given a third cockpit at the instigation of Russian fur traders and named baidarkas. They were used for hunting and trading voyages east of the Aleutians and as far south as Baja California. Today the closest approximations to the larger Aleut craft are the baidarkas built by George Dyson of Bellingham, author of the book *Baidarka* and founder of the Baidarka Historical Society. Using modern materials—chiefly nylon cloth and aluminum tubing—Dyson has built several kayaks with many of the original baidarka features. His triple seater is 8.5 metres (28 feet) long with a 76-centimetre (30-inch) beam. It is very stable and can carry a sail. Dyson's experimental fan sail design is most original: ashore the sail can double as a tent. Like its predecessors, this baidarka can carry some 270 kilograms (600 pounds) of equipment. Apart from the materials used, its greatest departure from traditional design is a sturdy foot-controlled rudder.

CHOOSING A KAYAK

Choosing the right kayak is like buying any other large-ticket item: the world suddenly becomes full of instant experts eager to give you advice and warn you of the pitfalls of this or that feature. Buying on the secondhand market is, of course, usually cheaper but fraught with dangers unless you know precisely what you are looking for. If you seek the advice of friends, you will usually buy the same boat as they have because they have grown to love theirs and can sing its praises loud and clear; they also have an investment in reassuring themselves—and you—that they made the right choice in the first place.

Buying direct from the builder is probably the worst way to get an objective opinion, though when your choice has been made, a discount can sometimes be arranged with the smaller builders who do not have a dealer network to support. This lack of objectivity does not mean that builders are dishonest. They are simply passionate about their creations and may believe that their design is the design for today's kayaker; their conviction can make them a little hard of hearing when you have special needs to be addressed.

By doing the round of designers, you will quickly realize that the so-called experts can disagree spectacularly on such fundamental features as the shape of the bow. I once heard a designer (redesigner might be a more appropriate term, since design today is simply a modification of existing design) being asked why he had put a long upswept bow on his kayak. He explained that it was to stop the boat from pearling (nose-diving in following seas). The customer thought about that for a while and then asked why the other boat he had built had a low bow. That too was to stop pearling, the designer explained a little sheepishly. Certainly there are few clearly right or wrong features—mostly trade-offs and preferences.

Probably the best way to choose a kayak is to visit a sea kayak symposium, one of the major sea kayaking clubs or a specialty store offering a wide range of models. At the store, seek the general guidance of a sales clerk but don't listen to anything the person tells you about how a boat handles—just take it out and try it. The problem with this system, however, is that a beginner will probably prefer a very stable kayak for a start; later, as he or she becomes more skilled, the stable boat could feel too dull. So rent some kayaks with an eye to purchasing. You may still end up choosing the stable boat in the end, but it won't be because you are afraid of the others.

Before you can expect to make sense of the hundreds of models of kayaks now available on the North American market, indulge in a little fantasy. Cast your mind back to the genesis of your interest in sea kayaking, that dream of how you see yourself in a kayak. Maybe it is a weekend tryst to the first secluded cove you and your partner come across; or maybe it is a King Farouk–sized challenge to nature with just you and your little boat duelling the ocean creamers; or maybe you wish to use the kayak for wildlife photography or an evening workout. Got the image? Well, hold on to it because now you have to use that image to find the right boat.

Unfortunately, there are at least two other factors that will complicate your choice: your budget constraints and your partner's(s') needs.

As I stated in the introduction to this book, the options available in the late 1990s have expanded impressively from those of the eighties. We still have singles, doubles, folding boats and rigid ones built of fibreglass, Kevlar, plastic, canvas/lath and nylon/aluminum tubing, plywood and cedar strip. There are both cheap and expensive kayaks, but it is the variety and quality of the new boats that set them apart from those of ten years ago.

Singles

The most popular sea kayaks are rigid singles—the freedom boats for those who seek independence or who are obliged through circumstance to paddle solo. Rigid singles are also the group with the most diverse designs, so the chance of finding the perfect boat for you is greatest in this category. Couples, however, should keep in mind that two singles will likely cost considerably more than a two-seater.

Doubles

A double is particularly appropriate if you and your partner are of significantly different strength or if the trip you plan is extremely arduous or if you are going to a remote area. After all, you cannot easily become separated from a companion in the same kayak, and two paddlers in a double are certainly a stronger unit than the same two paddlers in singles. Few doubles can be successfully paddled by one person under difficult conditions, however, with the exception of the downwind ocean crossings in which Lindemann and Gillet chose doubles (see Appendix A).

High Volume or Low Volume?

A high-volume single kayak is one with a volume of around 18 cubic feet, while a low-volume one runs from 10 to 12 cubic feet; there can be appreciable volume differences between two-seaters as well, but not to the same extent. Choosing the right-sized kayak is not quite as straightforward as choosing a pair of shoes, since most people select a kayak for the load it carries as well as for its fit. Others have a clear and unshakable preconceived idea of what a kayak should feel like, and they know exactly when they feel it. But choosing a kayak like a shoe is a pretty good place to start, since generally if you are a small person (under 68 kilograms, or 150 pounds), you will prefer a small boat, and if you are a larger person (say, over 80 kilograms, or 180 pounds), you are going to feel more comfortable in a larger boat. If you had no special load-carrying considerations, you would buy roughly according to such sizing.

For people who are 5 foot 2 inches and sport a pair of size 14 feet, the rule of thumb breaks down. You need a bigger boat to accommodate your tootsies. Even if you have no unusual physical attributes, you may choose a higher-volume boat so that you can carry plenty of fresh food along on your trip, or a few bottles of Chablis, or a box of camera equipment. People who fish for salmon from their kayaks should consider what they would do if they hooked into a 30-pounder. (They will be glad of the extra stability that usually comes with a higher-volume kayak and may judge the trade-off a good one.) Those who feel stiff-jointed and awkward getting into a kayak may also be glad of a little extra clearance in the cockpit and deck area.

Conversely, there are 190-pounders who get a great kick out of paddling fast in a sporty kayak, eating freeze-dried food and having waves wash over them every few seconds. They have absolutely no interest in taking pictures from a kayak unless they show crooked horizons intersecting the uplifting profile of their kayak midframe. For these people, too, the rules of high- and low-volume choices are accommodatingly elastic. If, however, you find that you are obliged to pile gear on deck because your boat's interior will not accommodate your needs, or if you find that you are viewing the waves from the wrong side more often than you should, try a higher-volume boat.

Rigid or Folding?

Put simply, you should choose a rigid kayak unless you need one that folds. Or you may prefer the aesthetics of a boat with the traditional internal frame—a boat that performs as silently as the original hunting craft and flexes in the waves like a living thing.

The advantages offered by rigid kayaks are numerous: for a start, there are more of them, so the chances of finding the right boat for your needs is going to be greater; they require less maintenance, less care around rocks and less concern about the effects of the elements; they are also usually much cheaper. The reasons for buying a folding kayak, however, are often as compelling: you may need to break the boat down for travel or to store it in an apartment. Such craft promise you the world of kayak touring in a backpack—Japan, New Zealand, the Aegean, the Caribbean . . .

The price for this versatility is not just measured in dollars; you must nurse your folding kayak over coral or barnacle-encrusted intertidal zones and wipe the sand off your feet and bags before placing them inside, since grit beneath the stringers will chafe the hull, rub away at the varnish or jam up the joints of an aluminum frame. Folding kayaks are simply fussier to own and maintain, something to think about as you reach for your cheque book. Assembly time for most folding kayaks is a fairly modest fifteen to thirty minutes.

Those who require more compactness than they would get from a collapsible kayak might consider the purchase of an inflatable kayak. (Audrey Sutherland of Hawaii has forced sea kayakers to take these stubby little craft seriously by paddling more than 8000 kilometres, or 5000 miles, of Alaska coast in one over several summers.) Apart from being lightweight, inflatable kayaks are the least expensive of folding craft.

For those who strongly prefer rigid kayaks yet need to reduce their overall length for storage, several manufacturers produce take-apart rigid boats. These boats, however, tend to be heavy, expensive—since they must be made of Kevlar—and prone to difficulties where they join.

Materials

Fibreglass kayaks are usually a combination of cloth, roving and, in some of the more cheaply constructed models, chopped matt. Matt provides stiffness and, when it is thick enough, strength, but results in a heavy and somewhat brittle hull. Most builders now use foam core or an internal keel of either foam or spruce to gain the hull rigidity required for strongly secured bulkheads and optimum kayak performance. The really high-tech boats are built with an initial layer of fibreglass cloth to improve abrasion resistance, followed by layers of Kevlar well stiffened with carbon fibre. Such boats are lighter, stronger and more expensive than their equivalent fibreglass models. Standard weight for a fibreglass kayak is around 25 kilograms (55 pounds) for a single and 40 kilograms (90 pounds) for a double.

The resin preferred by most fibreglass kayak builders today is vinyl ester, which is more flexible than the cheaper polyester resins and not as toxic as the tough epoxy resins. Most fibreglass kayaks are protected with a hard abrasion-resistant layer of gelcoat. This is the first layer to be sprayed into the mould and carries the pigment, which helps protect the resin and fibres from the damaging ultraviolet rays of the sun. Most kayaks come with a white hull, since white shows the scratches less than a dark colour. White does not, however, stand out well when the kayak is upside down amid breaking waves. The choice of colour for the deck depends on whether you want to stand out or blend in with your environment. The best colour for visibility is yellow, and the most visible boat is one that is yellow top and bottom.

The rotomoulded polyethylene kayaks are stronger and more economical than fibreglass models. Two principal types of material are used: linear polyethylene and cross-linked polyethylene. Linear is stiffer and cheaper than cross-linked and, in the unlikely event that you split it, it can be repaired with a plastic weld. Cross-linked polyethylene is softer and tougher and has a slightly waxy feel to it. The best whitewater kayaks are built of cross-linked polyethylene to withstand the impact of river rocks. Repairs, if needed, must be made with a patch rivetted over the damaged area. Different sandwich foam laminates are also available, offering greater stiffness than a single layer of polyethylene.

The disadvantages of polyethylene kayaks are that they are heavier (by about 4.5 kilograms, or 10 pounds) than most fibreglass models, and they scratch more severely than gel-coated fibreglass. The linear ones also seem particularly vulnerable to denting on roof racks in the hot sun, but dimples can usually be popped out with a stick wedged inside the boat. The life span of polyethylene kayaks, uv inhibitors notwithstanding, is also less than that of fibreglass kayaks, though the life span is going to vary greatly with the care taken when you store the boat.

Rotomoulded kayaks are made in an expensive nickel, steel or aluminum mould that is heated, usually in a gas oven, and then opened to receive a measured amount of plastic granules. This is where science ends and art begins; the mould is then rotated slowly and rocked end for end in such a manner that the melted plastic runs to an even thickness over the inside of the mould as it cools. As the newly formed boat cools, it contracts and must be handled carefully until it has set in its final form.

Wood kayaks are a relatively small part of the sea kayak market. Most are of the home-built variety, either constructed from a kit using sheets of marine-grade plywood stitched and then glued together or from thin cedar strips laid over a form and sheathed in fibreglass and epoxy. These kayaks are frequently of great beauty and often are surprisingly durable, given the right amount of maintenance. They are fun and inexpensive to build, the most common reason for choosing this type of boat over its less easily damaged fibreglass and polyethylene relatives.

Also popular among home builders are lath and canvas models, which can be built from plans and locally available materials. Such boats have an internal frame of wood with 12- or 14-ounce canvas stretched over it and then painted or varnished. The life of the canvas is around five years, at which time the boat can be stripped to its skeleton, the wood revarnished and a new skin fitted. These kayaks are lightweight, inexpensive and easy to build, though not exactly bombproof. A tougher hull can be created with the use of hypalon or rubberized cloth.

As we have seen, standard folding kayaks consist of a frame and removable skin. Frames are commonly made of wood or aluminium or a combination of both in Folbot. Ash is the most common wood for longitudinal frame pieces because it is both durable and flexible. Cross frames of birch plywood are used in Kleppers and Nautiraid. Feathercraft features a frame of high-grade aluminum with a baked epoxy coating and cross ribs of high-density polyethylene.

Wood has the advantage of being relatively easy to repair, though of course there is nothing to prevent you from using wood for temporary repairs to an aluminum frame in the field. The disadvantage of wood is that it can absorb water and swell. Aluminum, in contrast, suffers from a vulnerability to corrosion and electrolysis—particularly in warmer climates. All folding boats should be regularly disassembled to prevent them from metamorphosing into rigid ones. Small metal assembly parts are present on most frames and will need special care.

Today's most popular hull material is hypalon, with a direct tradeoff between hull weight and durability. Some manufacturers make an extra-lightweight model that uses nylon-covered butyl rubber, while others opt for a less expensive vinyl composite. Deck fabrics vary widely. Cotton is still used extensively, and though it is somewhat vulnerable to damage by ultraviolet radiation, it breathes, allowing air and moisture to pass through. This characteristic keeps the boat pleasantly cool in the tropics, since evaporation occurs off the inside, providing a natural air-conditioning system.

Nautiraid and Feathercraft rely instead on pack-cloth or Cordura because they are lighter than cotton, particularly when wet, and both are also waterproof, rot resistant and shrinkproof.

Hull Design

Hull shapes and their significance, I confess, are aspects of boat building that mostly elude my understanding. Why is it that one successful model is fish form (its widest beam forward of the cockpit) while another is Swede form (its widest beam aft of the cockpit) and yet another is symmetrical? What are the key features that make them work? My basic ignorance is not for want of trying to understand. I listen, along with the other kayak users, to the explanations of designers, and I marvel at their plausible reasons for why the hull was rounded just so, why this or that amount of flare was put in the bow to give added lift at speed and, of course, how each designer went about ensuring that his boat would not pearl as it surfed off the wave. I often find such talk disconcerting because I happen to know that the designer simply took someone else's design (or borrowed design), padded it out with bondo paste, added a foot of length amidships, changed the shape of the stern, adjusted the pitch of the deck, tried it out to see if it had improved any, and then attempted to rationalize the results.

To learn something objective about hull design and answer some of the more basic questions, *Sea Kayaker* magazine has sponsored a series of tests on popular models of touring singles within a given length and beam range. During the first testing of eleven kayaks, engineer and kayaker John Dawson supervised the program using the magazine's own facilities and the $2000-a-day test tank at the B.C. Research Institute in Vancouver. Various tests demonstrated that some boats behave differently from others and revealed some startling facts—for example, that raising the height of the seat by 2.5 centimetres (1 inch) could halve some kayaks' stability. It was also found, however, that some boats that looked radically different behaved almost identically. Almost nothing could be confirmed about basic hull design except for the most obvious stuff—for example, that long, narrow boats go faster than short, fat ones—and even these differences were not nearly as great as had been expected.

Computers have not yet provided us with the answer, either, since they consider only the wetted surface on calm water and not the effect of construction above the waterline, such as the profile of the deck. Too often when designers have relied on the computer for their inspiration, a dog was born—garbage in, garbage out and all that. We just don't know enough to start with. The focus of all our design intelligence to date has understandably been to try and make some sense of what exists, and we seem to be so far from understanding why one hull works and another does not that I doubt I will see the day when we can accurately project our knowledge to design radical new shapes (or perhaps radically ancient shapes) for boats. Today kayak design still lies mostly in the realm of art and living tradition, and perhaps it is better that way; at least it allows for some imaginative explanations. I also draw some comfort from the embarrassment that must have been felt by the designer of *Magic*, a 1983 challenger to the America's Cup, which, test-tank researcher Francis Clauser discovered, travelled through the water more efficiently backwards than it did forwards, rudder in place and all. So much for science and boat design.

Having made my reservations abundantly clear, let me repeat some of the popular wisdom that has gained credibility: long kayaks (up to around 7 metres, or 20 feet) are faster than short ones, given a powerful paddler (if the paddler is not strong, a long boat may actually be slower because of the greater wetted surface); wide ones are more stable and more difficult to lean than narrow ones; round-bottomed boats can be leaned more smoothly than flat-bottomed ones. (Despite optimistic rumours to the contrary, narrow boats have not proven themselves to be more seaworthy than wide ones.) Fish-form hulls are said to be more efficient than Swede-form ones by half the builders, while the other half swear it is just the opposite. A deep forefoot makes the boat hard to handle in wind, as does a high bow. A faintly V-shaped hull provides stiffness and aids with tracking when the V is carried aft of the cockpit. Rocker helps with turning; the more rocker, the more easily the boat turns but the harder it is to hold on a straight course. A fine entry cuts the waves cleanly but requires above-the-waterline buoyancy to prevent plunging. The stern should have both volume for buoyancy and a fine exit to minimize friction from turbulence.

RUDDERS & SKEGS

A rudder, operated by cables running forward to controls at the paddler's feet, saves effort on any sea kayak. It is a necessity on the larger doubles if they are to hold course in cross winds or be turned efficiently. A good rudder allows you to devote your paddle strokes to straightforward propulsion with an occasional support stroke. For years I paddled a single with no rudder, and I can remember times when, in order to stay on course in a cross wind, I paddled fourteen strokes to port for every one to starboard. A rudder alleviates this problem. In singles, however, a rudder should not be considered a turning device to replace the ability to manoeuvre with the paddle or to control major broaching problems. It saves effort in maintaining a course in cross winds, and though some additional drag results, the compromise is usually a good one.

Kayakers who are proud of their repertoire of paddle strokes are sometimes put off by rudders, as if it were demeaning to guide the kayak with the feet, and the problem of insecure footrests can be a serious one when rolling. But on a long voyage, or even a short one during adverse conditions, this device can save much wear and tear on belly and shoulder muscles. A well-designed rudder, usually of high-grade aluminum or stainless steel, can always be cocked out of the water where it will be less likely to become damaged and will not impede the ability of the kayak to be turned sharply while being leaned onto its gunwale. The best combination is to have a sea kayak that paddles well without a rudder but that has one anyway.

In doubles, rudder controls can be in either the forward (No. 1) or aft (No. 2) cockpit. The paddler in the No. 1 cockpit has an unobstructed view of the bow and what lies immediately ahead, whereas the person in the No. 2 position has a more commanding view of the whole boat and a greater sense of control. It is useful to fit auxiliary stirrups to the rudder cables so that they can be operated from either cockpit.

A rudder takes quite a hammering on a long trip and must be strongly built. It should be cocked for negotiating surf or for lying to a drogue and should kick up automatically on striking a submerged rock. The rudder assembly frequently becomes fouled when a kayak is used for towing, though this problem can be avoided by running the towline through a short, flexible whip above the rudder or providing a protective on-deck cage to deflect the towline. In surf, rudders can be downright dangerous to anyone in the water or anyone attempting to scramble aboard over the afterdeck.

I have to eat most of the disparaging comments I made about skegs in

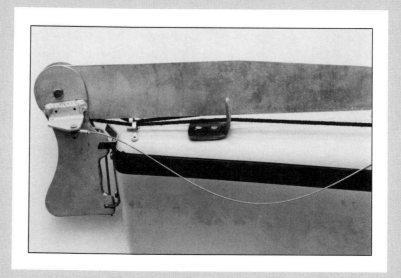

**Flip-up manually retractable rudder. Designed to swing through 270°
and lie along the deck.**

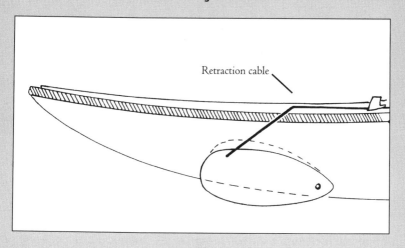

Retraction cable

Retractable skeg.

the earliest editions of this book. Since then, I have paddled kayaks with designs of skegs that worked well, and though I have yet to prefer them over a good rudder, I am impressed. The skeg amounts to a fixed rudder, which is occasionally adjustable and is usually designed to be lifted out of the water. It shifts the pivot point aft in smoothly round-hulled craft such as whitewater boats, and it enhances the tracking ability of more manoeuvrable yet "V"ed touring kayak hulls. The ideal placement for the skeg appears to be just aft of the seat, located in a boxed slot recessed into the keel line of the boat. The blade is raised and lowered with a cord leading back to the cockpit; thus, the amount of draught can be adjusted according to conditions. A skeg or a retractable dagger board so placed is almost never lifted clear of the water by passing waves, enhancing its effectiveness in rough seas. In addition, placing the new pivot point closer to the natural (central) pivot point makes the boat much more manageable in wind than it would be if the skeg were placed at the stern.

BUILT-IN BUOYANCY

Without special buoyancy systems, most boats will sink as soon as they fill with water. And even if they don't sink, they will float so low as to be unmanageable. The best buoyancy is usually the most buoyancy, and every opportunity should be made to maximize and back up buoyancy systems. The most effective one is a boat full of foam or air in sealed compartments. A number of other provisions for built-in buoyancy—including the air sponsons of some folding kayaks, the blocks of foam that some people permanently jam into bow and stern, and the water-tight bulkheads, pods and self-draining cockpits found in various models of rigid kayaks—are more practical because they leave room for gear and legs. The benefits of built-in buoyancy become especially obvious when one considers the number of inexperienced paddlers borrowing or buying used kayaks from individuals who may neglect to explain or emphasize the need for adequate buoyancy. Over the past few years, the rash of fatal and near fatal accidents involving insufficiently buoyant boats that sank or could not be re-entered have made this message even clearer. The disadvantages of built-in buoyancy are that it can wear, fail or prove insufficient—and this is why it should not be relied on without backup systems of waterproof gear bags.

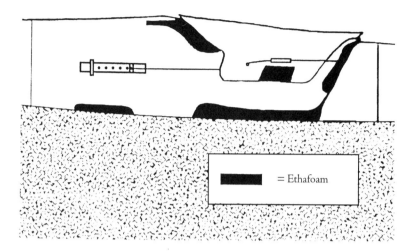

= Ethafoam

Bulkhead cockpit customized for comfort with Ethafoam.

Bulkheads & Hatches

Watertight bulkheads made from either fibreglass or foam slab caulked into position provide dry stowage and structural support as well as buoyancy. To be effective, bulkheads should be fitted as close to the back of the seat and as close to the end of the footrests as possible; this placement will also ensure a maximum of useable space for loading.

Equipment hatches may be either large or small. Large hatches—sometimes as large as 25 centimetres by 36 centimetres (10 inches by 14 inches)—are more convenient and practical than the smaller circular screw-in or pop-on varieties that range from 13 to 20 centimetres (5 to 8 inches) in diameter. The trade-off is that large hatches are usually less watertight than small ones. The choice is yours; how much seepage are you prepared to put up with for the convenience of a hatch that will take a good-sized waterproof bag in one gulp?

The Pod

Developed and promoted extensively by British designer Alan Byde, the pod is a rigid, low-volume capsule in which the paddler sits. Permanently attached to the cockpit rim, this watertight body chamber provides buoyancy control approximately 40 per cent greater than that provided by bulkheads fitted in close to the back of the seats and in front of the

The pod is essentially a watertight body chamber.

footrests of an equivalent boat. The pod's other function is to protect against fold-and-hold entrapment, a situation more commonly seen in white water, in which the kayak wraps around a rock or bridge support. Under pressure from the flow of the river, the kayak without a pod folds in two at the cockpit and may trap the paddler's legs, whereas the kayak with a pod tends to fold in front of or behind the pod, leaving the paddler clear to escape. This is a problem only likely to be encountered when touring boats are used on rivers.

The Self-Draining Kayak

During recent years a rash of sit-on kayaks has been developed for warm weather use and for playing around in surf. In these boats, the kayaker sits in a recessed body form in the deck. A pair of substantial holes at the lowest point of the recess allows the water to escape. The gear area is usually divided into fore and aft compartments accessible by large, practical hatches. Shortly after the turn of the century, Frederic Fenger's sailing canoe *Yakaboo*—a sailing kayak by modern-day definition—also featured a self-draining cockpit. Surf skis and wave skis have cockpit recesses so small that they don't even require a drainage hole, only the body of the paddler to displace the water.

SEATS

Few items are more personal than a kayaker's seat. One individual's source of comfort is another's medieval tool of torture. There are contoured foam seats and fibreglass bucket seats to fit skinny bums and fat bums; there are fabric seats that hang from the frames of folding boats, seats that can slide on plastic tracks, seats like convention hall chairs that are removable and must be tethered to stop their floating away during capsize drill, and seats that need a hole drilled through them so that water won't collect where you sit. There is, I regret to say, no perfect seat, nor is there a seat that will prove unacceptable to all people. I remember puzzling over one that looked like a Henry Moore sculpture suspended from the tight little cockpit rim of a foreign import. No one could get comfortable on the thing until one day a slim-hipped guy with a flat backside walked in and declared it the most comfortable thing he had ever sat on.

Maybe the main point to be learned from this is that as you assess a kayak you should pay only passing attention to the seat. After all, you can change it fairly easily by adding a little Ensolite here and a bit of foam there or ripping the whole thing out and replacing it with something that you feel good about. Don't pass up an otherwise ideal kayak because of the seat. Remember too that remaining seated for hours at a stretch isn't something you'll get used to right away, no matter how comfortable the seat; so don't expect too much.

The backrest is another part of the equation worthy of attention, as lower back support makes a significant difference to one's long-term comfort. When I go on a kayak trip, I usually carry so much gear that I end up throwing away the seat and backrest and then sitting on my wet suit jacket and a deflated air mattress, both of which I may want close at hand in an emergency. One of the drawbacks of this system is that you can easily destabilize the kayak by making your seat too high. As mentioned previously, raising the height of the seat by a couple of centimetres can halve the stability of some touring singles.

CUSTOMIZING YOUR COCKPIT

The objective in customizing your cockpit is to establish a snug fit for your hips, lower back, legs and feet so that your effort against the paddles is transferred efficiently into moving the boat. If your lower body flops around inside the kayak, you lose efficiency. Customizing can also provide comfort or at least minimize the discomfort of prolonged sitting in the kayak.

Ethafoam or some other nonabsorbent squishy material such as Ensolite can be glued over almost any surface where your body comes into contact with the boat, including the foot or rudder pedals, the bottom of the boat where your heels rest and the inside of the deck, where moulded knee pads provide a firm grip on the sideways motion of the boat. Occasionally, in some of the lower-volume boats, the deck is moulded so that the knee brace is extended into a full thigh brace as found in whitewater boats. Different thicknesses of foam may be glued inside this moulded deck to provide the right fit for different-sized individuals.

When customizing your seat, take care that the hip pads, attached to the side of the seat, are not so tight that they cause pressure pain. If you find your legs are "falling asleep" after some time paddling, experiment with a roll of Ensolite or a small gear bag under your thighs.

The best support for your back is one that firmly embraces your lumbar region while keeping your body upright. Many manufacturers offer a backrest that can be adjusted by a pull cord, which is then locked into a cam cleat alongside the seat. Be sure that this backrest is adjusted properly before you start padding out the seat.

Sometimes a painful pressure point appears where the spine touches the backrest. This problem can be solved by placing strips of Ensolite so as to restrict contact to the muscle on either side of the vertebrae.

SPRAY SKIRTS & SPRAY DECKS

A spray skirt is a skirt of neoprene or elastic-fringed nylon designed to prevent water from entering the boat through the cockpit. The smaller the cockpit, the less expansive the skirt and the smaller the chance that the surf will push it in, or so the theory goes. A large cockpit, however, is more convenient for entry and makes for easier loading and greater general comfort in the boat. In fact, it seems that a trade-off is not necessary in this case, since a well-designed, well-fitting spray skirt can be made to adhere firmly to the cockpit rim of a large-cockpit boat. If the spray skirt is fitted with a sturdy zipper that slides from chest almost to the deck, you can enter and leave the boat without removing the skirt—but even more important when the seas are very rough, a zipper gives quick access to your gear without your having to take off the spray skirt. It also enables you to close the cockpit the instant you see an approaching whitecap. A spray skirt can be difficult to put on the cockpit at sea, especially if your hands are cold, so it is good to be able to put it on the boat and leave it there. Once you have a zipper sewn into your spray skirt, you will wonder how you ever got along without one. (You may also find it hard to remember what it was like paddling with a dry crotch unless you have a waterproof zipper.)

A sturdy "panic loop" at the front of the skirt makes it easier to remove. The spray skirt should be attached loosely enough to be removed by a pull at this loop yet attached tightly enough to withstand the pounding of a breaker. Try pushing your knees up into the skirt. It should resist popping off, but not so much as to cause problems exiting in an emergency. Shoulder straps can prevent the skirt from riding down on your body and enable you to empty accumulating pools of water from the skirt with a shrug. A useful variation is the anorak, which fits around the cockpit over the top of the spray skirt or, like the old Inuit model, attaches directly to the cockpit, becoming a combination spray skirt and jacket. The anorak too may be fitted with a zipper, providing access to the interior.

Spray decks, found on many folding kayaks, are watertight covers for the enlarged cockpits. Because they cover a large area, it is important that they be securely attached to the coaming of the boat. Turnbuckles are suitable for this purpose, but ideally they should be combined with an additional waterproofing system, such as a tuck-in flap to prevent waves from forcing water beneath the cover. Expansive spray decks for single-cockpit doubles should be reinforced with a plywood frame between the cockpits to give added protection against breaking waves and to prevent formation of the annoying little pool of water that will otherwise gather between the paddlers. The plywood also gives the rear paddler a useful working surface for reading maps, eating meals or the like.

PADDLES

The paddle is probably the most misunderstood part of sea kayaking equipment today. In choosing a paddle, you must consider the boat it is to be used with; wider boats call for longer paddles, and narrow boats call for shorter ones. You must also consider the strength, height and arm length of the paddler, the choice of blade and the conditions for

Paddle styles: (upper) **Little Dipper, sea-touring blade;** (middle) **Arctic Wind, Inuit-style cruising paddle;** (lower) **San Juan, based on a standard racing blade.**

which the paddle is likely to be used. For a double, you must strive for a balance with the needs of the second paddler. It all boils down to a very complex set of requirements that makes choosing a paddle a very individual affair, which few kayak sales staff are equipped to help you with. Whitewater and racing paddles further complicate the equation because they are often advocated by cross-over paddlers.

Paddle shafts must be strong, oval and well cared for to avoid damaging your hands. Sea kayakers have traditionally used wooden paddles, but there has been a shift to synthetic ones since the 1980s.

Under normal touring conditions, tandem paddlers of the same size and strength would choose paddles of the same length. But one of the more common reasons for choosing a double is the imbalance between partners' strengths, and the choice of paddles can go a long way towards correcting this imbalance. The two variables are, of course, length and blade size (and of the two length is the more important). Thus, if you have a powerful 6-foot 4-inch, 250-pound paddler in the rear cockpit and her 110-pound asthmatic husband in the front, you can give them the same rate of paddling by supplying him with a short, narrow blade paddle and her with a long, large-bladed one.

To Feather or Not to Feather

When the blades are at an angle up to ninety degrees to each other, they are said to be feathered, and when the blades are in one plane, they are said to be unfeathered. There has been a major swing towards unfeathered paddles during the past ten years, but the choice is still mostly a matter of personal preference, or more often than not the preference of your particular kayak instructor. Notably, the sale of one-piece paddles to sea kayakers has almost stopped. If you are a beginner, I suggest using unfeathered paddles.

The pros and cons for both types are briefly as follows. Feathering reduces windage on the airborne blade when you are travelling into the wind. (It is also a natural angle for the high racing stroke when it is used with short paddles on very narrow racing boats.) With a strong following wind, however, it is to your advantage to have unfeathered blades and let the wind on the airborne blade help push you along. With a beam wind, unfeathered paddles are again the best choice, since they will catch less wind than feathered ones. Traditional Inuit and Aleut paddles, with slender blades, are never feathered.

I prefer unfeathered paddles under normal touring conditions, using feathered paddles only when paddling against severe head winds or when exiting through heavy surf where I would want to avoid smacking the back of the blade into the crest of a wave or where I might need a reflexive brace. This brings up a contentious point. In an earlier edition of this book, I suggested varying the angle of blades according to conditions. This works fine for the more stable doubles, but most people come unstuck when they vary the blade pitch in kayaks that depend on a reflexive brace for their seaworthiness. (I really appreciated this when I was paddling a particularly squirrelly surf ski in rough seas off Diamond Head in Hawaii. I quickly had to revert to the feathered blade on which I was weaned to avoid slicing up the ocean and going for a swim.) At sea, when the wind becomes too strong to paddle easily, unfeathered paddles are less likely to go spinning out of your hands as the wind catches first one angle and then the other. They are also less likely to catch a sideways gust, leaving you with the option of hanging onto your paddle and capsizing or letting go one end of the shaft and losing your stroke. If you have agile wrists, you will be able to retain your grip on the shaft and retrieve the paddle from the sea. If not, you won't have to worry about the angle of your paddle—you won't have one, unless you had it tethered. Another problem with feathered paddles is that over long periods they increase the chance of tenosynovitis, which results from overuse, particularly if one is using the twisting motion that feathered paddles require or if the wrist does not form a straight line with the forearm. In fact, in view of their few advantages and serious disadvantages, it is a wonder that feathered paddles ever became popular with touring kayakers at all.

Blade shape is another great mystery to most people, and it helps to realize how shapes evolved in order to better judge the most appropriate paddle type for the boat you use and the sort of kayaking you do. The broad square-ended blades, for example, are traditionally whitewater paddles, which appear to have evolved from the old square-ended oars popular early in this century. They were broadened to enhance control for slalom courses and to provide holding power in aerated water. The paddles are usually short and feathered to help negotiate the narrow gates of a slalom course.

The large-bladed asymmetric paddle is the most powerful blade because of its size and the fact that the angled tip balances the area of the immersed blade on either side of the spline so as to eliminate any twist. (Twist is also eliminated with a narrow blade.) This paddle is designed for flat-water racing boats that weigh 7 to 9 kilograms (15 to 20 pounds). It is also ideal for light, fast singles when wind is not a factor. It is less than ideal for doubles, which can weigh as much as 225 kilograms (500 pounds) when fully loaded. Here the efficient blade that works so well for the light boat becomes a liability to the joints and muscles of the user. This is a case where the narrower paddle comes into its own.

The narrow paddle evolved in the Arctic, and variations of it were used by all Native paddlers, not because they were incapable of manufacturing wider blades, as is sometimes suggested by casual observers, but because the paddles were not vulnerable to wind and had little impact on the joints and muscles of the endurance paddler. A wide range of traditional sizes and configurations exist, most of which have yet to be copied by the manufacturers of today's store-bought paddles.

Waterproof bags come in many sizes.

BAGS & CONTAINERS

Sea kayaking has almost unlimited potential for people who like putting things in bags and sealing them tightly. A good system for waterproofing equipment is crucial, and in cold climates your life may depend on it. Today there is a wide range of waterproof bags of different sizes and materials on the market, some designed exclusively for use in sea kayaks. Most seal by means of a flap and dome closure or roll-down top with snap buckle arrangement. Less expensive, and disproportionately less effective, is a series of plastic garbage bags placed one inside the other with necks folded over and tied. If you use garbage bags, they should be protected by a regular canvas bag and you should carry plenty of spares, since they are prone to tear during repeated loading and unloading. Wider boats usually have spaces on either side of the seats that can be used efficiently if narrow bags are chosen to hold items you may require while paddling. This method is much safer than carrying bits and pieces on deck and more convenient than carrying them loose inside the boat. Items such as flares, VHF radio, flashlight, diving mask, sunscreen, camera and, of course, lunch can all be stored here, and provided that the bags are securely attached to the boat, they will not be lost should you capsize.

Several manufacturers make tapered waterproof bags that fit nicely into the bow and stern of the kayak and that can be blown full of air after they have been loaded. These are usually sealed by means of a fold-down flap with a Fastex closure and are mostly appropriate for kayaks without bulkheads or those featuring hatches large enough to stuff the bag through. In the absence of bulkheads, such bags should be backed up by a cockpit sock (see below).

Be sure that the tapered bags you use are of sturdy material, that the inside of your kayak is clear of sharp edges and that you have the means to attach the bags to the kayak so that in the event of a capsize your equipment will not float away. If you are using standard tapered air bags for buoyancy, make sure that they are large enough to occupy all of the space you are not using for your legs or your gear in waterproof bags. Small air bags placed at either end of a large boat just occupy valuable storage space and create an axis around which a flooded boat can turn, making it tricky to re-enter without overbalancing again. The ideal location for buoyancy in such a case would be along the gunwale so as to provide a pontoon effect when the boat is awash. (Ontario's Georgian Bay Kayak Ltd. has developed such a buoyancy pontoon device, which can be used to prevent a capsize from occurring or speedily deployed to stabilize a kayak after a capsize.) When you are relying on inflatable gear bags and air bags, make sure that the inflation tubes are long enough to allow you to top up the bags orally while they are in place, necessary when a temperature drop causes a loosening of the bags inside your boat.

The cockpit sock is one more bag for the last baggable item, the paddler. The sock is a pod-shaped waterproof bag, set into the cockpit after the boat is loaded and attached by its elastic rim to the coaming before the spray skirt goes on. As with the pod, if the paddler bails out, only the sock fills with water. Rudder controls can be operated readily through the sock. During trials with two socks fitted to a large double devoid of bulkheads, we were able to re-enter and resume paddling within one minute, whereas a rescue in the same boat with only air bags fore and aft failed. It has not proved necessary to invert the socks, which in modern hardshell kayaks are held in place by a strong vacuum.

The design of food bags will depend on the type of boat you are using. If you are loading your food through a fairly small hatch, you may decide to pack the food containers loosely and use a bag only for carrying them from boat to campsite. In the larger boats, containers may be carried in a wide-mouthed sack or mesh bag, enabling you to rummage about inside the bag for the tin that has migrated to the bottom. It is a good idea to have everything stored in some kind of bag. Apart from securing gear during a capsize, it makes carrying easier when your campsite is some distance from the point you were obliged to land.

Special attention should be given to a dry bag for your documents. On the market are several inexpensive plastic and vinyl bags, but these usually have a life span proportional to their economy—not much of a saving when you find your passport or logbook reduced to papier-mâché. Strongly made bags with grommets that allow them to be tied in place are especially useful. So are bags with a separate flotation chamber that can cushion fragile gear or keep it from sinking and being lost.

REPAIR KIT

Ideally, each boat should carry its own repair kit containing patching materials for deck and hull—whether it is fibreglass or fabric—as well as needles, thread, assorted stainless steel bolts, nuts and clamps, aluminum or brass rivets and screws of various sizes. Tools will vary according to the construction of your boat but might include long-nosed pliers, a bradawl, screwdriver, small hacksaw, sailmaker's palm, whetstone and spare fittings, and a waterproof zipper suitable for the spray skirt together with some neoprene cement or waterproof glue. A few metres of copper wire and some tough monofilament stainless steel wire are also handy, and enough braided stainless steel wire to replace both rudder cables. Most useful of all is a roll of duct tape or divers' airhose tape, which is capable of holding the whole show together (and frequently does). The repair kit should be stored, of course, in a waterproof container.

SAFETY EQUIPMENT

The following list includes a good deal of safety equipment. To carry it all would be ludicrous, but each article has its use. You should assess the

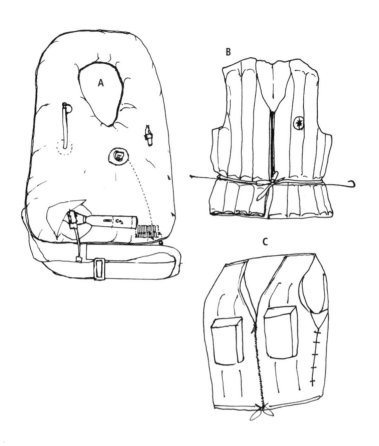

(A) The inflatable Mae West jacket, and (B) PFD (Personal Flotation Device).
Comfortable models of the latter are no longer hard to find
and frequently come with useful pockets (C).

problems you are likely to encounter and take what you are most likely
to need, bearing in mind that adequate buoyancy for your boat, a Personal Flotation Device for yourself, a bailing device and a spare paddle
are standard fare for sea kayak safety, along with coast guard–required
light and signalling devices.

Life Jacket or Personal Flotation Device (PFD)
A nonswimmer would be foolish to go kayaking without a life jacket,
but those who go down to the sea in kayaks should know how to swim.
The chief value of a life jacket is that it makes swimming unnecessary,

allowing the person to stay hunched in the HELP position (heat escape lessening position) and so almost double survival time in cold water.

Of the many life jackets and buoyancy aids on the market, I prefer the old Mae West variety, as used on commercial aircraft, or the diver's buoyancy aid. Whether stowed or worn, these can be kept totally deflated and out of the way until needed, and then inflated instantly by CO_2 cartridge or more slowly by mouth. Deflated, they are comfortable to paddle in and they fold away into a compact parcel about the size of a lunch box. At long last these vests have been approved by the U.S. Coast Guard, so you no longer need to carry a bulky padded one to appease the authorities. Better than that, several manufacturers, anticipating the obvious, have come out with a line of clothing that incorporates the inflatable feature into otherwise normal outdoor clothing.

Although bulkier and generally less comfortable than deflatable vests, regular padded life vests do offer a measure of protection against weather and cold water. At the same time, many of the traditional roles of the life jacket are performed more efficiently by a wet suit or dry suit, and these provide increased protection against the real killer, which is hypothermia. A deflatable life jacket can be worn handily in conjunction with such suits, and you can swim efficiently by deflating it, or rest when you please by giving it some air. The deflatable jacket's disadvantages are that it requires careful handling to avoid punctures and it is useless if you are struck unconscious before reaching your CO_2 charge—as might happen in surf. Standard PFDs, being more prevalent, are more economical, and good comfortable designs are now easier to find. Although some models feature sewn-on pockets, enabling the wearer to carry emergency items, such PFDs may not carry coast guard approval. Sewing tabs or pockets onto an approved life jacket may void approval.

Freon "Air" Horns

When I was in the business of selling marine survival equipment, an irate customer returned one of the popular models of "air" horn with the complaint that when he needed it to attract the attention of a passing yacht after capsizing his kayak, the horn, after an initial optimistic squeak, decreased to a wheeze and a sigh. Surprised, I pressed the button and nearly deafened us both. The customer was adamant. We took it down to the water for more tests and found that when it was wet, the expanding gas quickly iced up the jet, choking off the sound. This may be less of a problem in hot weather, but I wouldn't bet on it. Stick with a pea-less whistle attached to your PFD.

Pumps & Bailers

Ideally, a sea kayak needs two bilge pumps: a foot-operated, low-volume pump and a hand-operated, higher-capacity pump. Each pump has its own function.

The foot pump (mostly needed only on folding kayaks, since they have a tendency to leak slightly at the stitched seams) with a capacity of about 4 litres (1 gallon) per minute, should be mounted so that its intake is at the lowest point of the boat. Its purpose is to keep pace with the seepage from waves washing over the boat or from small leaks in the hull. The foot pump comes into its own during rough conditions when you are frequently taking seas over the deck or when for some other reason it is unsafe to pause and bail—for example, when there is a strong wind onto a lee shore or when you are in a difficult head wind. Without the foot pump, your boat fills gradually and becomes less stable. You must bail, yet you cannot afford to stop paddling. You do not have to be on a thousand-mile journey to find yourself in this situation; you can encounter such conditions on many a day trip.

With a capacity of 38 to 45 litres (10 to 12 gallons) per minute, the hand pump is your pump for emergencies. It can be used to drain off routine seepage, but you must stop paddling to do so. Depending on the model, it can be operated through the unzipped spray skirt, mounted semipermanently through the deck behind the rear cockpit or stored inside and then taken out and attached to a permanently placed hose with an outlet beside the cockpit. The main emergency use for this pump is to drain the kayak after a flooding.

Other bailing devices may include your toilet-pot, which we trust will have a generous capacity and can help if you capsize in calm waters, while a sponge will afford you the luxury of reaching the last drops. Hand pumping a narrow kayak after a capsize presents some practical balance problems, since it requires the use of the hands both for pumping and balancing. Tricks such as using the pump with one hand while bracing with the paddle across your shoulder and down the other arm cannot be relied on in rough conditions. Emergency sponsons deployed early in the emergency make far more sense. Tasmanian kayakers have been using battery-operated bilge pumps since the mid-eighties and claim to be able to empty a flooded kayak in a matter of minutes, but these devices have not caught on with the average North American paddler. The great beauty of such a system is that the boat is emptied rapidly at the flick of a switch while the paddler has both hands free to brace until stability is regained.

Flares, Lights & Reflectors

Each boat should carry its own set of flares. Ideally, this would include several twin star pocket flares with independent launchers, which may be used as a follow-up to a distress rocket. A couple of large parachute flares such as the Schermuly rockets should be your means of initial contact. The available range includes a very effective maroon star signal flare and flares with radar reflective payloads.

The more flares you carry the better, within reason, but the minimum for a trip on which there is a chance that they will be needed is two parachute flares handy and attached to the boat and three pocket flares on your person. I suggest that you plan on three per person, though many people would consider this excessive—until they needed them. One smoke flare per boat and a strobe light for night location is also very reasonable. The solo paddler would do well to have all these backups.

The routine I recommend for an emergency, such as a capsize in cold water where there is a chance you may not be able to complete a self-rescue in a few minutes, is to fire off your biggest flare right away. When you confirm in your own mind that you are indeed in trouble—and before you begin to feel too cold—fire off the second rocket. These big flares can be seen from as far as 10 or 15 miles, and it could take as long as an hour for someone who has seen it to reach you, so don't despair and don't go firing off your pocket flares unless you can see the rescue boat. The pocket flares are to attract the attention of a rescuer who is fairly close. Such flares do not have a very high visibility, since they are in the air only briefly and attain an altitude of no more than 150 metres (500 feet). (The big rockets can reach over 450 metres [1500 feet] and stay aloft some forty seconds.)

When choosing pocket flares, avoid the miniflare packs that have a single launcher and a row of cartridges with screw-in heads. Although these appear to give a greater bang for the buck, they are too fiddly to operate with cold hands, and once you have fumbled and dropped the launcher, you can't do much with the shells. To a lesser extent, the same can be said for the Very Pistol. If you must use this type of flare gun, tie everything together and then to the boat or your person.

For pinpointing your position once the search has been called, you can also use a smoke flare, a strobe or, for an aerial search, marker dye for the water. On sunny days a mirror to attract the attention of distant aircraft and boats can be very effective.

A waterproof flashlight is another handy aid—useful for alerting motorboats to your presence, invaluable for night landings and a coast guard requirement for night paddling. The best I have found is the plastic two-cell diver's light with the screw-on hood. On especially dangerous coasts I sometimes carry an additional, more powerful eight-cell light with the switch taped in the "off" position. Another useful light source is the glow stick—a flexible plastic tube containing chemicals and a glass vial. The contents are mixed by bending the tube to break the vial and shaking. The chemical reaction produces a green light, which will last eight hours in temperate climates (more in the tropics and less in the Arctic). Glow sticks provide enough light to make one kayak visible to another almost a mile away, and they enable you to read charts and compass without difficulty. They are not affected by water and produce no heat.

While travelling at night, you can improve your chance of being seen with a radar reflector. This can be conveniently displayed aloft on a fishing rod. It is easy to make a multifaceted diamond-shaped reflector that folds away flat for storage. Its value is limited on the open ocean, since ships will be on the wide range of their radar, but in foggy channels, such as those on the British Columbia coast, fishing boats will more readily detect you with such a device.

Checklist of Additional Safety Equipment
- Transistor radio, for weather forecasts
- A cellular phone or VHF radio, for kayak-to-kayak communication and emergency contact with ships or shore
- Tow-line, rigged and ready for deployment
- EPIRB (Emergercy Position Indicating Radio Beacon)

- Air mattress, emergency sponsons or paddle float as a life-saving device and for additional flotation during pump and re-entry
- Helmet, for dangerous surf
- Solar still or desalinator, especially for tropical voyages
- Dry suit or wet suit, in temperate and cold climates (fins and a mask with snorkel might prove more useful in the tropics)
- Drogue or sea-chute, sea anchor

Radios

A hand-held VHF (Very High Frequency) radio can provide communications to help cope with a wide range of emergency situations. In addition, it can be used for weather reports and telephoning out from coastal wilderness regions, to reassure anxious family members and to prevent unnecessary searches. The radios, which range in strength from one to five watts, have line-of-sight capacity, which usually translates into 10 to 30 miles, depending on the heights of the transmitting and receiving points. They are vulnerable to blind spots caused by mountains and are normally only available in marine band frequencies.

Licences are required for their operation in Canada and the United States, but the requirements are simple and not expensive. To date, several lives have been saved by the timely use of VHF radios carried by kayakers. Almost the entire North American coast is covered by a network of relay stations positioned on prominent mountaintops. I once received a telephone call from a kayaker cruising off the remote Brooks Peninsula. He was a couple of miles offshore with 2.5-metre (8-foot) sea running. His signal was picked up by a telephone relay station and connected to the international network. Another source of contacts is the plethora of commercial and pleasure craft that cruise the coast tuned to channel 16, the international standby and contact channel. These vessels can be requested to relay messages on their more powerful radios.

Aside from its emergency value, a major reason for carrying VHF radios is for contact between members of the group. If yours is a fairly large party, the first and last boats can be used to hold the group together. (A lower frequency and less expensive CB [Citizen's Band] radio could be used for communication within the group, but CB radios are far more vulnerable to splash damage.) Also, most of the North American coast is served by a marine weather service that transmits constant weather information invaluable for route planning. This service can only be picked up using VHF, and only the VHF frequencies are continuously monitored by coast guard and other vessels.

EPIRBs

Emergency Position Indicating Radio Beacons, or EPIRBs, are strictly emergency signal beacons that can be either manually or automatically activated when a rescue is called for. There are three classes of EPIRBs: A, B and C. A and B transmit on both 121.5 MHz and 243 MHz, which are monitored by air traffic control as well as the coast guard and the military. C transmits on VHR channel 16 and then switches to channel 15 for a homing beacon. (It is a relatively weak signal that shuts down automatically after twenty-four hours.)

A and B are monitored not only by passing aircraft, but also by the SARSAT system (satellite navigation system), which monitors the waters off North American and European shores and can identify your position to within 5 miles. It requires at least two passes of a satellite to fix your position, resulting in a response time of up to three hours, but improvements are imminent.

An EPIRB is a neat trick to carry in your grab bag of backups. Unfortunately, EPIRBs are technically illegal for inshore use, and though they are very effective, the coast guard is resisting their more general use because of the ease with which they can be accidentally turned on, thus initiating an unnecessary and expensive search. The kayakers of my acquaintance who carry EPIRBs do so on the understanding that they would happily pay a fine for carrying an illegal EPIRB if it saved their lives. Some kayak outfitters even rent out EPIRBs for about twenty dollars a week.

One of the more dramatic rescues to be initiated by an EPIRB took place off the Oregon coast in the mid-1980s when the marathon kayaking team of Steve Landick and Verlen Kruger ran into trouble. (Verlen capsized, and his boat was blown away by the wind.) Steve turned on his EPIRB and then began assisting his companion to shore. In about twenty minutes the coast guard helicopter was upon them, and Verlen was whisked away to hospital. There have been other successful rescues from remote areas from the Aleutians to the Baja—and a number of instances where, because the emergency occurred in a relatively popu-

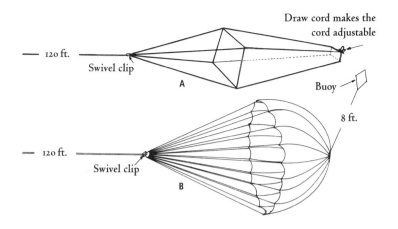

(A) A drogue, and (B) a sea-chute. The mouth of the drogue should be about 46 to 60 centimetres (18 to 24 inches) across, whereas the diameter of the sea-chute might be 1 to 1.5 metres (4 or 5 feet).

lated area, nobody bothered to respond to the signal, believing it was yet another false alarm. Cellular phones may also be considered for urban paddlers.

Drogue, Sea-Chute & Anchor
A drogue (sea anchor) is a necessary item on any journey with open sea to leeward; this includes interisland passages and coastal kayaking with prevailing offshore winds. Its most likely function is to reduce wind drift at sea, though it may be used to stabilize entry through surf. Steve Dutton, who paddled the West Coast of the United States in 1993, reported great success using 13 metres (42 feet) of line between his boat and the drogue, though I imagine the length would vary according to the wave length of the day. He also successfully crossed the surf line with two boats in series, separated by a similar length of nylon cord.

The drogue should be ready for instant use, the end attached to a strong point on the boat. It can then be led through a loop at the bow and back to the deck, where it is folded and held in place by shock cord or stored in its own rapid deployment sleeve on the foredeck, as is the case for the DriftStopper, a fine commercially available sea-chute. The drogue is attached to the boat by approximately 37 metres (120 feet) of

43

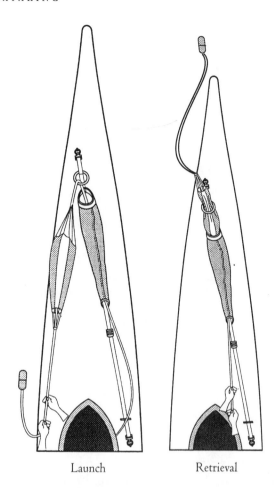

Launch   Retrieval

The DriftStopper drogue for reducing wind drift.

nylon parachute cord, which, when not in use, is carefully coiled and tied to prevent tangles and then tucked inside the folded canopy.

The best material for standard sea anchors seems to be heavy-duty ripstop nylon or similar fabric that is lightweight and will resist rot if it is stored damp. For a loaded double, an effective size is 90 centimetres (36 inches) long with an entrance of 50 centimetres (20 inches) square and an apex aperture of about 10 centimetres (4 inches) square. A swivel at the junction of the line and the drogue traces will reduce the tendency to tangle. Most drogues designed for yachts have a trip line attached to their apex, but a trip line is not necessary with a kayak. If the drogue becomes too heavy to retrieve, you need only paddle a little to ease the tension on the line.

A sea-chute is a larger alternative to the sea anchor and is built exactly like a regular parachute. It is more effective at stopping wind drift, and indeed it can be so effective as to cause considerable stress in a big sea. With a large sea-chute set at sea, it is important to have a full length of nylon cable so that there is plenty of stretch to absorb the shock. It is also advisable to attach a float to the crown of the chute by a 3-metre (10-foot) line. This device prevents the chute from sinking too deeply and holding you down into a wave. A short-term alternative to a specialized sea-chute is a parafoil with a restraining float. Using a parafoil in water can be very effective but may eventually harm the parafoil.

A bottom anchor is hardly standard equipment for most kayaks, but it can be useful if you need to sleep in your boat near shore—either because you are unable to land or because for some reason the land is inhospitable. A small Danforth or Bruce anchor with about 4.5 metres (15 feet) of chain is suitable. It can be attached to the already rigged sea anchor warp. The anchor also comes in handy if you plan to fish or dive from the kayak. George Dyson frequently anchors his big baidarkas offshore to avoid the hassle of dragging them out of the way of the tide or to avoid the mosquitoes and blackflies ashore.

CLOTHING

Paddling generates heat, and even in cold climates it usually pays to dress lightly so long as the spray skirt is in place and you are wearing a windproof, waterproof outer garment. The inside layers can be a combination of light underclothing of either polypropylene or wool and a

Matt Wallis/Kokatat

This full dry suit has waterproof seals at neck and cuffs.

light pile or woollen jersey. Rubber boots are convenient but should be removed for all-day paddles to discourage the formation of mushrooms inside. (Regular dustings with antifungal powder will work wonders on these.) On coastal trips that call for frequent exiting through breaking beach waves, wet suit booties with hard soles may be a practical option to reduce the trauma of getting your feet wet. If you stop paddling long enough to cool off, have something warm at hand to put on. You will need additional clothing as soon as you get ashore, when the closed kayak is no longer insulating you against the cold.

Where there is a likelihood of capsizing (and many people argue that the possibility is always present, and therefore you should always dress for a swim), consider wearing a wet suit or dry suit as opposed to an anorak and legging combination. The most popular style of wet suits are the Farmer Johns (or Farmer Janes). These are tightly fitting overall-style 3-millimetre (⅛-inch) neoprene trousers with a bib and high back that offer one-piece thermal protection to trunk, crotch and legs. The upper part may be folded down to the waist for summer paddling. A wet suit functions by holding in a thin layer of water, which is quickly warmed by the body and insulated from the sea by the layer of foam rubber. Wet suits are not ideal for trips involving six hours of paddling day after day, since they become pretty ripe in a short time. Another point to consider is the necessity to relieve oneself; it can be a tricky business to remove a wet suit if there is a sea running and no place to hop ashore.

A 3-millimetre (⅛-inch) Farmer John can be expected to add thirty to forty-five minutes to your functional survival time swimming in cool, temperate waters. A neoprene jacket with hood and long sleeves can probably almost double this time, but it is not practical to paddle in and is usually only kept as a backup to be pulled on in the water. *Note*: In cold water conditions, you will find it almost impossible to put on the wet suit while swimming, and the importance of anticipating the areas of likely capsize can hardly be overstressed.

The dry suit is a loose-fitting vinyl one- or two-piece suit with latex waterproof seals at all openings and, in one-piece suits, a heavy-duty waterproof zipper across the chest or back. The thermal protection of a dry suit depends on the clothing worn underneath, and therein lies the problem: to be really effective in 10°C (50°F) water, it will probably require more clothing than you normally feel like paddling in. A dry suit is, however, considerably more comfortable than a wet suit and is probably best thought of as a garment that increases your functional self-rescue time in the water even without the full complement of clothing underneath and one that improves your comfort on rainy days ashore.

A modification of the dry suit is the semi–dry suit made of waterproof nylon with adjustable neoprene cuffs and neck seal. Like the dry suit, the semi–dry suit depends on the underclothing layer for warmth. It is, however, not entirely watertight and will admit a certain amount of water through the cuffs and chest zipper when worn in the water. Its effectiveness depends on restricting the flushing through of the precious body-heated water, and it is less efficient at this than either the wet suit or the dry suit.

The paddling jacket is popular among today's sea kayakers and is often worn in combination with a Farmer John. It consists of a waterproofed nylon windbreaker with cuffs and neck seals that can be closed against the water. It usually comes fitted with a large kangaroo pouch for carrying personal flares and other useful items, such as waterproof matches, a compass, or a knife. More elaborate versions have detachable hoods as well as underarm vents to minimize the condensation that inevitably occurs. (I have yet to find a breathable fabric that is reliably effective in the sea. Most become clogged with salt and grime and lose their waterproof quality within a couple of weeks of coastal use.)

Layers of synthetic pile underclothing are popular for cold weather trips, but where there is a lot of rain or the waves are giving a wet ride on long trips, I revert to wool. On a six-month trip in Patagonia, which lasted through midwinter, I finally abandoned my nylon pile underclothing in favour of locally purchased woollen long johns and pullover.

One of the joys of warm water kayaking is warm hands. In cold climates you will need pogies or gloves. Pogies are gauntlet mittens designed to cover the closed fists rather than the open hands. They are constructed with a small opening at either side of the fist and a sealable flap across the knuckles so that you can run the paddle shaft in one side and out the other. Pogies will protect your hands while giving you a satisfying barehand grip on the paddle. Many varieties are now available, in either neoprene or nylon, lined or unlined. A neoprene mitten with the palm cut out is also available.

For cold rain and sleet, ordinary leather workman's gloves are usually adequate, and the wet leather gives a good grip on the paddle shaft. I have experimented with silk inner and rubber outer gloves, neoprene gloves and woollen ones, Millermitts (fingertips cut out) and fancy driving gloves, but simple leather work gloves still seem to be the most practical.

Some kayakers also like to wear spats. These are neoprene tubes that seal the cuffs of your anorak. They make short trips more comfortable but tend to encourage saltwater rashes on longer trips. I have several times started a trip with them only to discard them later and allow the water to flow in and out of my anorak sleeves. Spats are redundant, of course, with dry suits and are already sewn onto paddling jackets.

This semi–dry suit splits at the waist.

In the tropics, clothing is mostly for protection from the sun, which for the unprepared can be as deadly as the cold of a northern winter. Cotton is preferable to synthetics for the very reason that it is a poor choice in cool climes, namely, that it holds water, is slow to dry and offers little thermal protection when wet. Clothing should be rinsed daily in fresh water if possible to remove accumulated salt. If you are one of those daredevil souls who can look death by skin cancer in the eye, you may get by with just a swimsuit during the day; but keep a long-sleeved shirt close at hand for when the sun gets too fierce. A wide-brimmed hat is important no matter how well thatched you might be, and a bandana that can be pulled over the nose and mouth will protect those vulnerable parts. A waterproof anorak and light woollen jersey or comfortable shortie wet suit should be kept handy for rainy or windy night crossings. You may be surprised how cold such a night can be once you have become acclimatized to the tropics.

If you expect to encounter difficult surf, you may want a protective helmet.

LOADING A KAYAK

Normally volume, not weight, is the limiting factor when loading a touring kayak. Although the manufacturer may claim that a boat will carry 115 kilograms (250 pounds), the volume of items such as tents, wet suit, food, clothing and sleeping bag may reduce the effective load to as little as 45 to 70 kilograms (100 to 150 pounds) in a small kayak. A large double can comfortably carry 115 to 135 kilograms (250 to 300 pounds) of regular expedition equipment.

How a kayak is loaded is largely a matter of personal preference, but there are some general points to bear in mind. The kayak should ride evenly in the water for normal cruising comfort. A bow-heavy boat will plunge into waves and be awkward to steer in a following sea, whereas a seriously stern-heavy one will behave badly in side winds. If you know you are going to be punching into a head wind all day, however, it is to your advantage to make the boat light on the bow so that it will rise easily to the waves. Load the objects you will require least frequently in the extremities of the boat, and leave those required at sea or during a lunch stop to be packed last. Everything, both inside and outside, that is not stashed away in bags should be lashed to the boat. A caution here: a kayaker who recently capsized on an extended trip discovered that his boat could not be flipped upright because of the weight of the gear hanging from various strings beneath it, including an anchor! Apart from the high risk of entanglement, the system failed because all the gear had to be cut away before the boat could be successfully righted.

Spare spray skirts, fittings and emergency food supplies should be pushed as far forward as they will go. With boats that don't have hatches, you may want to tie a trailing cord around the neck of these bags so that they can be withdrawn without your having to crawl inside the hull. Heavy objects such as canned food and water containers should be stored along the keel of the boat, amidships, and some heavy object such as a diver's weight belt should be kept until last for the final trim. Heavy objects in a partially loaded boat should be secured so that they will not shift if you lean or attempt to roll the kayak.

The Deck Cargo

A well-loaded sea kayak carries the absolute minimum on deck. Nothing that is not firmly tied down should be there unless you can afford to

Nautiraid

Loading kayaks can be an art form, particularly for the military.

lose it. Some people like the deck crisscrossed with nylon webbing and shock cord. Convenient as it may be, though, elastic shock cord is not reliable enough for permanent attachment in rough water, and you will eventually lose equipment stored under it.

It is my opinion that the only objects on deck during a kayak journey should be spare paddles (in secure holders); a drogue, fully rigged and stored beneath a map case, which is made fast by means of small cleats at all four corners; and a kangaroo pouch (easily glued to the spray cover) for miniflares, sunglasses, sweets and the like. Perhaps the only object loosely held by shock cord could be a canvas sack to hold fish caught during the day.

A seagoing kayak should have secure loops at either end to which are attached 3-metre (10-foot) bow and stern painters. (The bow line could serve as a paddle leash.) These painters are normally tied off to cleats on each side of the cockpit(s). A variety of additional sturdy cleats can take the shroud, stays and sheets of a sail rig. When paddling open water or lee shores, I rig a drogue or regular anchor ready for immediate deployment.

Don't carry your water bottle on deck. It is far too valuable to risk losing, and besides, it would heat up in the sun. Rocket flares and flashlight are best stored close inside where they cannot be carried away by a wave or knocked off by another kayak when you are rafted up and where they will stand a better chance of staying dry.

The afterdeck is a tempting place to deposit your treasures, since it is the area least swept by the sea, but it is also the place where you are least likely to notice equipment breaking free. You can even carry rucksacks on the afterdeck of some kayaks, at the price of stability, but this practice is not advisable during rough or windy conditions and certainly not on open water.

If you plan to rely on a paddle float for self-rescue, you will also require rope or webbing paddle holds to secure your outrigging paddle. For Sea Wing sponsons (see "The Sea Wing Self-Rescue," page 93) you will need to have the appropriate deck fittings in place.

Carrying a Loaded Kayak

Frequently you will have to move a loaded kayak up or down the beach, a hazard for both boat and self. A loaded double often weighs as much as 180 kilograms (400 pounds). Dragging that much weight can damage the hull, and having to push and pull such a heavy load up the beach could strain your back, even if you slide the kayak on seaweed or roll it on small logs.

If you have four people in your party, the best way to carry a loaded boat is to have two people on each side support its weight on two straps made from nylon webbing slung about 1 metre (3 feet) in from the bow and stern. These straps may be as short as 1.2 metres (4 feet), with toggles for the hands or long belts that run over the shoulder and are held in the offside hand. In either case they enable you to carry the boat more safely, as your powerful leg muscles do the heavy lifting.

One person at each end is much less desirable but often necessary because companions are not handy to help you or because the surf is too hazardous to leave one boat in it while lugging the other. This method of carrying is probably responsible for more injuries to muscles and discs than anything else on a kayak journey. It can also put great stress

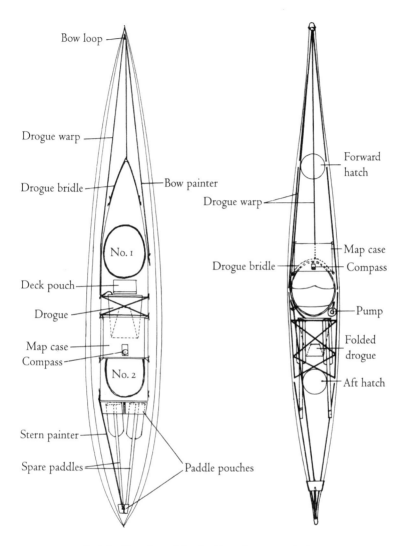

Deck loading of a cruising double and a narrow single.

on a boat, not to mention relationships. If possible, remove the heaviest gear from amidships before lifting. Good-sized hand toggles at bow and stern will make your carry more comfortable.

One person, or two people with a strop, can also move a heavily loaded kayak up the beach by taking one end of the boat and walking it around 180 degrees and then returning to do the same with the other end. As soon as your boat touches the beach, you can begin this process by lifting the bow and floating the stern up the beach on a wave. To reduce damage to the pivot point, slip a piece of board or an inverted skillet underneath and let the boat turn on that. Remove or cock the rudder to avoid damage.

A set of wheels that can be taken apart for stowage inside the boat is a very useful item for carrying a kayak on and off ferries.

KAYAK MAINTENANCE

The amount of time you spend on kayak maintenance will depend on what type of kayak you have. As already mentioned, folding kayaks require the most attention, whereas a rudderless plastic or fibreglass kayak requires the least.

UV the Destroyer

Probably the most destructive element for a plastic or fibreglass kayak is direct sunlight. Ultraviolet rays alter the composition of the hull material so that it becomes brittle and eventually weakened. The process will likely take six to twelve years (we don't really know with modern plastics, since they have yet to stand the test of time), depending on the strength of the sunlight, and the composition of the hull material and protective layers such as gelcoat or UV screen waxes.

Ultraviolet rays can be even more destructive to soft skin boats. I have seen folding kayak decks that were literally falling apart after less than a year's exposure to tropical sunshine and salt water.

To protect your kayak from the ravages of ultraviolet light, store it carefully in the shade when not in use and polish fibreglass kayaks with an ultraviolet-inhibiting wax. I know of no way to protect canvas from ultraviolet rays, though some of the new fabrics found on modern folding boats have improved UV resistance.

Water the Infiltrator

Plastic and fibreglass boats are mostly immune to damage from water, but folding boats and lath and canvas kayaks are another matter. Water soaks in through any small scratch in the varnish and may travel inches on either side. Fungus soon follows, and in no time greyish stains mar the golden hues of the ash and birch. Water left on the skin of canvas boats is a breeding ground for fungus and rot, which can destroy a skin in weeks. Certain death for a folding kayak is to leave it upside down on the lawn over winter or to store it outside so that autumn leaves lie wetly on its shaded surface.

When you have finished using your folding kayak, dry the skin on the frame (to avoid any chance of shrinkage), dust down the inside with French chalk and then store it in a cool, dry place such as the attic of your house or in a cupboard. If there are rats or mice around, store the skin in a mouseproof box, since the little bleeders sometimes develop an expensive taste for synthetic rubber. The frame should be inspected at the beginning of each season for signs of water seepage, and every few years the old varnish should be sanded off and new coats applied.

Salt the Consumer

Salt corrodes and consumes your metal fittings. Aluminum-framed folding kayaks can seize up in a matter of months if left assembled in tropical waters. You can almost watch the little cauliflowers sprouting out of the affected joints. Dismantle the boat every month or so and wipe the metal-to-metal joints with an oily rag. On one trip I had to replace all the aluminum rivets on the frame of an Aerius 20 after only four months of kayaking in the tropics. Foot pedals and rudders need constant attention to prevent them from their seizing up. Combining metals distantly spaced on the electrolytic scale results in sometimes spectacular electrolysis as one metal consumes another. Sacrificial zinc anodes in the bilge might be a consideration if you are doing a long tropical trip with an aluminum-framed boat.

Heat the Exacerbater

All of the above destruction becomes a more serious problem as the temperature increases. Decay and corrosion are much slower in the Arctic. With heat, electrolysis speeds up: fungus grows on everything that sits still and lots of things that don't; metals ulcerate in a matter of weeks. Prevention requires that you treat your folding boat with fungicides, wash it down with fresh water and let it dry off as often as possible in a well-aerated shady space. Plastic and fibreglass kayaks only really need an occasional rinse out with water and diluted fungicide and some WD-40 on moving parts such as the rudder and rudder controls.

Checking for Leaks

Leaks can be difficult to find, particularly in fibreglass kayaks. Begin by checking the hull for small impact fractures. These can appear as soft spots in the gelcoat or a spider web of small cracks. No hole may be visible, but under pressure, water will find its way through. This type of leak can be repaired with a small fibreglass patch on either side of the fracture.

If no fracture is found in the hull, check the following possibilities:

1 Seams—Kayaks with plastic extruded seams between the deck and hull are difficult to build without leaks. To locate leaks, run a hose around the seam and watch to see where the water comes through. If that does not work, you may have to fill the kayak with water. (Support it well first.) Mark the spots and then patch them on the inside.

2 End plugs—This is a solid area at each end of the kayak designed to strengthen the tips and provide a solid anchor point for rudders, bow loops, and so on. The plug is formed by pouring a mixture of fibreglass resin and micro-balloons into the end of the vertical kayak. Sometimes the plug cracks as it cools, and when holes are drilled into it, water can seep in through the hair cracks in the plug. This problem can be fixed by making a second pour of a small quantity of resin.

3 The coaming—The coaming is usually attached to the deck of the kayak with an epoxy putty. Sometimes the putty cracks, falls out or was never put in properly. A hose squirted up under the lip of the coaming will reveal any leaks, and fresh putty can then be applied without having to remove the whole coaming.

4 Bulkheads—To check the bulkheads, fill the midsection of the kayak with water and mark any leaks with a felt pen. Repairs are made with either fibreglass patching strips or Sikaflex caulking compound applied to both sides of the bulkhead.

Note: With all the above repairs, the kayak surfaces must first be dried carefully.

Storing for Winter

After your folding boat is dried, powdered and tucked away under your bed, store your plastic boat right side up on a flat surface with small wedges under the bow and stern to maintain the rocker. Don't put it on two sawhorses for three months or you may find that you have some permanent grooves across your hull in the spring, particularly if you are storing the boat in a heated room. Storing outside is not good for any self-respecting kayak either, particularly in snow country. I know of some rather sad-looking kayaks dug out from under a pile of wet snow that fell from the roof of a house that was supposed to be offering protection.

Car Topping

For most of us, the roof of our automobile is going to be the riskiest place we are likely to place our kayak. The potential for total destruction of the boat is considerable; for example, you have the overhang—frequently not visible in the rear view mirror. You back up in order to extricate your vehicle from a parking space and drive the stern of your kayak into the brick wall of the supermarket. If you drive a small car and paddle a large double, it is probable that sooner or later you will impale a Winnebago at a traffic light. I have personally broken a kayak from whiplash when I drove over a curb, not realizing that an inch of rain had accumulated in the bilges overnight.

But perhaps the most spectacular way to do in your kayak is to leave the bowline trailing so that the front wheel of your car drives over it. Even at modest speed, the effect is devastating.

As a final possibility, consider the brace of kayaks that you notice floating alongside you on the freeway. These boats, which originated on your roof, are floating free because your bargain roof rack has chosen this moment to release its grip on the gutters of your car. Combining an overload problem with a failure to secure the boats fore and aft or a reliance on rubber bungies is definitely something to avoid.

Paul Caffyn riding in on a wave on the coast of New Zealand.

CHAPTER TWO

TECHNIQUE

PADDLING

The key to paddling a sea kayak is to develop a relatively effortless stroke. This will not be possible against strong head winds, but for most other situations, the ideal stroke eases up on the power as the boat reaches its optimum cruising speed, usually between 2½ and 3 knots. Depending on the paddle used, this stroke is usually a moderately wide, balanced push and pull, with the paddle shaft held about 45 degrees to the horizon, lower in strong wind. The hands are normally held about shoulder width, widening when you want to "change down a gear." They grip the paddle lightly, with the upper hand opening slightly on each push, applying just enough grip to control the angle of the blade with the lower, pulling hand. The wrist of the pushing hand is kept straight to minimize the risk of an overuse injury. For cruising, most of the effort is from the waist up, using a combination of body rotation and arm push and pull. The back is braced lightly against the backrest, knees wedged in firmly beneath the deck, and the feet are braced against the footrest, pointing slightly forward. The legs and feet are important both for balance and as the roots of power for the stroke. In narrower kayaks, the wide bracing of the knees and thighs is more critical than in large, stable kayaks, but in both, flopping about inside the boat decreases efficiency.

You may get some radically different advice on paddle technique, depending on who you learn from. Several schools now teach flat-water "box" or "rotation" racing strokes to sea kayakers, in which you keep the elbows straight as your body rotates. Although this technique is undoubtedly efficient for lightweight racing boats, using wing paddles, it is not the best stroke for a heavily loaded touring boat over a long day. Chances are that even the instructor who teaches such a stroke will revert to a less contrived style after a few hours of that silliness.

The method I suggest is to reach forward an easy distance with the paddle so that it enters the water at no more than blade depth. By pointing forward slightly with the shoulder, you insert the right amount of rotation into the stroke. Maximum power is exerted during the middle third of the stroke, sweeping the blade out slightly (as demanded by the length of the paddles if they are not to go too deep). This outward sweep will give increased stability. Begin to withdraw as soon as the blade enters the final third of its stroke by simply reaching into the next stroke with the opposite paddle blade. Do not apply power during this last third of the stroke, since it wastes energy by lifting water. The leading arm should punch steadily forward—elbow not quite straight—levering the blade through the water against the pull of the other arm. The fingers of the upper hand should be relaxed and open, the fleshy part of the thumb and palm pushing against the shaft of the paddle, wrist straight. On long trips, avoid paddling with unnecessary force. Remember, you are seeking the optimum stroke, which is the one that expends the least amount of energy for the cruising speed of your boat. In doubles, seek a harmonic rhythm with your partner and the condition of the sea, and try not to succumb to the temptation to race the boat alongside you.

In a group, your travel speed is going to depend on how everyone is feeling as well as on the prevailing conditions. During the day, your energy will ebb and flow. Sometimes, for no apparent reason, you will feel like going for it; other times, you will barely be able to push one paddle ahead of the other and you'll wonder why you didn't take up sailing instead. Ride high on the good times by all means, but take care not to burn yourself out by overdoing it. Plodding on with leaden paddles becomes somewhat easier too with the knowledge that the next stage is bound to be a good one.

A good trick to try near the end of a long day is to imagine that you now have to turn around and paddle all the way back again. (It's great to realize you don't have to.) Frequently, your energy will evaporate as soon as you make a landfall, and until experience has taught you better, you will be quite convinced that you are incapable of paddling another mile. But if you had to paddle back, your energy would last. You really have a choice: to let go or to hang on to that energy. The more you hang on to it, the more amazed you will be by the apparently infinite amount at your disposal.

Alone on the sea, your paddle rating (cadence) will be as variable as the conditions and your mood. In a head wind, it will be long and slow, sometimes under thirty strokes per minute, and you will apply power nearly all the way. With a fresh following breeze, you will be doing over sixty, using a chopping, shorter stroke, and your boat will race along. Your seating position too will vary—first forward and then back, on one cheek and then the other—anything for a change.

With wind and waves abeam, lower your stroke and lean into the wind slightly. The resulting wider sweep stroke on the leeward side will alter the rating slightly. These adjustments will occur automatically as you get used to the conditions. If the waves are big and breaking, you can acquire a great deal of stability by accentuating the regular paddle stroke in the breaking crest, and this technique may alter your rating as you hang back or jump your stroke to anticipate the whitecap.

Variations in the rating may also occur when you are running with a good following sea. The waves will alternately push your boat with the crests and then drag heavily at it in the troughs. This speeding up and slowing down can be exhausting, particularly if you dissipate your effort by paddling hard on the upward movement of the wave. Surfing these waves is good fun, but unless the waves are just perfect, over distance I have found it is usually best to strive for a steady rhythm.

Chaotic seas, such as those off steep-to lee shores, demand a very rapid rating; you may almost have to sprint through them. Quite likely you'll feel like doing that anyway. You should make your stroke short and quick, providing extra stability in the unpredictable waves. A faster rating leads to faster reactions, readier support strokes and less time spent in unreadable water.

Apart from regular forward and backward strokes, which offer most of the stability a sea kayaker requires, there are variations known as paddle braces, which you would be wise to master.

PADDLE BRACES

Paddle braces are strokes that maintain the balance and control of the kayak. Their importance and relevance increase as the beam of the kayak diminishes and conditions become rougher. They run the gamut from the reflexive slap support for times when you nearly "trip" to the deliberate sculling support stroke. They are valuable skills for all paddlers, particularly those with singles sporting a beam of less than 64 centimetres (25 inches), though even with a beamy double, a sound brace can make the difference between coming through the surf line on top of or alongside your kayak. To be effective, braces must be an automatic reaction to a situation on either side of the kayak, be it the sudden cresting of a breaker or the twist given your kayak from crossing an eddy line. They are the techniques by which you turn the paddler/kayak combination into a seaworthy unit.

Sculling Support Stroke

This stroke (see page 69) provides a constant support for a stationary kayak. It stabilizes the boat for operations such as re-entry. The procedure is to lean the boat slightly to the side on which you intend to gain support, which should be the weather side when conditions are rough. (Leaning downwind increases the chance of capsize.) The paddle is stretched abeam the boat and the blade sculled back and forth on the surface, face down, taking enough weight to give stability. This action is most effective if hands are moved about 45 centimetres (18 inches) back along the shaft towards the airborne blade. This stroke requires plenty of practice so that it won't cut water and send you swimming. It is a useful stroke for emergencies or where an extraordinary amount of stability is required.

Slap Support

As its name suggests, this is a straightforward recovery stroke in which you smack the paddle face (or back) onto the surface to regain lost or threatened balance. It is not used frequently by sea kayakers, but it is a necessary reflex to develop. The only tricky part is to be sure to slap the face, not the edge, of the paddle onto the water; if you have been varying the feathering of your paddles, your reflex slap may not be of much help to you. A more common variant of this stroke is to blend the slap into a regular stroke, thus providing recovery power without breaking rhythm. The paddle blade will return to the surface at an angle, so in fact your slap support will lead easily into a sculling support stroke.

The Floating Paddle Brace

The floating paddle support enhances stability for a move such as rearranging your seat or retrieving a water bottle from inside your cockpit. It is particularly helpful for beginners who find themselves sitting in an unfamiliar or unstable kayak. Simply float the blade of your paddle out on the surface of the water at a right angle to your boat. The shaft at the base of the near blade rests on the coaming, while the control hand, wrist held straight, holds the paddle near the centre of the shaft. This has a stabilizing effect both psychologically and physically. The paddle is well placed to scull gently back and forth or to provide a softly sinking platform if you need sudden support. A most useful feature of the floating brace is that you can remove your hand from the near end of the paddle to perform simple tasks.

The Low Brace

This is a brace suited to gaining support when a small breaking wave catches you suddenly abeam. Thrust the blade (with a spoon-shaped paddle, use the back of the blade) out onto the turbulence while leaning some of your weight onto the shaft, much as an alpinist will gain three-point support by leaning on an ice axe during a glissade. The strongest brace is one using the straight-backed fist pushing downwards onto the paddle shaft close in to the paddler's waist and in the stern quarter. The result is a very stable position so long as the boat is sliding sideways and the paddle blade remains on the surface.

The High Brace

The high brace is better suited to coping with stronger breaking waves such as surf, where, once you are lying abeam the breaking waves, your paddle can be thrust into or onto the turbulent internal hydraulics. It differs from the low brace in two principal ways. First, during a high brace, the face of the blade is the working surface. Second, the paddler's elbows should be held in as close as possible to the body so that the hands hang off the shaft rather than pushing down on it as in a low brace. This second point is critical to executing the brace safely.

This brace has sometimes been shown held high so that the paddler is literally hanging off a paddle held above his or her head. This technique has resulted in a large number of shoulder dislocations. The strongest

Above: **The High Brace. Support is from a downward pull with the power face of the blade. The elbow of the non-bracing side is kept in close to the body and the hand is below eye level.** Below: **In the Low Brace, support is from a downward and forward push with the back of the blade. Wrists are kept straight for strength.**

position to place the paddle is in the forward quarter. Any backward angle on an outstretched arm will increase the risk of dislocation.

A high brace can be incorporated into a normal paddle stroke sim-

Above: **The Sweeping High Brace. Leaning makes turning easier by raising the kayak's bow and stern from the water.** Below: **The Sweeping Low Brace (Reverse Sweep). A steeper blade angle gives more turn, but less support for the lean.**

ply by turning the blade from the vertical to the horizontal position if a wave hits in the midst of a stroke. It can be argued that there are really only two strokes—forward and backward. The forward strokes use the face of the paddle, while the backward strokes use the back of the paddle. Every stroke—and every brace—is some modification of these two basic movements

Greenland Sculling Braces

John Heath, an authority on Inuit kayaking techniques, has brought to light various sculling braces traditionally used by Greenland paddlers. Unlike standard braces, where the purpose is to help the paddler avoid immersion, Greenland sculling braces explore the halfway zone between up and down in a way that leaves the torso largely immersed. There is the Greenland Side Sculling Brace and the Back Sculling Brace. (Another method, the Chest Sculling Brace, has been excluded from this discussion because the bracing position required can only be sustained for very short periods.) I leave the description of the Side Sculling Brace and Back Sculling Brace to John Heath:

> In the Side Sculling Brace, the kayaker lies in the water more or less on his side, with the paddle at right angles to the axis of the kayak. The torso is twisted slightly with the upper shoulder nearest the kayak, and one leans as far aft as one comfortably can, both of which serve to keep body weight near the kayak. The paddle is extended outward from the kayak at right angles, as seen from above, and most of it is under water at an angle to the surface—as seen from either end—of about 30 degrees, although the angle can vary widely. The hands hold the paddle across the chest with both palms facing up against the face of the inboard blade, knuckles facing the paddler. The inboard hand, which will serve as a pivot point for the sculling motion, grips the blade near the inboard end.
>
> Everything said about the Side Sculling Brace applies to the Back Sculling Brace, except for the body and paddle positions. In this brace the shoulders are twisted in line with the theoretical centre line, or axis, of the kayak, and since the paddle is held across the chest, it then extends towards the bow, parallel to the axis, instead of at a right angle to it. The body position also positions the paddle more or less parallel to the surface.
>
> The torso need not be held close to the kayak, because with the shoulders twisted in line with the kayak axis, it is easy to keep

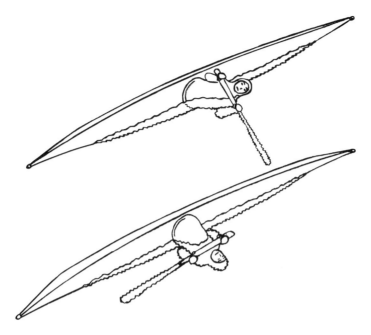

Greenland sculling positions.

most of the upper body except the face, hands and abdomen under water. The buoyancy thus gained enables one to loaf for several minutes using this brace.

MANOEUVRING

An efficient rudder is a great asset to a kayak at sea. As previously discussed, it saves energy by eliminating the need to constantly lean the kayak or break the paddle rhythm for corrective strokes. It also reduces your chances of pulling a muscle through uneven effort. But you should not rely on a rudder for manoeuvring single kayaks. Rudders break, and under certain conditions, such as steep following seas, rudders are lifted clear of the water when you need them most. In these situations, a simple repertoire of strokes will handle 90 per cent of your needs, and you should learn them thoroughly.

Sweep Stroke

To adjust your course to starboard, just ease up on the starboard paddle stroke and sweep a little more widely with the port stroke while tilting

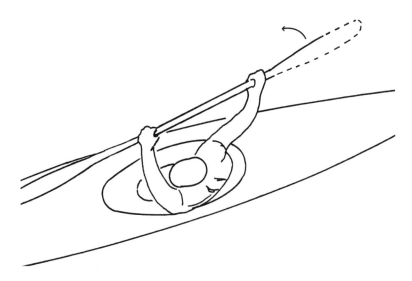

Stern rudder under way—boat turns to starboard.

the boat gently onto the port side, effectively altering the underwater profile so that there is more rocker. To alter course more drastically, skip the starboard stroke altogether and sweep wide to port with the kayak hard over on the port side.

Stern Rudder

This stroke will give you a sharper turn when the boat is gaining momentum on a wave or at the end of a spurt of power paddling. A stern rudder involves reaching back with the paddle so that the back of the blade presses hard at the passing water, pushing the stern of the kayak away from the paddle side. You lose headway with this stroke.

Reverse Sweep

From the stern rudder position, you can further sharpen the turn by leaning out onto the paddle while at the same time pressing down and sweeping the blade out and forward across the surface of the water, easing off power as the paddle enters the forward quarter.

A reverse sweep alternating with a forward sweep on the opposite side will normally turn a single kayak in its own length and is known as pinwheeling.

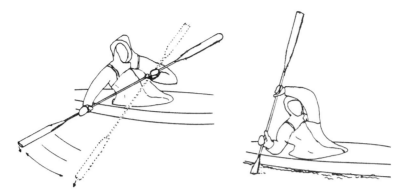

The Sculling Support Stroke (left) **and the Sculling Draw Stroke.**

Cross-Paddle Turn

The turning circle of a double may be tightened by a cross-paddle turn. In order to turn sharply to starboard, for instance, the rudder is held hard over (or lifted out of the water) while the No. 2 paddler leans back into starboard stern rudder position and then executes a reverse sweep. At the same time, the No. 1 paddler does a forward sweep on the port side. This procedure will normally turn a laden double in its own length.

Sculling Draw Stroke

On occasion it is desirable to move a boat sideways. The stroke required resembles the sculling support stroke in many ways, but you bite deeper with the paddle while hanging off the shaft in much the same way as you would during a high brace. Keeping the blade in the water at an angle of about 75 degrees, draw a series of Zs, one on top of the other, and you will draw the boat abeam through the water. This manoeuvre, best suited for doubles, since it does not require coordinating leaning the kayak, is useful to bring one boat alongside another for a lunch stop or a discussion of charts or to pass something across. An indispensable stroke when positioning your boat to assist a swimmer or capsized fellow kayaker, it is also handy for docking.

Draw Stroke

This stroke is particularly useful for singles and may be used in the same situations as the sculling draw stroke as well as at those times when it is necessary to move the kayak sideways slightly as part of your forward motion. In this case it is incorporated at the end of an otherwise normal forward stroke to draw the stern of the kayak around slightly and thus help correct mild weathercocking (the tendency moving kayaks have to turn into the wind). When the kayak is stationary, the regular draw stroke may be used to pull the entire kayak sideways through the water by leaning the kayak and reaching out with the paddle and then drawing the blade towards you. The blade is returned to full reach again by either twisting the blade and slicing out or by lifting it clear of the water and placing it as far out to the side as you can comfortably reach.

TURNING IN WIND

Turning a kayak in strong wind can be a serious problem for kayakers and involves a variety of the previously mentioned strokes, smoothly and automatically blended together and sometimes combined with creative strategies. A kayak left to its own devices will normally lie abeam the wind and waves, since this is the position where wind and wave action play equally fore and aft. When you wish to go some direction other than directly across the wind and waves, you are going to be fighting this tendency. The most difficult angles are between 40 and 70 degrees off the wind. Directly into the wind is usually more manageable, though a moment of inattentiveness may cause you to be quickly turned side on. The problem is that when you turn into the wind, your bow will lift clear of the waves, exposing it to more wind force than the stern, which, at that moment, is deep in the trough. In addition, the breaking crest pushes the part of the kayak it hits first, turning the boat until equilibrium is established. This effect and the circular motion of water within a wave creates a convergence of forces resisting your attempts to turn.

At the crest of the wave there is frequently a moment when both the bow and stern are clear of the water and a timely sweep stroke, topped off with a draw, will bring you around beyond the critical angle of 40 degrees. If this technique does not work, try leaning the kayak hard away from the direction you wish to turn as you apply your sweep.

The rudder's main job is to help hold a course in wind by eliminating weathercocking, but it can also help with turning. To be effective, however, the rudder needs to be passing through the water at some speed, and under strong head wind conditions, the water speed may be so slow that it becomes a pivot around which the entire boat will turn downwind (if you wish to head downwind, of course, you are away laughing). If you have no rudder or it is broken, you can maintain a great deal of control by carefully timing your strokes to take full advantage of the crests and troughs, sweeping and drawing at the optimal moments. It is not something you can learn from this book or any other. To gain this skill, you must go out in wind—an onshore one—and play in the waves to develop the instinct and skills you must have.

As conditions become more severe, particularly if your objective is to maintain a course somewhere in the range of 40 to 70 degrees off the wind, you will need to resort to lopsided paddle stroking. Before I discovered the value of a rudder, I had been obliged to paddle some crossings almost entirely on one side, occasionally even throwing in a stern rudder stroke or a reverse sweep. A better strategy often is to head slightly to windward of your destination, thus allowing yourself the relative ease of paddling in the zone that is less than 40 degrees off the wind. You can then "fall off" the wind when you come abeam your destination, thus mostly avoiding the most difficult angles for dealing with wind.

Kayak designer and merchant Matt Broze has done some valuable analysis of handling a kayak in wind without a rudder. His favoured method of breaking out of the "hove-to" position is to take full advantage of the boat's natural tendency to weathercock. Boats that resist weathercocking forward will usually be vulnerable to weathercocking backwards, and this tendency can be used to help you turn. Simply get up speed across the wind and waves and then sweep to enhance the natural tendency the boat has to weathercock.

Sometimes, as Matt gleefully points out, the rudder can be of greater value out of the water than in, since a rudder that is laid along the deck will increase the windage of the stern and help bring a recalcitrant bow around.

During Matt's experimenting, he also discovered that if both you and your partner are having difficulty with turning into a strong wind, a towline attached between the stern of the stronger paddler and the bow of the weaker one can help both, since the rear boat pulls the stern of the first boat around, while the bow of the second boat is, in turn, held into the wind.

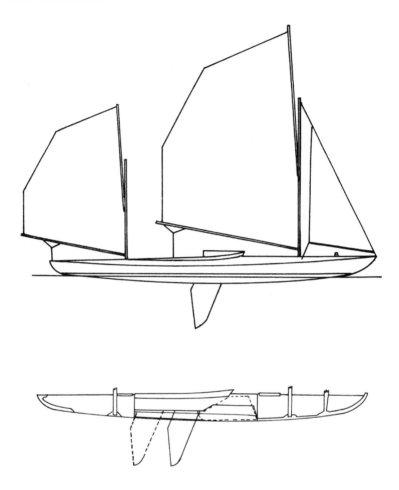

The Yakaboo: Frederic Fenger's ketch-rigged single kayak,
17' long with a 36" beam.

SAILING

To a kayaking purist, paddles are for paddlers, sails are for sailors, and
motors are for maniacs. Even purist sea kayakers will agree, however,
that an improvised sail on a kayak can be of great benefit in some situations, particularly in the tropics, since it enables the paddler to conserve
strength and cut water intake by reducing effort. In truth, kayak sailing
is a sport in its own right, deserving of its own how-to manual. It is a
sport that was once very popular in the United States and Europe and
can be a lot of fun. Sailing can provide relief on long trips; indeed,

many of the longest sea kayak expeditions have relied on sail. In 1923 Karl Schott paddled and sailed a foldboat down the Danube to Greece, around the Mediterranean to Suez and across the Arabian Gulf to India. In 1928 Franz Romer sailed across the Atlantic in a specially built 6.5-metre (21-foot) single, and in 1956 Hannes Lindemann repeated Romer's feat in a double. In 1987 Ed Gillet sailed and paddled from Monterey, California, to Maui, Hawaii, in a hardshell two-seater. The three transoceanic crossings took between fifty-six and seventy-two days each (see Appendix A).

If you intend to sail your kayak for more than running with the wind, some modifications will be necessary. A keel, a centreboard, lee-boards or at least some substantial ballast is needed. Several manufacturers sell sailing rigs and leeboards specifically designed for their own models of kayak, and several innovative outrigger devices are available for the generic kayak.

A most remarkable example of a sailing kayak was the *Yakaboo*, designed by the American Frederic Fenger in the early twentieth century. The 5-metre (17-foot), home-built craft boasted such features as a self-draining cockpit, watertight bulkheads with hatch covers, a mobile, retractable centreboard and 2 metres (6 feet) of sleeping space. It carried 7.5 square metres (80 square feet) of canvas on twin gaff-rigged sprit sails and could sail itself so well that on Fenger's 1911 trip from Grenada to Saba in the West Indies a rudder proved unnecessary. All alterations to course were achieved by manipulation of the main sheet and centreboard, and Fenger sailed to windward successfully, crossing the rough interisland passages of the Lesser Antilles against the trade winds in approximately half the time it took my friends and me when we paddled the route sixty-seven years later.

In 1969 a friend and I followed the path of three survivors from the Australian Commando Group X, who had tried to escape by kayak after a raid on Japanese Singapore during World War II. (One made it to Timor before being caught and executed.) Our kayak, like that of our predecessors, was not rigged specifically for sailing, but a square of parachute silk hoisted on a spare paddle provided a welcome relief from paddling in the scorching heat of the South China and Java Seas. Twice we travelled over a hundred miles between landfalls—journeys we would probably not have attempted without the sail. On another trip, in the

Caribbean in 1977–78, we carried sails as a backup in case a storm from the Windward or Leeward Islands blew the party out to sea. Rather than attempting to fight the northeast trades and the equatorial current back to the islands, we planned to rig a tent fly on the spare paddle and then turn and run 500 miles southwest to Venezuela or Colombia. As it happened, we held our course and no tent-fly sailing was required.

Parafoil Sailing

The parafoil, developed by Jalbert of Florida, is ideal for sailing a kayak. It eliminates the need for a mast—that source of purchase that can result in a sudden capsize when normal sailing rigs are fitted to kayaks—and it packs away to the size of a shirt. The boat is literally drawn along by the pull on the string. Given that in a head wind it is usually more efficient to paddle than to tack, the use of a downwind rig such as a kite will offer no serious limitations. In fact, the parafoil can offer assistance to a loaded kayak up to 80 degrees off the wind.

Generally, kites come in two sizes—about a square metre (9 or so square feet) and 1.4 square metres (15 square feet). I have also owned a 30-square-footer (almost 3 square metres), which could almost lift me off the ground in a 25-knot wind, but 15 square feet is adequate to pull even a loaded double when the wind is 10 to 20 knots, and this size is about as big as one can launch from the boat. To launch these smaller kites, turn the kayak downwind on the rudder and then hold open the tubes on the leading edge of the kite. As wind fills them out, the kite lifts and the lines trail through your fingers to the apex and then eventually to the single line.

Smaller kites are easier to launch than larger ones and can be set successfully in winds as low as 5 knots. Under such conditions, however, the kite has no pull and is more of a frustration than an asset. (If you wish to use winds of this strength, you would be better off with a spinnaker-type sail.) For kites of 15 square feet and over, 10 knots is the minimal useful wind, though some assistance can be gained from a 7-knot breeze. In winds exceeding 20 knots, however, you may do better with a small kite stabilized with a tail.

It certainly helps to have a rudder on the kayak for parafoil sailing, though it is possible to steer with the paddle if you attach the parafoil cord just forward of the cockpit. This technique can be dangerous,

George Dyson's extremely seaworthy three-man baidarka,
whose sail doubles as a tent.

however, since, in contrast to regular sailing, if you did happen to capsize, your kite would keep on pulling and you could find yourself on a long swim after an upside-down kayak that has just been relieved of your weight. Some safety suggestions for using a parafoil are as follows:

1 Don't attach the kite string to the kayak without also tying yourself to the boat.
2 Always attach your paddle to the boat (it is too easy to lose it from the deck lines), and always carry a spare.
3 Keep a sharp knife or safety cutter handy in case the kite has to be released suddenly.
4 Use a lightweight spool so that the kite will fall and not fly on if released.
5 Attach a small piece of styrofoam to the kite tail to prevent it from sinking should it fall into the sea.
6 Avoid pulling hard on a submerged kite, since you may damage it.

For proper flying, the kite must be correctly adjusted. This is best done on land with about 9 metres (30 feet) of line out. All the bridle lines (shrouds) should first be evenly tensioned. This procedure requires repeated launchings and readjustments. Try to tighten the lines evenly on opposite sides of the kite. If you find that it flies off to one side, loosen off the lines on the favoured side or tighten those on the opposite side. The angle of flight can also be adjusted by shortening or lengthening horizontal rows of shrouds. The optimum angle of flight is about 60 to 70 degrees: if the angle is too high, the forward pull is reduced, and if it is too low, the kite swoops and plunges excessively. A tail made of strips of cloth will help stabilize the kite in high winds.

The ideal place to attach the kite string to the boat will vary according to the angle off the wind you are attempting to run. For example, if you are planning to run downwind exactly, attach the line close to the bow. As you move off the wind, the point of attachment is moved back until it is at the cockpit. You can move the point of attachment by running the line through a clip that is fastened to a rope loop that can be pulled forward or back. Hold the kite reel in your hand to retain a feel for the pull being exerted on the boat and keep a knife handy to cut the line free if you are unhappy with the way things feel and cannot pull the kite in.

Although the kite may be flown on 500 feet of line or more, it requires a lot of work to bring it in again; 75 to 100 feet is usually adequate.

SURFING AT SEA

In a following sea, when the combination of wave size, wave shape and boat speed is just right, your kayak will catch the wave and you will find yourself surfing. With practice, you will learn to judge the right moment to throw your weight forward, paddling hard to hitch such a ride. The telltale sign is your bow. Anticipate the moment at which it will burrow into the trough of the wave that has just passed and then haul on the paddles as the next wave lifts your stern and, eventually, your bow. As your bow breaks free, you will start to surf, you can help by throwing your weight back while increasing your rating as the boat starts planing. Then for 90 metres (100 yards) or more you can be swept along in front of the wave—at up to three times your hull speed.

The wave passes; your run dies, and the boat drags down the back of the wave into the trough and it is time to catch the next wave. Watch your bow, put on full power and throw your weight forward again as your bow begins to drop.

Surfing can heavily tax your strength, but it is fun and it is a good way to pick up miles at sea. There will come a time, however, when the fun ceases, the waves suddenly become unmanageable (bad weather seems to sneak up less obtrusively from astern) and you realize, with sudden misgivings, that instead of your playing with the waves, they are playing with you. If you have a boat loaded with fancy equipment (not least your feet) that you are anxious to keep dry, and if the water looks cold and the land is still miles away, you will probably want to alter the rules of the game. When the next big wave builds up on you, stall by backpaddling a stroke or two just at the point where, before, you would have thrown your weight forward. This move should not slow you down too much, and it will help prevent that agonizing uncontrolled descent and the distressing high-speed broach across the face of the wave, with your weather paddle clawing up the slope towards a wall of green and white that is about to envelop you.

If you still find your boat being picked up by the waves (a turn of the tide could be steepening their faces) and if you are no longer able to brace comfortably into the breaking crests, you may have to consider a holding action. Turn and face the oncoming crests, paddling into them as they break, and allowing yourself to be blown backward (with occasional help from your paddles). If the wind is strong enough to blow up a sea like that, you will probably still be making in excess of 2 knots with your course lying to sternward. Open sea waves can carry very hard-hitting crests. The only ways I know to tackle the really big ones are as follows:

1   Paddle right through them.
2   Take them side on with your paddle stuck into the turbulence, just as you would come through beach surf.
3   Lie to a drogue.

Once, in very rough water during a night crossing of the Mona Passage, between Puerto Rico and the Dominican Republic, our kayak was hit by the full force of an ocean breaker while I was busy handpumping the bilges. (We had no foot pump.) I sensed the presence of the crest above us and managed to zipper the spray skirt closed just as the wave struck. It came down exactly on our stern, and the force was numbing—as if we had just been struck by a ship. We were swept forward at a phenomenal speed, breathless in the wall of flying spray and totally out of control, managing merely to wing a paddle out on each side as a token gesture. There were four of us in two doubles, and we had been keeping close company. When we shakily regained our equilibrium after that wave, our boat was so far from the other boat that we could barely make out each other's lights.

CHAPTER THREE

SEAMANSHIP, SELF-RESCUE & ASSISTED RESCUES

Seamanship is the art of living according to the rules of the sea. It is what this book is all about, and it requires, along with knowledge, a healthy respect for the sea and a knack for expecting the unexpected. It means committing yourself to the problems of the voyage, from initial planning through final execution, with a complete acceptance of responsibility for your actions. Seamanship is the measure by which you partake of the wisdom of the sea.

DAILY PLANNING
Daily on a kayak trip of any length, you will face the questions of whether and when and where to paddle. These are fundamental questions, always worth re-asking. And as always where the sea is concerned, there are no fixed rules; the variables make every situation totally different. Your choices will depend on the strength of your party, where you are in the world, where you are on the coast, your sense of the weather and the nature of your intended landfall, how far you will have to paddle to your destination and how much farther you will have to paddle if you miss it or are unable to land. Timing may be a critical factor, and you may have to choose between a night or daytime trip. A major factor to consider will always be the weather and, more specifically, the wind: its direction, strength and likely development. Tides, currents and surf may also play a prominent role in your thinking. That said, there are some general rules, which you break at your peril. These include the following:

1 Don't set off on a trip with someone unless you have a good idea of his or her level of competence.
2 Don't set off downwind if you are likely to have to return against that wind within a certain time frame.
3 Don't commit yourself to going on a trip with unfamiliar equipment, don't rely on other people to have the safety equipment, and don't set off—even for a day paddle—without a weather forecast.
4 Don't leave without making sure that everyone knows what is going on and is comfortable with the level of exposure to risk.

Ideally, your group will get together for a predeparture discussion of conditions and the day's schedule. This is the time to talk over all possible problems and decide on a bail-out plan. An escape route should be an integral part of any day's planning. Sometimes one is simply not available, and it is particularly important that you realize this fact before you set out, not after an emergency occurs. Such knowledge will greatly affect your assessment of risk and your subsequent decision to travel or to stay on shore that day.

If your group consists of equally experienced members, you will all be able to decide on the best of several probable alternatives. If, however, only the leader is knowledgeable, this meeting becomes critical in a different way. It allows the group to learn from the leader and understand the reasons behind the decisions. The problems may require less laborious discussion in experienced groups, but a bail-out plan should still always be established and a rendezvous point agreed on, to be used if the group is accidentally split. Unintentional separations can occur even in the calmest water, so before leaving the shelter of a bay, you should agree on your exact destination and a compass course. Even if you can see the land you are paddling to, rain and fog may quickly obscure it. Everyone in the party should know the course and the goal.

When circumstances allow, it helps to take a day's pause before a big crossing. Spend the time resting, watching weather and currents closely, talking with locals and eating plenty of good food. Getting the boat and equipment ready in advance is a part of the mental preparation, as is talking over details of the route with your companions—if you have not already worn the subject out. Take some time to compose yourself and quietly go over the chart so that when the moment to push off arrives, you are totally focussed on the problems at hand.

TAKING ADVICE

Don't be intimidated by reports of currents that run at terrible speeds, but don't dismiss them either. Just treat all advice on currents with suspicion. Few boaters can report accurately on the speed of currents they have experienced, and seldom do their estimates err on the slow side. This may be because in a motor vessel they usually have far more power available than you do. Likewise, your faithful copy of the government coast pilot or sailing directions must be regarded only as a general guide to inshore navigation, not as a bible. For all their survey ships and research stations, navies and coast guards often know precious little about currents.

The best you can do when planning a major crossing is to combine all you have heard and read with what your eyes tell you from the cliff top. Judge each source of information critically against your own experience and then make your decision. Don't let anyone do it for you unless you are listening to a kayaker more experienced than you are, or to someone whose credibility you know to be utterly beyond doubt. Yachters' advice must be tempered with your knowledge of kayaks. Commercial fishers tend to be scornful of sea kayakers, and their advice is often full of gloom. Skippers of oceangoing ships seem to be either all for you or totally against you. My experience has been that their advice is usually sound, but remember that they don't know the inshore effects of currents and their ships behave quite differently from a kayak in rough seas. Landing sites, in particular, are a subject on which you cannot unquestioningly accept the word of those who have not studied the coast from a kayak. It may be helpful, though, to cross-examine yachters by asking such questions as: "Can you get ashore in a dinghy?" or "Is it safe to swim in the surf off that beach?" This approach may alter their frame of reference and yield a more useful answer than the general question, "Is there any protection on that shore?"

Remember too that visibility from a kayak is far less than from a yacht or fishing boat, so a sandy cay or rocky reef visible at 15 miles according to yachters may not be visible until 7 miles from your boat.

GROUP TRAVEL

If you are travelling as a group, always stay close enough to maintain communication—unless you have made some other arrangement that everyone clearly understands. During darkness, staying close enough usually means staying within earshot of the other boats and being able to see their lights clearly. Daylight allows travel within hand-signalling distance on fine days, but you should be close enough to respond to likely emergencies during rough conditions.

Although each kayak should carry a compass and chart and each person should know the course, it is usually best if one boat leads and the others follow. This procedure will help to eliminate the tendency that crews or individual paddlers have to pull apart, each convinced they are on the right course. I regard this arrangement as very important. Diverging compass courses can result from compass differences if some metal or electrical circuit is nearby, but mostly they occur because one paddler compensates slightly more or less than the others for the effect of each passing wave. It is the sort of thing that can become irritating for everyone concerned, and quite often no one is clearly to blame—yet the distance between boats can become so great that communication is hampered, and someone ends up having to paddle back half a mile to maintain that communication. Another advantage to having one boat follow the other is that should the lead boat wander off course, the deviation can quickly be corrected by the other paddlers. It is good for morale if the role of lead boat is changed frequently or if one of the physically weaker paddlers takes the lead.

It is the responsibility of the lead boat to see that no one is left too far behind, though the actual task of keeping the boats together may be assigned to the last boat. If you have more than two boats in your group, try to keep one of the strongest paddlers or teams of paddlers at the rear to help in emergencies and to encourage weaker members. Juggle the crews of doubles so that no boat has two weak paddlers. The point of having a team is the additional security the presence of other boats can offer and the pleasure of their company. If you are all going your own ways and not looking after each other, these advantages are cancelled out and you might as well have made your voyage alone. When travelling as a small group on a windy day, an ideal formation is a line, with each boat spaced two boat lengths astern and two to windward of the one in front. This formation enables each paddler to watch the nearest boat astern while at the same time keeping an eye on approaching waves. Your blind spot in wind lies astern and to leeward.

The National Outdoor Leadership School (NOLS) has been running a sea kayaking program since the seventies and has developed a system of travelling in tight pods of either eight or sixteen paddlers, in a combination of doubles and singles, usually with a student to staff ratio no greater than 4:1. The school's experience is relevant here because it teaches students how to run their own trips as distinct from tour companies, which handle all logistical problems on behalf of their clients.

The NOLS group travel guidelines for instructors advise pods to always stay close enough to be able to communicate verbally with the rest of the group, either directly or by message relays. This arrangement ensures that the entire group will be able to respond to an emergency while leaving the actual distance between boats to vary according to conditions. In following seas the guidelines allow a wider spacing to avoid the risk that one boat will surf onto another. With the larger pods, positions are designated, such as a point boat to set the course and take the lead. The point boat is usually the slowest boat, ensuring that the whole group can keep up. The strongest paddler is at the rear and must be capable of herding strays back into the flock. When conditions are marginal, a flank boat on either side of the pod is set in place to assist with this task.

RESCUE

Fundamental to safe sea kayaking is a reliable method of self-rescue. It is not good enough to rely on the platitude that there is safety in numbers. Often there is, but it is a fool who bases his or her capsize recovery entirely on the assistance of companions. The following pages will discuss the Eskimo roll, alternative methods of self-rescue and, finally, assisted rescues.

The Eskimo Roll

For those with suitable boats, this is the first line of defence against falling out of an upturned kayak. It is, however, a mistake to rely on the Eskimo roll alone, and one should always be capable of performing an alternative self-rescue. Remember, needing to roll is usually a sign of failure to manage the conditions, and those same conditions will be there to greet you when you come up. Your backup system should be secure enough to cope with the conditions that knocked you down. Also, no matter how deft your roll, if you capsize while you have the spray skirt open and your arms inside the boat rummaging for your lunch (a very likely time to capsize), rolling is not going to help you much.

Some kayaks roll easily (some roll too easily!), and others can be rolled only with great difficulty. Some of the surviving traditional Eskimo kayaks are plainly not designed to be rolled, and it seems clear that the Eskimo roll was by no means a universal technique among those who invented and perfected the kayak. Polls have shown that less than 10 per cent of the seakayaking population have a reliable roll under emergency conditions. If you find yourself in the remaining 90 per cent, be sure that you have a bomb-proof backup method.

The Pawlata Roll

There are many ways to roll, and it does not matter very much which one you choose so long as you can do it consistently with your loaded boat if you plan to rely on it. Probably the simplest and most reliable is the Pawlata or extended-paddle roll. It is possible to coordinate it for use in doubles, but the practice is not common. For slender singles, the Pawlata is ideal, since at sea you have plenty of time to position your paddle carefully, a luxury that whitewater kayakers do not always enjoy.

To learn to roll properly, you are going to need a little help from your friends or, better still, from an instructor. When you are upside down with water up your nose and your world out of focus, it is extremely difficult to be your own best critic on the finer points of the angle and depth of the paddle blade. There are several exercises that can make your first roll a less desperate affair; for a start, you can get used to escaping from an inverted kayak—just in case you should change your mind about rolling some day. Capsize the boat and control your panic. Count to five slowly and then feel for the spray skirt release tab. Count another five seconds and then pull the spray skirt free and do a gentle, unhurried forward roll out of the boat and up to the surface. It is good to know you can come out of your boat without tearing away the deck or leaving your kneecaps behind.

Next, with a friend standing waist deep alongside and holding your

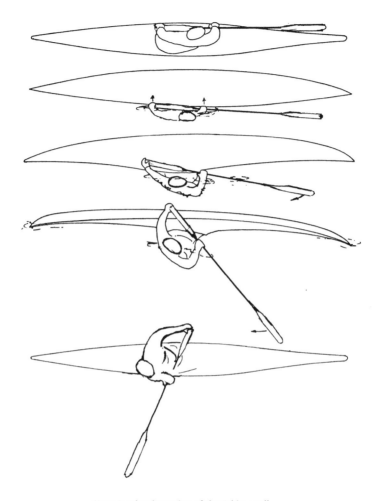

Hans Pawlata's version of the Eskimo roll.

hands, capsize and pull yourself upright again. You will find that it pays to flick the hips sharply, leaving the head and shoulders to follow. Do this until you can come up easily and without a struggle.

When it's time to make your first attempt at rolling, you can make life easier for yourself by slipping a piece of buoyancy such as a paddle-float over your sweep blade and then set up:

THE SETUP: Lean forward, hold the near blade of your paddle in your left hand and, with your right hand, hold the shaft at about the midway point. Place the paddle along the deck, extended blade towards the bow on the port side, the blade horizontal and facing upward. Turn and drop your right wrist so that the back of your hand faces outward.

THE SWEEP: Capsize the boat and, when you have stabilized upside down, sweep the blade of your paddle towards the surface. At the same time, lean out towards the paddle while pushing the left hand forward and up.

THE ROLL: Levering the blade against the water at the same angle as that used for a sculling support stroke, sweep the paddle out from the boat. Your head and shoulders will be drawn closer to the surface. As your body begins to break water, pull down hard with the right hand, give a flick with the hips, leaving head and shoulders until the last moment and then sculling forward with the paddle for final support.

I would like to rely on the knowledge and experience of John Heath to supplement this section on the Eskimo roll with three examples of techniques developed by Native kayakers: the Standard Greenland Roll, the Greenland Storm Roll, and the Alaska King Island Roll. The solid lines indicate the starting position for a clockwise roll. Holding the paddle as shown, lean forward and to starboard until the kayak capsizes. Turn the illustration upside down and you will get a fish-eye view of the fully capsized position. To right yourself from this position:

1 Position the paddle to a planing angle by rolling your wrists.
2 Sweep the paddle outward in a planing arc, thus lifting your body to the surface.
3 Complete the roll by lifting your hands while applying opposing hand pressures and dragging the blade inward.

The Storm Roll
This roll is of interest because it leaves the kayaker in a stable, forward-leaning, low-profile position at the completion of the roll. As the name implies, it evolved for use in storms, and knowledge of this technique probably saved the lives of a large number of Greenlandic hunters. Explains John Heath:

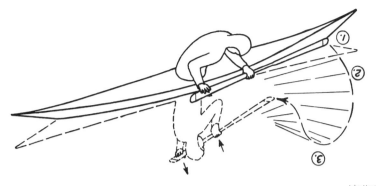

John Heath

The Standard Greenland Roll.

This method brings one up leaning well forward with the paddle extended to one side in a paddle brace. By keeping low, with the paddle extended, one can rest, or scull if necessary, to prevent another capsize.

The basic movement of the Storm Roll is similar to the Standard Greenland method in that it consists of a sweep and a lift by using the paddle as a lever.

But in the Standard Roll, the torso sweeps back with the paddle and the lift is done in a chinning attitude with the palms facing upward. In the Storm Roll, the torso does not sweep with the paddle, and the roll is finished with the paddle against the foredeck with the palms facing downward.

1 To practise the Storm Roll, lean far forward and keep the torso, head and arms as low as possible. Hold the paddle flat against the side of the kayak, below the starboard gunwale, parallel to the water surface and as far forward as possible with the right hand holding the blade near the end and the left hand holding it short of the middle. (This applies to a Greenland or other narrow unfeathered paddle.)

2 Capsize to the right.

3 To recover, push the aft end of the paddle forward, upward and inboard so that the knuckles brush the bottom of the kayak, keeping the blade flat against the kayak. At the same time, the left hand is brought outward in a sweep past the head, with the

leading edge of the working blade at a 5- or 10-degree planing angle to the water surface. As the right hand moves across the kayak bottom, the kayak rolls under it, so that the roll is completed with each hand at its respective gunwale and the paddle extended to the left in a brace.

The critical stage of recovery is illustrated below.

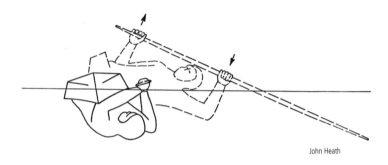

John Heath

The start (solid lines) and finish (broken lines) of a planing sweep are shown head-on. Success is almost certain if you have surfaced by the time you have completed the 90° sweep.

The King Island Roll

This roll was developed by King Islanders, who usually used a single-bladed paddle. It is included here because many kayakers carry a two-piece sectional paddle on the afterdeck, where it is accessible to roll up with if the main paddle is lost. Also, if a paddle breaks, the paddler can use the King Island Roll with the remaining blade.

Before capsizing, the paddle is held horizontally in front of the body, with the blade to the left, parallel to the water surface. Capsize to your right.

Turn the illustration on page 89 upside down, for a fish-eye view of your capsized position. The arms are extended during, or immediately after, the capsize.

Other Rolls

With practice it is possible to roll up with all manner of aids, such as a flat board, a knife or even your hands. These techniques have evolved

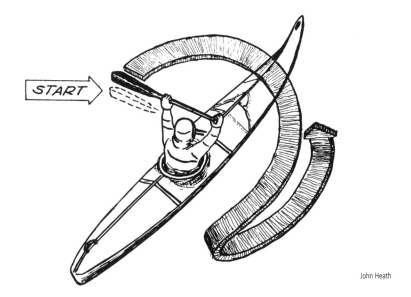

John Heath

To right yourself, sweep the paddle forward along the path shown by the arrow (illustration viewed upside down), the leading edge of your blade towards the surface of the water in order to gain lift.

from necessity, and any one of them can be considered a backup to the failure of some other system. The need to roll at all, however, usually indicates that the paddler is in major trouble and that the overwhelming conditions will remain after the roll has been completed. Unless the cause of capsize was falling asleep, the paddler is going to be in a weaker position than before the roll. The real value of a repertoire of rolls may well be the development of such fine paddling skills that there is little likelihood that the rolls will ever be needed.

Note: A 1.5-square-foot Ethafoam sandwich about 2 inches thick slipped over the paddle blade will greatly assist with early practice rolls by keeping the paddle close to the surface and providing solid support. This float can then be stored close in behind the paddler where it can be reached and used to hand-roll the kayak if a paddle is lost or broken. An emergency CO_2 inflatable Roll-Aid is also on the market. This device may be secured within easy reach and provides an "instant" float for a backup roll.

A list of instructions such as the preceding is a poor and probably bewildering substitute for learning from an expert who can see your mistakes and guide you clearly. Most instructors will have their own favoured variations of the roll. What matters is that you find a version that you can successfully perform when you have to.

Other Recovery Methods—Some Good, Some Not So Good

In this book I would like to emphasize self-rescue techniques other than the Eskimo roll because a backup technique is mandatory for sea voyages, given that relatively few sea kayakers will ever roll successfully and because workable alternative techniques are too often neglected.

The alternatives taught by most kayak schools in the past involved the use of one or two other kayaks in a variety of routines with code names such as T, TX, H and HI. These techniques, misleadingly known as deep-water rescues, basically involve hoisting a flooded kayak across the decks of two others. They have their place as training for novice parties in calm water with empty boats and on rivers whence they evolved, but they are poor first-line techniques for the touring kayaker who cannot roll. They cannot be reliably performed with a loaded boat, and they are unreliable during the sort of conditions likely to cause a capsize. I have myself instructed unsuspecting Outward Bound pupils in these techniques, using the unconvincing line that "with a little more practice you will be able to do it in rough water." That is wrong and dangerous advice.

I repeat: under rough conditions with loaded kayaks, most one-kayak-across-the-other, swimming-pool coaching methods of rescue simply do not work. Fresh from the factory, a sea kayak may weigh as little as 18 to 23 kilograms (40 to 50 pounds). Laden with gear and awash from a capsize, it can easily weigh 450 kilograms (1000 pounds). A quarter of that weight cannot be lifted by two kayakers in calm water, much less be controlled in a raging sea.

Another method sometimes advocated for sea work is the Eskimo bow rescue. In this procedure, the capsized individual (we'll refer to a man) remains seated in the inverted boat, confidently thumping the upturned hull to attract the attention of his pals. He then sweeps his arms backward and forward in the hope of finding a friendly bow upon which to hoist himself smartly out of the water with a flick of the hips and, doubtless, a loud gasp. Again, this can be a great exercise, it promotes bonding, and was probably very practical when groups of Inuit were wrestling seals from kayaks and one capsized, or when combined with one of the Greenland sculling positions described by John Heath on pages 66–67. The weakness of the method is that in a touring situation it would normally take a good deal more than thirty seconds for a companion boat to be manoeuvred into a position of assistance. I doubt that anyone who has accidentally capsized at sea will hang around upside down hoping that his mates will make it before he runs out of air.

If you are using this technique to spot for someone learning to roll, you might prefer to align the boats in parallel rather than to form a T. With this formation, it is easier for the victim to find the rescuer's boat, and it reduces the chances that an over-eager rescuer will impale the victim's boat (or worse, his arm) with his bow.

Another technique commonly advocated is the re-entry and roll for the kayaker who, though capable of rolling, has failed to do so. In this case the individual who has come out of her kayak dives, faces the stern while gripping the paddle on her favoured setup side and then re-enters the boat upside down by doing a backward somersault (provided the gear has not shifted to prevent this). Depending on the boat, the spray skirt may or may not be replaced with one hand. The paddle is then manoeuvred into position and the roll executed. *Note:* The odds of a successful roll can be greatly increased by attaching a paddle float to the sweep end of the paddle.

The re-entry and roll is another of those techniques that are good training and work fine in warmed swimming pools or for skilled paddlers who have been careless, but it is really a step beyond competence at rolling and highlights the paradox that if you can do it, you will almost certainly have precluded yourself from the necessity to do so. Furthermore, the conditions that caused the capsize in the first place will still be there when you come up, and chances are that the cockpit will have scooped up a tubful of water that destabilizes the boat. It is by no means a method for those who, because of exhaustion or extreme conditions, have been knocked over and just failed to complete the much simpler Eskimo roll. Like the now thoroughly debunked drown-proofing system for swimmers advocated in the seventies, it hastens the onset of hypothermia by calling for the re-immersion of the head and neck.

Remember, the self-rescue method that you rely on should get you out of the water fast and leave you in a more stable position than you were in when you capsized.

Cold Water Self-Rescues

During capsize drill in 10°C (50°F) water, even wearing a Farmer John wet suit and paddling jacket, Vancouver paddler Duncan Murray discovered to his amazement that he had lost the functional use of his arms and fingers after only seven minutes in the water. In tropical waters this loss of dexterity would be unlikely to occur for three or four hours or more, so obviously your margin of safety is going to be drastically affected by water temperature and your technique for getting back into the boat will depend on the temperature of the water you are in.

During a cold water capsize the priority, after having air to breathe, is to reduce the rate at which your body loses heat. This means getting your torso out of the water as soon as you can. Start the process by recognizing that you are in a potentially life-threatening situation. If you were not already wearing your wet suit jacket, grab it along with the largest rocket flare you have and haul your upper body out of the water across the upturned hull. Fire off the flare while you still have the dexterity to do so and then struggle into your wet suit jacket or whatever other protective clothing you have.

Your next move will depend on the type of boat you have, the amount and placement of buoyancy, the rescue aids you carry and the methods you have practised; and practise them you must, for it is not enough to simply carry a pump and a rescue aid. You must be able to use your aids readily under moderate conditions if you are to have a hope of using them effectively under extreme ones.

The more stable your kayak, the easier the self-rescue, all other things being equal. The more buoyancy you have, the more stable the boat when it is awash. A beamy single with a pod or sea sock is going to be a lot easier to re-enter than a narrow single with loose-fitting airbags, or, worse, with no buoyancy at all.

A most sobering exercise is to dump your kayak and try to re-enter it with 15 centimetres (6 inches) of water in the cockpit. Even with none of the destabilizing slosh and splash inside the boat, you would still find it difficult to maintain your balance astride the cockpit. When you adopt the more efficient low-profile technique of hugging the afterdeck while you insert your legs inside the cockpit and then twist your body into the seat, you will still find it hard to re-enter. Given the sort of conditions that cause a capsize in the first place, it will soon become clear that you have a ready formula for disaster, since each time you fail (and get colder) diminishes your chances of success on the next attempt. Your priority is to get out of the cold water and stabilize the kayak enough to pump it out. Here's where the rescue aids come in.

The Sea Wing Self-Rescue

The Sea Wing self-rescue has been developed and determinedly promoted by Tim Dyer of Georgian Bay Kayaks despite a somewhat skeptical response from many sectors of the trade. It takes an idea incorporated into folding kayaks—the lateral air sponsons—and makes it available to any kayak on a demand basis. The device, called a Sea Wing, consists of twin external air sponsons, which can be deployed below the gunwale alongside the cockpit so as to offer enough stability to re-enter a kayak over the bow or stern unassisted.

METHOD: The system must be set up in advance, and female Fastex or similar clips should be in place on deck and the webbing pre-adjusted for your boat. Feathercraft, which markets a sporty, narrow folding kayak, includes a Sea Wing as part of the price of the boat. Here are the instructions given to customers:

1 After capsizing, wet-exit the kayak but do not right it. Locate your paddle and slide it under the deck rigging. Swim to the side of the kayak to which the Sea Wing is attached. With the kayak still overturned, pull the Sea Wing out of the storage bag. Pull the sponson that is clipped onto the stern deck forward, clip its forward end to the prepared D-ring.
2 Inflate the sponson about half full (about five puffs).
3 Throw the uninflated second sponson over the hull of the kayak.
4 Right the kayak by rolling it towards you.
5 Attach the stern and bow clips to the D-rings provided.
6 Inflate both sponsons fully.
7 Re-enter the kayak by straddling the stern and pulling yourself forward.
8 Pump the water from the kayak.

Courtesy of Feathercraft

The Sea Wing Self-Rescue.

Note: To maintain enhanced stability while paddling after a capsize, use a piece of shock cord looped around the entire device, including the boat. Placing it near the front of the air bladders will greatly reduce drag. One model of Sea Wing comes with suspended nylon webbing loops, which enable weak or excessively cold paddlers to use their strong thigh muscles to hoist themselves out of the water.

ADVANTAGES: The great advantage of the Sea Wing is that it leaves the paddler in a more stable position than before the capsize.

LIMITATIONS: The system must be rigged in advance if the rescue is to be performed rapidly; it is a bit fiddly and may not be easy to deploy with very cold hands. Being inflatable makes it vulnerable to puncture, and big people may have difficulty with the limited amount of buoyancy if they insist on climbing over the side, as is common in other rescues. Such people might consider using it in conjunction with the paddle float, discussed in the next section.

SUMMARY: The Sea Wing is a solid idea, which, with refinement, could become a mainstay backup for solo kayakers or for leaders who want to increase the stability of an incapacitated or novice paddler.

Outrigger Self-Rescue (The Mariner Self-Rescue)

This rescue, developed by Matt and Cam Broze, involves using a rigid foam paddle float or twin-chambered inflatable bag designed to slip over the blade of the paddle as an outrigger to provide enough stability for the paddler to re-enter the kayak, attach the spray cover and pump out the water. It requires carrying the paddle float device together with a deck-rigging configuration capable of quickly securing the paddle blade to the boat.

METHOD:

1 Right the kayak by pushing up and away to reduce water entry.
2 Attach the paddle float to the blade and to the kayak with shock cord.
3 Secure the paddle blade to the afterdeck (downwind).
4 Position yourself forward of the paddle shaft and then swim your upper body onto the stern deck, face down, with most of your weight supported on the paddle float.
5 Insert one leg into the cockpit and then the other and twist around into the seat.

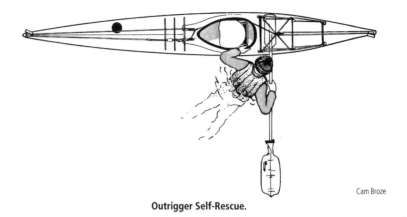

Cam Broze

Outrigger Self-Rescue.

6 Reattach your spray skirt while leaning the kayak onto the float.
7 Pump out the boat through the closed spray deck.
8 Retrieve your paddle and keep the float inflated and handy for possible use as a hand-rolling aid.

APPLICATION: Suitable for self-rescues in moderately rough water by competent paddlers in singles or doubles.

LIMITATIONS: The rescue requires practice to clarify the routine and develop a feel for the balance, since the boat can still capsize on the side that does not have a supporting outrigger. In addition, when there are strong currents against strong winds, this rescue is nearly impossible to complete. In surf you would do well to concentrate on getting ashore. Heavy individuals should check to make sure there is enough flotation to support their weight as they re-enter. The inflatable bag is more vulnerable to damage than the bulkier solid foam paddle float.

It should be clear by now that I favour self-reliance as both your first and second line of defence against a capsize. This is not to deny the value of systems that use the presence of others when they are around but rather stresses that you need to have a backup system of rescue that you can perform alone and that leaves you in a more stable position after the capsize than you were before it.

There is one more self-rescue worthy of mention for the athletic paddler. It is generally referred to as the cowboy rescue, or the cowgirl rescue. I once had a novice woman paddler capsize in the harbour, and using this technique, she hopped back into the kayak in seconds unassisted. Turns out she was a black-belt karate instructor.

This rescue requires the boat to have a large cockpit, and ideally it should be one that when inverted can be emptied by pushing down on the stern so that the bow rises and the water can be spilled almost completely. This technique will only work with some boat designs.

After you have emptied the boat, you straddle the stern of the now normally floating kayak and hug your way up the boat until your butt is overhanging the seat. Keeping the legs in the water will enhance your stability for this crawl . A paddle can be used for support at the next stage, which involves sitting up and dropping your backside onto the seat, legs over the side grasshopper style. Retrieve extraneous limbs and store them inside the kayak.

ADVANTAGES: Speed.

LIMITATIONS: You must be particularly athletic and have a suitable boat. Such a boat has a high-volume stern, a bulkhead close in behind the seat and a peaked foredeck that won't trap water. The cockpit should be large and cut low to facilitate breaking the air seal.

ASSISTED RESCUES

The Assisted Re-Entry

Probably the most obvious way to deal with capsized paddlers is to simply come alongside, help them re-enter their kayak and then stabilize their craft until they have pumped it out and recovered their composure. This rescue is the most straightforward assisted rescue and is particularly useful when orchestrated by a strong and skilled paddler. In an instructor/student situation an alert instructor can pull a flailing student out of the water in moments and calm him or her face to face in a secure raft formation.

METHOD:

1 The rescue boat comes alongside the capsized vessel, bow to stern on the opposite side from the swimmer.

2 After making sure that the victim is okay and his paddle secured,

right the boat and clear the inside of gear that may have shifted, interfering with leg room.

3   Reach across the cockpit and grasp the coaming strongly. When you are ready, instruct the person in the water to launch his body onto the afterdeck, face down, knees level with the seat. If necessary, assistance can be provided with a firm pull on the person's belt or the seat of his pants. (It is remarkable how much propulsion can be supplied in this way!)

4   The victim then squirms down into the cockpit and turns into the seated position. The rescuer retains a grip on the cockpit until the victim is comfortable and secure. If the victim is shaky and at risk of capsizing again, consider fitting his boat with a sponson or remaining rafted until he has calmed down.

LIMITATIONS: A problem can occur with particularly heavy capsize victims or those with poor upper body strength who have difficulty clambering onto the stern of their own boat. In such a case, consider the use of the next rescue.

Paddle Stirrup Method (PS Rescue)

This rescue is valuable on group trips with a mixture of skilled and unskilled paddlers, particularly where upper body strength—or lack thereof—may be an issue.

METHOD:

1   The rescue kayak pulls alongside the capsized boat on the upwind side (either bow to bow or bow to stern; I prefer the latter since it gives the person directing the rescue a more commanding leadership position).

2   Both paddles are laid across the upturned hull and held in the crook of the rescuer's arm. She then reaches across the hull and rights the boat.

3   A sling made with about 2 metres (6 feet) of floating rope is slipped over both paddles close to the far side of the flooded kayak using a cat's paw knot.

4   The capsized paddler swims to the downwind side of the two boats, puts one foot in the sling, steps up and, while lying face down on the stern of his own kayak, slips one leg into the cockpit and then the other with a turn around into the seat.

5   The spray skirt is fitted and the boat pumped dry.

Grant M. Thompson

The PS Rescue.

APPLICATION: The sling method is a particularly good rescue for those with very cold hands and arms, since it relies upon the powerful leg muscles to lift the swimmer out of the water and into his or her boat. It is also a good method for an experienced paddler to administer to a heavy notice, since it is simple and can be done with a fully loaded kayak just as readily as an empty one. The sling may also be used in conjunction with the paddle float self-rescue. The rescuer remains in a stable position throughout the rescue and can assist and orient the shivering wretch who has just been hauled from the ocean.

LIMITATIONS: This rescue is limited to moderate, choppy conditions because of the hazard of having two boats rafted in close while the seas are rough. It requires a piece of equipment (the rope loop), and there is always the risk that the person in the water will poke his or her leg through the sling and become snared. In addition, the risk of breaking or damaging paddles exists when heavy people are to be rescued.

Pump & Re-Entry (Doubles)

There are two versions or stages to the doubles pump and re-entry method. The first works well for moderate seas and has been used by the Special Boat Section of the Royal Marines since World War II. Stage 2 is essentially the same technique adapted for use in heavy seas or very choppy water.

STAGE I

1 Once capsized, each partner checks that the other is swimming clear, that both paddles are accounted for and that the boat is not in danger of being blown away.

2 The No. 2 (stern) person gives his or her paddle to No. 1, who swims to the bow. No. 2 then mantleshelves onto the upturned hull amidships, reaches over, grasps the far gunwale and flips backward into the water, pulling the kayak over with him or her.

3 No. 2 then re-enters by climbing astride the afterdeck while No. 1 steadies the boat by hugging the bow.

4 No. 2 then steadies the kayak with a sculling support stroke while No. 1 lies across the cockpit and then, facing down and backward, slips into the cockpit and twists into the seat. As far as possible the person re-entering should check first to make sure that dislodged gear is not blocking access.

5 Spray skirts are secured; the boat is pumped and bailed dry.

If you are in a lightly loaded double, there is a useful (warm water) alternative for step 3 of this method. Both kayakers dive and come up with their heads inside the boat and their shoulders in the cockpits. They inflate their life vests when necessary and then grip the coaming and give a synchronized push on one side while holding firm to the other. A light boat flipped in this way will have less water inside and will therefore be faster to pump and more stable to re-enter. A double fitted with sea socks takes on almost no water at all.

If a second kayak is standing by during re-entry, you will be able to brace your paddles across the two boats, steadying the empty craft and giving you a convenient grip as you hoist yourself out of the water. Or you can use a Paddle Stirrup rescue.

The sea, however, has a way of playing havoc with the straightforward antics of this stage. You may find that waves constantly sweep over the waterlogged kayak, defying your attempts to pump it dry. The problem is invariably that the boat is too low in the water. In warm climates, one or both of you is going to have to get back into the sea to lighten it. In cold water, you must have a wet suit or dry suit on to consider such a move. If you have no such thermal protection and do not have an inflatable raft or air mattress, your best bet is to stay in the boat, sealing it as best you can—and pumping like hell.

STAGE 2: THE EXTREME PROCEDURE

1   If the boat rides too low with your weight on board, re-enter the water, leaving the spray skirts in position on the boat. (Spray skirts with zippers make this procedure especially easy.)

2   Unless fresh water is going to be in short supply, your water containers should be emptied and then shoved back inside to give extra buoyancy. Air mattresses can be partially inflated inside the boat, and heavy objects such as weight belts and canned food can be ditched or transferred to another boat. All of these steps are taken so that you can pump water out faster than it sloshes in, and of course the tighter your boat seals, the fewer problems you will have.

3   No. 2 ties off the No. 1 spray skirt so that no water can enter (the bow painter can be used for this) and then ties off the No. 2 spray skirt around the hand pump—unless you are using a built-in hand

or electric pump, in which case both spray skirts are tied off.

4 Only when the kayak is pumped dry and floating high should you attempt to re-enter it as described in Stage 1. If instability due to the amount of water inside the boat is your problem, you may be able to improvise a sponson arrangement by lashing a waterproof gear bag to each side of the coaming with a line beneath the kayak.

A second kayak can help considerably during the pumping operation (particularly by keeping the swimmers out of the cold water), but be prepared to handle it unassisted.

Note: Buoyancy is the critical factor in any pump and re-entry operation. Anything you can do to increase it will help.

Earlier in this chapter I mentioned a series of group rescues, which, although I personally don't trust them for laden kayaks, have their place on club trips, particularly with lightly loaded boats under moderate conditions. These include the TX, the HI and the most questionable All-In Rescue.

The TX Rescue

This is a fairly quick rescue for two paddlers, one of whom capsizes well within the level of capabilities of the other. It was developed for whitewater kayaks but can also be used by an experienced paddler who comes upon someone in difficulties in a canoe or kayak, since the system does not depend heavily on the experience of the capsized paddler.

METHOD:

1 The capsized boat is left inverted so as to trap as much air as possible as it is manoeuvred into a position at a right angle to the hull of the rescuing craft.

2 The rescue paddler snatches the bow of the capsized boat over the foredeck of his or her own kayak as quickly as possible so as to minimize the amount of water entering the cockpit.

3 The swimmer helps manoeuvre the upturned kayak across the deck of the rescue boat, rocking it from the bow to help remove the excess water.

4 When the boat has been drained, it is rolled over and slipped back into the water. The kayak can then be re-entered using an assisted rescue or the assisted re-entry or the Paddle Stirrup method.

Grant M. Thompson

The TX Rescue.

LIMITATIONS: This method is a poor choice for loaded boats, doubles or rough conditions. It can also destroy spray skirts and fibreglass kayaks and can injure fingers and hands.

The HI Rescue.

The HI Rescue

This is a rescue for one of three kayaks. It got its name not because everyone involved sits waving at beachside spectators but because the boats, when seen from a rescuing helicopter, will look either like a squished **H** or an impacted **I** (or maybe a **K** or an **N**, depending on the frequency of large waves). This procedure can also be used to rescue kayakers or canoeists outside your group since, when conditions are fairly calm, it can provide a stable platform.

METHOD:

1 The capsized boat is kept upside down.
2 The two companion boats come alongside, collect the unfortunate's paddle and form a bridge between their two cockpits with the bundle of three paddles.
3 The capsized boat is hauled between the rescue craft and then lifted across the bundle of paddles assisted by the swimmer, who is hanging off the bow of one of the rescue boats. Rocking, timed to coincide with passing waves, will remove most of the water from the boat.
4 The boat is then turned over and relaunched between the two "nurse" kayaks.
5 The paddler re-enters the kayak.

APPLICATION: This is a fine rescue for teaching a group of novice paddlers how to work together or for building character. With practice, it can be performed quickly under moderate sea conditions.

LIMITATIONS: The method is not appropriate for loaded boats, doubles or rough conditions. It can damage the paddle shafts, in extreme cases even breaking the whole bunch. If the swimmer lets go of one of the rescue boats in a strong wind, the whole contraption could take off, further delaying the rescue.

The All-In Rescue

This rescue is designed for the situation in which an entire group is blown over by a gust of wind. It is assumed that all are close enough to pull their boats together. A weak assumption to say the least!

METHOD:

1 After all the boats have been dragged into a group, select the one that is riding highest and use it as the fulcrum for a modified TX rescue.

2 With one swimmer on each side of the most buoyant boat, heave the bow of the boat to be emptied across the upturned hull.

3 When the cockpit is sitting on the hull of the pivot boat, rock gently to empty both ends of water. (Take care not to let air escape from the pivot boat.)

4 Right the emptied kayak and assist the paddler into it, using a stirrup from a paddle held across the two boats.

5 The rest of the boats are then emptied using the TX rescue or a pump and re-entry Paddle Stirrup rescue.

Note: It is necessary to get the strongest, most competent paddler out of the water first, since that person will need to do the remaining rescues. The next person back in a boat should probably be the most hypothermic.

APPLICATION: This is a desperate, last-ditch method for group rescue. Its usefulness is considerably greater in warm water than cold, since you will have hours to pull the kayaks together in the tropics.

LIMITATIONS: This is definitely a flawed rescue. My principal reason for including it is to highlight its limitations, since it is sometimes still advocated by people confusing classroom exercises with the realities of the sea. For a start, it is extremely unlikely that any party that is all blown over at one time will be close enough to pull the boats together. To attempt to do so would just waste valuable time and energy that would be better used performing self-rescues. Second, it has almost no chance of being performed with a loaded boat, let alone a double. Third, it leaves people floating idly in the water waiting their turn. In cold water these people only have ten to twenty minutes of being functional, and when their time comes for a TX, they might as well be using stumps instead of hands. Even training with this method runs the risk of creating some potentially tragic illusions about safety.

The most useful procedure for a situation where all the boats are blown over by a squall is to have every person perform his or her own self-rescue, enabling the successful ones to go around and assist the rest with whatever rescue suits that particular situation.

Grant M. Thompson

The curl is useful for emptying a seriously flooded boat.

The Curl

The curl is a useful technique, apparently developed by English instructor and author Derek Hutchinson for draining water from a partially waterlogged kayak, a condition known as Cleopatra's needle, which, if not treated promptly, might leave you sans kayak.

METHOD:

1 The cockpit of the partially submerged kayak is hooked with the hand or foot of a swimmer gaining support by holding onto the bow of a rescue boat, and slowly lifted until it lies parallel to the rescue boat. This manoeuvre need not require a great deal of strength so long as none of the boat is lifted out of the water.

2 When the cockpit of the submerged kayak is close alongside and slightly in front of the rescue boat's cockpit, the swimmer leans across the rescue boat's deck and, turning the flooded boat on its side, grasps the cockpit rim, palms uppermost, elbows braced on the rescue boat. If the swimmer has trouble with the amount of leverage, she should try sliding back until her wrists are supported on the deck of the rescue boat. With the two boats touching, the swimmer

slowly leans back, breaking the air seal and allowing water to flood gently out of the cockpit. If care is taken with the use of leverage, and enough time is allowed for the boat to drain slowly, most of the water can be eliminated.

3 During the last phase, the rescuing kayaker can assist by leaning gently away from the now partially emptied kayak so that almost no strength is required by the swimmer.

APPLICATION: This procedure is useful for a seriously flooded kayak, but only, of course, when there is a second kayak standing by. It can be incorporated in a number of rescue scenarios where it may be necessary to remove most of the water from a boat with poor buoyancy before attempts are made to re-enter it.

LIMITATIONS: The curl works better with small light singles than with large doubles, since the latter require both paddlers to "curl" simultaneously in separate cockpits across the rescue boat.

Swimmer Rescue

If a kayaker has to rescue a swimmer, there are several alternatives, depending on the type of kayak being used, the size of the individual being rescued and the skill of both parties. Basically, all techniques involve getting the swimmer out of the water and onto (or into) the kayak. This approach is much faster than towing a person and greatly reduces heat loss.

METHOD:

1 Be sure the swimmer is neither panicking nor likely to disobey your directions.

2 Hold the kayak stern to the wind. This position gives you a view of both the swimmer and approaching waves as you look back.

3 Instruct the swimmer to crawl over the stern of your boat onto the afterdeck to a point where his or her head is close to your back. Your passenger should be lying face down as low as possible with his or her legs over the side to enhance the stability of the kayak.

4 Paddle to safety.

APPLICATION: This method can be used for rescuing a kayaker whose kayak has sunk as well as for rescuing a swimmer or board sailor in difficulty. Long distances can be covered, especially if the swimmer's legs can be lifted out of the water.

LIMITATIONS: As previously stated, much of the success of this operation depends on the kayak, kayaker and swimmer involved. Kayaks with low, buoyant sterns are more suitable than those with peaked, low-volume sterns. An agile, lightweight person is obviously going to threaten the stability of the kayak less than someone who is heavy or clumsy, and a beamy double kayak is going to require a lot less balancing than a narrow single. A great deal also depends on the paddling skill of the kayaker, since someone with a really strong brace could get through surf with an epileptic walrus on deck. There is also doubtless a limit to the degree of turbulence in which it is practical to attempt this rescue, though this too can be countered by the determination and skill of those involved or by the use of special equipment such as inflatable pontoons or a paddle float.

The swimmer's ability to crawl onto and balance on the afterdeck of the kayak will also be affected by the degree of hypothermia present. If the swimmer is barely able to move, you may find it easier to assist if he or she crawls up onto the forward deck. This position does not enhance the handling of the kayak, but it gives you a better idea of the victim's condition. Rudders and equipment on the afterdeck can also injure or impede a victim's efforts.

Note: Any self-rescue or group rescue must be practised in rough water and controlled conditions to be sure it works for you. For group rescues, practice sessions should give participants an opportunity to experience the various methods from the perspective of both the rescuer and the victim.

Coastal B.C. has a maze of islands, which demands careful navigation.

CHAPTER FOUR

NAVIGATION

This chapter is not designed to teach basic navigation. For that I recommend *Fundamentals of Kayak Navigation* by David Burch. This chapter assumes that you are familiar with chart and compass and have a degree of competence in basic navigational skills. The focus of the chapter is on special difficulties and how to solve them using minimal equipment. The kayak, remember, is the smallest, simplest oceangoing craft there is. What I have to say here may well raise the eyebrows of navigators schooled in the methods of a modern navy, but the kayak handles very differently from a motor vessel. The apparent "bush navigator" approach of the following pages is not meant to repudiate precise navigation; rather, it is an acknowledgement of its limits when applied to kayaks at sea.

Most kayak navigation is done by dead reckoning, which in my terms is navigation as an art rather than a science. It involves the use of nautical charts, a watch, dividers, a compass and a protractor and a great deal of knowledge of weather, tides, currents and wave patterns, all rolled into what eventually becomes an elusive "feel for the sea." You will also need another commodity that can't be found in the chandlery—the knack of turning the answers to old problems into the solutions for new ones. Good dead reckoning means being constantly aware of your approximate position and then using the techniques at your disposal to check and clarify that position. To be unsure of your position on any part of a routine coastal paddle is inexcusable. From your chart, you should be able to anticipate the next problem or the next safe landing. If you find yourself making repeated navigational errors, then brush up fast on your map and compass work.

TOOLS OF THE TRADE

Nautical charts are too large to handle in a kayak. They should be cut or folded carefully into one-foot squares and waterproofed on both sides with clear adhesive plastic. Take care always to include a section of the corresponding latitudinal degree markings so that you can accurately measure distance. Where possible, include a compass rose and make a note of relevant warnings to mariners. For plotting on a plastic-covered chart, use a chinagraph pencil, which can be erased with a cloth or the back of your hand.

British Admiralty charts are usually reliable for deep-water readings and sometimes for shallow-water ones, but you cannot always depend on them for the latter, nor can you rely on the existence of old landmarks. I have known charts on which not only towns but also whole islands are omitted, lights are misplaced and marked channels are nonexistent. Perhaps the early cartographers reasoned that the waters were too shallow to interest navigators, but inshore details are of paramount importance to the kayaker. National Ocean Service charts are usually more accurate, since they are often drawn from aerial photographs. Ordnance Survey or topographical maps are more reliable for land detail such as roads, buildings and contours, and where they exist, these maps may be used in conjunction with your chart. Check the date on the chart or map.

It is not good enough to hold your chart to the deck of the kayak by a piece of shock cord. You cannot afford to lose it, of all things. A waterproof folder with a clear plastic window through which the chart can be viewed should be attached firmly to the boat forward of the cockpit. If shock cord loops are fitted to its rear corners, this cover can extend over the spray skirt, where it will offer added protection against breaking waves while holding the chart in the most perfect position to be read as you paddle. The basic orienteering compass is adequate for a kayak. It can be slipped inside the map case through the Velcro-sealed entrance at the rear end of the case. It will eliminate the need for a protractor and is accurate enough for you to paddle to within 5 degrees of your intended course—a degree of accuracy that is as good as you can reasonably expect from a kayak. Orienteering compasses are inexpensive, and because they are flat, there is little chance of their being knocked overboard or getting in the way of your paddle.

Keep a pair of brass dividers in the map case so that you can quickly and accurately check distances during the day. It is a good idea to do this frequently against the clock until you have developed a firm sense of speed without constantly having to calculate it.

A diver's watch is ideal for a kayaker and is vital for estimating distances at sea. There are many inexpensive models that are quite adequate.

A Radio Direction Finder (RDF) takes navigation beyond dead reckoning, but it is a useful aid to navigation in certain parts of the world. The coasts of Europe and the United Kingdom, as well as those of the Bahamas and North America, are covered with set frequency transmitters, and if you carry a small RDF in your kayak, you can fix your position by tuning in on two of these.

The Global Positioning System (GPS) has a range of pocket-size waterproof microcomputers that use orbiting satellites to fix your position to within a hundred metres (328 feet) or so. They can also tell you your speed, the time remaining until your arrival, the distance you have travelled and the distance you still have to go, as well as give you a graphic display of your course deviation. In other words, they are the ultimate magic box for the nerd who never could get the hang of a compass and all that sea. They now may be purchased for around $250 and are addictive. The down side is that they leave you totally at the mercy of those who control the satellites.

A sextant and tables is another, dare I say, primitive aid for those crossing open ocean or running the risk of being blown out to sea. I have never carried an RDF, a GPS or a sextant on any of my trips, though I could have used them on a number of occasions to confirm my dead reckoning. The sextant may also be used for calculating distances by measuring the angles to summits of known altitude, but the bulk of the instrument and its tables makes most kayakers think more than twice before bringing one aboard.

Hannes Lindemann carried two air force surplus sextants on his Atlantic crossing but finished the epic trip by dead reckoning after losing both in capsizes. (Let's face it, if you keep heading west, you're bound to hit land). Ed Gillet had better luck; he managed to maintain his course to Hawaii precisely and arrived with both his sextants. He also carried an early version of a Personal Locator Beacon (PLB), but it was fried by contact with the electric wonders aboard a friendly U.S. gunboat and caused no end of grief to those ashore when they lost his signal.

TAKING RANGES & BEARINGS AND
ESTIMATING SPEED & DISTANCE
IN THE WIND

Most sea kayaking is done within sight of land, and the simplest method of locating your position is by ranges or transits. Choose a pair of stationary objects that you can see and that are shown on your chart; then watch for them to range, or line up, as you paddle by. A line drawn through the objects on your chart will match the range line through the objects, and your position is necessarily somewhere along that line. If you can gauge the distance to the objects, you can gauge your position. If you combine the range line with a compass bearing on a third object, the intersection on your chart of the range line and bearing line will give you your position exactly. Even without the compass, you may be able to find two simultaneous ranges, and the intersection of these two lines will again give you a plot of your precise position (see page 115, example A). Buoys, remember, are likely to move, and should therefore not be used for ranges or bearings if accuracy is required.

Attentive coastal kayakers draw up dozens of mental transit lines as they paddle along. They will notice one object passing another on the shore, and not only will they have fixed a mental range line but they also will be able to estimate from it how fast the current is running and how much the wind is affecting them. In short, through a vast number of what eventually become automatic ranges, kayakers can gather a total picture of their progress.

The use of a compass in a kayak introduces some new and exciting ways to make mistakes. Only if you always pack your kayak the same way and always keep the compass in the same spot can the compass deviation be reliably known. The fact is, though, that you will probably have to move the compass around in order to take bearings. And if you put your flashlight on deck to examine the needle that is to guide you through the foggy dark, your needle will probably be following you instead of the other way around. The solutions to these problems are to load all ferrous metals and radios well clear of the compass and to use a chemical light. If you minimize the objective deviation hazard, you will be able to dedicate yourself to a sometimes far more fecund source of error—your use of the instrument.

Some orienteering compasses can be conveniently adjusted to com-

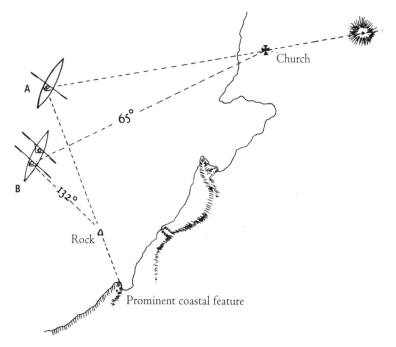

**During coastal travel, keep tabs on your location by a
series of fixes using ranges (A), bearings (B), or both.**

pensate for local variation. Take care to correct either the compass or
the bearings you take with it, but not both.

Normally a navigator would transfer the bearing to the chart with a
parallel rule, and it would be nice to have one aboard, but most kayakers
don't and will try to do it by eye—with the aid of two fat fingers and a
thumb. This is another source of considerable error! As a substitute for
the awkward parallel rule, a perspex grid about 10 inches square can be
stored conveniently inside the map holder. Or you may choose to use a
combination protractor-plotter instead, correcting all bearings to true
and working the protractor against a convenient longitude line.

A useful way to get an approximate idea of your position during a
crossing is to get your line of travel by means of a bearing on your point
of departure or destination; you then estimate your distance along this
line by multiplying your time by your known speed of travel. The obvious weakness in this formula is the great variability of "known speed of
travel." The following table lists a series of estimates based on a stan-

dard ten-hour paddle with approximately five minutes of rest each hour and about half an hour for lunch, except if there are high head winds, when the estimates assume that you must snatch food while paddling. Corrections for current must naturally be made according to conditions. A beam wind will usually affect your course, not your rate of travel, unless it is so strong as to interfere with your paddling. Winds forward and aft of the beam naturally have an effect on your speed, which varies according to their angle.

	Wind Speed in knots	Kayak Speed in knots	
	20 — 30	1.50 — 1.25	
HEAD WIND	15 — 20	2.25 — 1.50	
	10 — 15	2.50 — 2.25	
	5 — 10	2.75 — 2.50	
	0 — 5	3.00 — 2.75	
	0 — 5	3.00 — 3.25	
	5 — 10	3.25 — 3.50	
STERN WIND	10 — 20	3.50 — 4.00	} Surfing
	20 — 30	4.00 — 5.00	

OPEN CROSSINGS

The open ocean is normally a friendly environment for a sea kayak. Waves are regular and predictable, and winds and currents tend to be constant. Island hopping, which often includes open water, can be trickier, however. You may have a variable current or tidal flow to contend with, disturbed seas on each side of the crossing near land that is exposed to bad weather, and exposure to the big waves of the open sea. Part of your planning when island hopping is to gain a clear picture of what the tidal flow will be doing. If local tide tables prove inaccurate, keep a close watch on the ebb and flow yourself. Follow the phases of the moon so that you will know when to expect the strongest flows. When you are on the move constantly, you will become as familiar with the phases of the moon and the state of the tide as you normally are with day and night.

Paddling a kayak from one island to another across open sea poses some of the more serious navigational problems you will normally have to face. Let's assume your group is camped on a calm bay on the sheltered side of an island and you plan to paddle 25 miles to a high island due north, a major crossing by paddling standards. You know that there is a steady 1-knot current running from east to west and that the wind is forecast at 10 to 15 knots from the east-northeast.

A knowledge of your cruising speed under various conditions is vital. This information is best obtained not from the foregoing table but from frequent observations and calculation of your average speed over a whole day of reasonably constant conditions. A measurement of your speed over an hour or two is meaningless for longer-distance calculations.

Let us say that in the past you have calculated your average speed to be 2.5 knots under conditions such as our hypothetical crossing. You know therefore that the 25 miles will take you ten hours. (I would call that eleven just to be on the safe side.) It gets dark at seven o'clock in the evening, so you want to be in by five—in case you have to search for a landing or you find yourselves delayed. Counting back eleven hours, your scheduled departure will be for six o'clock in the morning. If your group takes the normal two hours to get away in the mornings, that means getting up at four o'clock.

To estimate the allowance you will have to make for that 1-knot current: take a piece of note paper and draw a line BC of appropriate length for the current, at 1 knot to the inch. At a right angle to BC, draw a line BZ of indefinite length. Now lay the ruler so that the zero mark is at C and your paddling speed (again at 1 knot to the inch) is on the line BZ. Mark the point where the lines cross as A. The angle BAC is your necessary correction, and the length of AB tells you how far over ground you will travel in one hour.

Alas, life is not so simple. Because of your slow cruising speed relative to the current, not to mention the current's variability, you cannot rely on being able to maintain this course. There is usually an allowance to be made for wind, but even neglecting that for the moment, you must take the calculated correction for current as a guide only—one that has to be constantly checked.

Let us assume, for example, that you depart on schedule and paddle down the sheltered coast to the nearest point of land to your destination. After a brief pause to see that the bilge pumps are sucking water and that the spray skirt is correctly secured, you head out into the rough

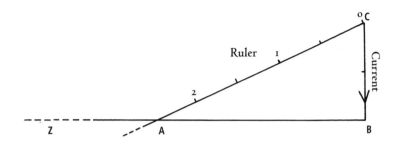

water. Coming from the open sea, the waves are 2 metres (6 feet) and lumpy off the headland because of the current and rebound effect. Paddle steadily on your intended course (in this case due north plus or minus the magnetic variation for the area plus the angle BAC) for a distance of about half a mile. That should take you about ten minutes. Then sight along the shaft of your paddle to your destination (or your departure point, if your destination is beyond the horizon or is obscured). Hold the kayak to your course (as corrected for current) while making this sighting. Then lay the shaft of your paddle across your compass; you should get a reading against the shaft that corresponds to the uncorrected compass course plotted on your chart. If it does not correspond, correct the set of your boat to the current until it does. Watch carefully for changes in the current flow. Do you expect it to ease up or change direction with a change of tide? If so, you should know when to expect that change.

Note: It is prudent to err on the upwind side of the current and wind during the first part of such a crossing, since it is much easier to correct for an overestimation of current than for an underestimation. Once you have decided on a set for the crossing, check it at least once an hour using your paddle shaft. The presence of shoals can greatly affect the speed of the current—pushing a 1.5-knot surface current to as much as 4 knots on occasions. Your chart should show these shoals. Their worst effects can often be avoided by skirting them upstream.

Should rain or haze obscure land, you must combine your total knowledge of all forces affecting your passage and then hold your course accordingly (or pull out your GPS). Have faith in your reasoned decision. The inability to see where you are going can rapidly undermine confidence if you are not prepared for it. Changes of current are difficult to spot unless they are related to some stationary object, such as land or

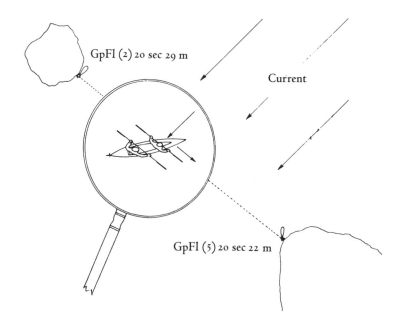

GpFl (2) 20 sec 29 m

Current

GpFl (5) 20 sec 22 m

Ferry-gliding across the current.

a buoy, but an experienced eye can sometimes detect them from the altered shape of the waves. In fog, your ears will alert you to the proximity of surf, and in rain, visibility is normally sufficient to avoid danger.

Here is an unhypothetical example of navigating by the paddle shaft. There is a 21-mile crossing from Trinidad to Tobago in the West Indies, known as the Galleon Passage. It has a steady current of 2 to 2.5 knots. Our party paddled it at night, going from Toco lighthouse on Trinidad to Scarborough lighthouse on Tobago. Both lighthouses were visible the whole way except during brief squalls. Our allowance for the current was frequently as high as 70 degrees from our intended course. Total crossing time: nine hours. Although use of the compass became necessary in squalls, most of the time we simply lined up the two lights along the paddle shafts and varied our set to keep them in line—exactly as a river kayaker would ferry-glide from one bank to another.

A different approach was needed on the next leg of that journey, where the distance was far greater: 80 miles of open sea to Grenada, in the Windward Islands. Departure was from a point 65 miles east and 50 miles south of Grenada, paddling due north so as to allow the current to carry us onto the island. This was considerably safer than ferry-gliding, since it gave more sea room to correct for unexpected delays—which could not have been made up had we been down-current. Besides, rain obscured our destination until twenty-five hours after leaving Tobago. As soon as we made a land sighting, we adjusted the course to keep upweather of the island, thus assuring seaway for the latter stages of the paddle—a particularly necessary precaution in this case because of a shoal to the southwest, which caused the current to accelerate with nasty overfalls and gave us a poor chance of fighting it back to the island.

MORE ABOUT WIND

Wind can affect the sea kayaker even more than current, but sighting and paddleshaft navigation work for judging its effects as well. The east-northeast wind on our hypothetical crossing a few pages ago could be tricky for a northbound kayak because of the tendency to turn into such a wind (a rudder helps). In this example, however, you would be paddling almost exactly east-northeast by virtue of the allowance you are making for the current, so you need not correct course for the wind at all. You need only take into account that your average speed will be somewhat reduced. The wind, we said, was forecast at 10 to 15 knots, so you could expect it to cut your speed by at least half a knot.

Should the wind swing more to the east, however, you would need to increase the angle of your set by a few degrees to compensate. Just how much allowance you make will depend on a variety of factors, including the weather outlook. Are you trying to gain seaway (getting upweather of your destination)? Has the wind been on the increase? And what is the condition of your party?

If the island to which you are paddling is steep-to and mountainous, be prepared for disturbed gusty winds near the shore, with williwaws, downdrafts and blasts coming from odd directions as a result of the funneling effect down valleys. One such downdraft is the infamous White Squall off the southern end of the island of Dominica, which, when we were there, struck an 18-metre (60-foot) yacht so savagely that she was laid hard over. Water flooded through her open hatches and she sank in seconds.

Landforms such as Cabo Froward in the Strait of Magellan so disturb the flow of winds that williwaws, twisters and appalling downdrafts are almost daily occurrences. Indeed, in blustery weather half a dozen or more williwaws may play about the cape at one time.

You cannot expect real progress against a wind in excess of 30 knots. You will barely hold your own against one of 40. But if you paddle at sea long enough, you will sometimes have to contend with even higher winds, especially in squalls, when you may have to settle for a ride backward until the gust eases—at which point you can resume your forward crawl.

One of the worst aspects of really strong head wind is that it prevents you from pausing. Assuming your normal speed is 3 knots, a 1-knot headway in a strong wind means that you will be blown back at 2 knots if you stop. Seen another way, it means that half an hour's pause in a strong wind demands another full hour of paddling just to regain your previous position. Such conditions can be soul destroying, and these are the situations in which you will be grateful for a small-volume, foot- or battery-operated bilge pump, or a large sea-chute, or both.

Normally one would be well advised to avoid making interisland crossings such as our hypothetical one in winds exceeding 20 knots if they are from the forward quarter. From anywhere astern, however, such a strong breeze may be a great asset—although you will still need to make allowances for drift, depending on how close abeam it is blowing.

NAVIGATING IN THE PRESENCE OF COASTAL WINDS

In general terms, coastal paddling may be classified according to whether the wind is onto the land (a lee shore) or off the land (a windward shore).

Unprotected lee shores are normally dangerous. They are usually visited by heavy surf and may be bristling with rock or coral reefs. The safest thing to have under the surf, of course, is a nice sandy beach. Whenever you are obliged to paddle a lee shore, plan your arrival for certain daylight and choose as a landing site a sheltered cove or an area protected by an offshore reef. It may not always be possible to achieve this goal, and heavy surf may make landing at your intended destination too risky. In that case—if there is no nearby alternative—you have either to continue paddling throughout the night and find a safe landing at dawn, or to search until dark, then anchor offshore and wait until dawn to see what your choices are. Be warned, however, that you should not count on your anchor if the wind is strong, and it is extremely dangerous to attempt to land on an unknown lee shore in the dark.

The sea off a lee shore is usually rougher than open sea, and chaotic rebound waves develop if the coast is at all steep-to. If it is a gently sloping beach, the waves will steepen long before they break. Stay well beyond the line of breakers and keep a weather eye open for the rogue wave that may peak farther out than the rest.

Although it is undeniably dangerous, the lee shore does not hold the same terror for kayakers as it did for the sailors of the old windjammers, whose ships were often swept onto the rocks when they ran out of seaway. Even modern yachts that can beat effectively to windward must take care never to be caught in a gale on a lee shore. You are less at the mercy of the wind in a kayak, but being caught on a lee shore during gale conditions could force you to run unfamiliar surf if there are no good landings within reach, and that is a situation to be avoided if possible. Lee shores without protected harbours should be attempted only when the weather is stable.

Windward shores are more forgiving. The water is calmest here, and hazards are more easily seen and avoided. When approaching a small island from upwind, you should land if you can on the windward shore. Even if you are able to land on a lee shore because of moderate conditions, you may get stuck there if the wind freshens during your stay. When approaching an unfamiliar island in the dark, always do so from the windward shore.

The danger of windward shores is the sometimes strong offshore wind that can blow small boats to sea. The inexperienced may make a fatal miscalculation when they see that the water "looks so calm" close in to land. The farther out you get, the rougher the sea may become and the harder it may be to return. If the wind is really strong, you may not be able to return against it from only a few hundred metres offshore. You can paddle a windward shore during high winds only by staying very close to the land. Under such conditions, don't be tempted into taking the short route across a wide bay.

DEALING WITH COASTAL CURRENTS

The sea is seldom without a current along the coast of an island or continent, and you can save a lot of effort if you know what this current is doing. Some excellent computer programs are on the market today, including Nautical Software, which offers minute-by-minute tide and current information for dozens of locations around North America—for the next hundred years (just what you need for long-range planning!). Printouts of tidal information can be in either a graphic or table form and can be prepared before you leave home.

Although annoying, a contrary current on a coastal paddle does not necessarily condemn you to stay in camp. It usually means that you should paddle close ashore to gain the benefit of eddies and backflows (though this may not be possible on rough lee shores). Even where there is a contrary current close inshore, it is frequently slower than farther out to sea. In some cases, shelter can be gained from strong currents by paddling inside the line of kelp or inside a coral reef. If you are going with the current, however, it is faster to stay well clear of the shore. Entering bays in this case only causes you to get caught up in backflows.

The trick is to know when to paddle close ashore and when to paddle out and, if you are paddling inside the current, to know just how far you have to enter the bays to avoid the head-on current yet not to lose distance by entering the counterflow too deeply. Your instructions are written on the surface of the sea. Once you realize they are there, they are not difficult to read. Belts of current can be seen from their effects on the water surface, enabling you to turn tightly into a current flowing your way. Close inshore, snags, kelp, lobsterpot buoys or lines of flotsam reveal the flow of back eddies that can be of assistance to you. As a cyclist's knowledge of hills and road surface becomes more intimate than a motorist's, so your knowledge of currents will become more intimate than that of other mariners. Few other craft can navigate in water less than 15 centimetres (6 inches) deep. And the kayak's slow cruising speed and light weight make an occasional bump on a boulder quite inconsequential if the sea is calm.

NAVIGATING ESTUARIES & HEADLANDS

Rounding a steep-to headland produces the greatest difficulty for those travelling against the flow of the current. It is off the headland that the current runs strongest and closest to shore. Usually there is no alternative but to sprint around into the relatively still water of the next bay. On a rough lee shore, the current around a prominent headland will produce very turbulent conditions well out to sea. The winds will be stronger, and williwaws may occur. In short, headlands are crisis points in coastal kayaking.

Estuaries also produce a variety of surprises for the unwary. Most problems occur in the higher and lower latitudes, where tidal variations are greatest and current speeds can get very high if the estuary extends far inland. Where it enters open sea, the tidal outflow from what may basically be a small stream can acquire the proportions of a mighty river. In some places, speeds can exceed 15 knots. Overfalls, upsurges, bores and whirlpools develop, and where the flow meets big ocean swells, rollers form a barrier of destruction. When approaching unknown estuaries, look well ahead for the white water and then do what you must to avoid it.

Ferry-gliding is the normal way of crossing a fast tidal flow in an estuary. If you have to make ground against the flow and can't wait for a tide change, stay in as close to shore as you can. If you are going with it, get out in the middle and enjoy the ride. When entering a fast flow from still water, either enter at an angle considerably sharper than that which you will adopt to ferry-glide the stream or lean downstream as you enter the current. This prevents water from piling up on the deck and causing a capsize.

NAVIGATING AT NIGHT

Try to avoid paddling by night along unknown coastal waters unless there is a bright full moon or the coast is well marked with lights and lighted buoys. As already mentioned, there are times when night paddling is desirable, but these are usually for open sea crossings or familiar waters. Extra care must go into the planning of night crossings if you are paddling towards an unlit shore. If you can arrange to depart before dark, do so because it will allow you to check your drift against the land before you lose sight of it.

Paddling with your head bowed to the compass all night can be unpleasant. It can also be unsafe, as you will to some extent lose your feel for the sea and increase the risk of seasickness. When the stars are visible, it pays to select one in line with your course and paddle towards it fifteen minutes or so at a time and then select another if the movement of the heavens requires you to do so. Few things can be more enchanting than paddling across open water on a starry night with bursts of phosphorescence glittering on your paddles and streaming off the wet deck. On cloudy nights, you have little choice but to paddle with your eyes to your compass, but when the wind is steady, you may get relief by simply holding a constant angle to the wind and waves. But beware of gradual shifts in the wind, made noticeable by its coming to odds with the waves.

The collision rules do not mention kayaks, but they require of a rowboat, "whether under oars or sail, to have ready at hand a lantern showing a white light, which shall be temporarily exhibited in sufficient time to prevent a collision." In addition to a diver's flashlight, I advocate that each boat carry a chemical "glow stick." When we first experimented with these glow sticks, we carried them on the stern of each kayak. In a following sea, however, the light was frequently beneath the water for seconds at a time and on one occasion, a huge fish struck one kayak a blow, which the unfortunate paddler described as like being rear-ended at a traffic light. (I have since learned that glow stick lures are popular with deep-sea fishers.) After that, we wore the lights in our hat bands. This increased the effective range of the sticks and provided us with a fine light by which to read the compass.

The great unwritten rule of the sea says that kayaks must get out of other people's way. Lighted or not, your kayak is too small to be seen easily, and you won't appear on most radar unless you are flying a radar reflector. Neither a reflector nor anything else will give comfort in the presence of fast craft such as speedboats, hydrofoils or Hovercraft, whose very speed sometimes makes their course almost impossible to predict accurately enough for a kayaker to take effective evasive action. In these cases you will have to rely on your guardian angel and white light and hope that they are keeping a good watch. This is not to say that big ships cannot be scary and don't travel deceptively fast. They do; but a ship's course is more constant, and at night you can tell its direction by the lights—red for port, green for starboard and the bow light always 4.5 metres (15 feet) lower than the masthead light. You know all is well so long as you can see only the green or the red light with the two white lights spaced comfortably one before the other. When you see both red and green, and the two white lights one above the other, it is time, or past time, to move quickly.

SNIFFING UP LAND

When paddling over the horizon to a large city or town at night you will usually see the loom of the lights—a glow in the sky—long before you see the lights themselves. The chart will usually indicate the outline of the town, and you can take a useful compass bearing on the glow in the heavens. The loom of a lighthouse too is usually visible well beyond the limit of visibility of the light itself. Your chart will indicate the range at which the light, not the loom, can be seen on a clear night. Lights in places such as the Bahamas, Latin America, Southeast Asia and the Middle East cannot be relied upon, however.

Convection clouds are flat-bottomed fluffy clouds that form above low landmasses in the tropics. The morning sun heats the land faster than the sea, and the hot air goes straight up, forming a cloud when the dew point is reached. In the Bahamas, you often see a fluffy replica forming directly above the landmass; cloud replicas are most distinct around noon. These airborne models can be so accurate that they show the individual bays that lie below. By late afternoon, the image will usually have merged into more general cloud, but such clouds too may tell a tale because their bellies reflect the pale turquoise water of the Banks.

Mountain clouds (cumulus rain clouds) often hover around the peaks of high islands, especially in the tropics, on otherwise clear, cloudless days. They too may be seen long before the land itself.

Winds and waves may also indicate the presence of obscured land. A flat island may not be visible from a kayak more than 5 miles distant, but look for waves that seem smaller than you would expect from the existing wind over open sea. If the waves are smaller, their fetch (that is, the distance over which the wind raises them) may be shorter, indicating the presence of an island or reef to windward.

An old transistor radio containing an internal dipole antenna can be used to locate the direction of a known radio station. Rotate the radio until it gives the best reception. The station then lies on a line at a right angle to the dipole. With luck you will know which way to head along this line.

CHAPTER FIVE

WEATHER

Generally speaking, kayakers set their own limits on the weather—or, more precisely, the wind—in which they choose to paddle. I don't know the limit of a well-found sea kayak, though I have approached what I believed to be my own limit a number of times. Yet the limits are always nudged forward with the use of better equipment and the application of more skill and determination. Who can say where the limits lie, or even be sure there are limits at all? I suspect that this is sometimes the hidden quest of the dedicated sea kayaker—the answer to those unanswerable questioners who, without hope of comprehending, ask why you paddle in the first place.

I say only that if you feel compelled to push your limits in wild weather and rough seas, you must not set out to do it on trips with less experienced people. If you are organizing a group, it pays to view weather defensively. Situations with odds acceptable to one person testing mind, body and soul at sea are often best avoided by a heavily loaded flotilla crossing from one island to another.

It is nice to know, however, that should you be caught in a real blow, all is not lost. There is an excellent chance of survival in a well-found kayak if the paddlers know what they are doing and nobody panics. I once ran before a storm into harbour at Picton, New Zealand, where the weather station was recording winds of 96 knots! We were not blown away and did not lose our paddles or anything else. In fact, the heavily loaded boat handled beautifully. We just clutched the paddles, crouched low and guided the kayak into harbour on the rudder. In the Windward

Passage north of Haiti, four of us in two boats were once caught 20 miles from land in a tremendous storm at night. Preceded by a waterspout over 300 metres (1000 feet) high, the wind at one stage did a full 360-degree turn in one hour, and the rain and flying spray were such that it was almost impossible to see the light on the other boat, though it was so close that there was a constant risk of collision. Lindemann and Romer survived days of fierce storms at sea when they crossed the Atlantic, and many an epic has no doubt been silently endured by hundreds of dedicated sea kayakers the world over. What I am saying is that with care, knowledge, skill, the right boat and plenty of faith in yourself, you can come to terms with the sea in most weather.

If you have doubts about the conditions, usually the best thing is to paddle out and look. Remember, seas are often more chaotic and difficult near headlands and on steep-to lee shores, so you may have to go out a way into the open sea. If you are a party, however, and you as leader have any doubts at all, be prudent. Return and wait for better weather. You can be pretty sure that those with less experience will be having far more doubts than you, and their very lack of confidence can only increase their vulnerability. (Some novices, in contrast, are totally fearless even when faced with disastrous conditions, and these people can be equally dangerous to themselves and their companions.)

Part of your trip planning should be a visit to your library to study the weather patterns of the area, in particular the nature of the prevailing winds. Local mariners usually know nothing about the capabilities of kayaks, but they too can be full of valuable tips on the weather. They can tell you the special weather warning signs of the region—mist forming on such-and-such peak, or the significance of an unusual shift in the wind. Their descriptions of local weather are also likely to be more vivid than the dry jargon on official forecasts.

Let's face it, though, value your forecasting ability as you may, your most reliable and commonly available aid in predicting the weather will be your radio. Before entering an area, record the times and frequencies of marine weather forecasts. Get a weather check before any major crossing or lee-shore paddle. In civilized parts of the world, a phone call to the local weather bureau, coast guard or airport will supply you with exactly the information you require, but if you are in the wilderness, you will have to rely on what you see around you to forecast your own weather. (Sometimes even in remote areas your radio will pick up useful satellite information on the location and movement of air masses.)

WIND ORIENTATION

Weather systems entering the area, bringing shifts of wind that would make a crossing or exposed lee shore hazardous, will likely be your prime concern. Nature provides warnings of these approaching systems. High cirrus clouds usually indicate the approach of a low-pressure system still a day or two away. Lenticular clouds threatening more immediate high wind, or a suddenly forming high haze, may also reveal a new weather system pushing in. Still other signs are a haze ring around the sun or moon or layers of cloud running at different angles to each other.

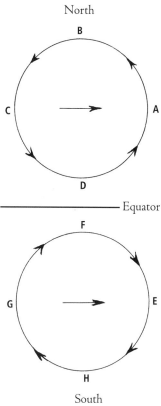

In the Northern Hemisphere, depressions contain winds at the lower levels that blow counterclockwise, whereas at higher altitudes (5 to 16 kilometres, or 3 to 10 miles), winds flow more or less steadily from a westerly direction. Thus, by examining the movement of upper and lower cloud levels during unstable weather, you can locate yourself relative to the depression and make an enlightened guess at future weather trends.

In the diagram on this page, the horizontal arrows represent the prevailing high-altitude westerlies, and the circles show the wind patterns of low-pressure systems nearer the earth's surface in the Northern and Southern Hemispheres. At point A, if you stand with your back to the wind, you will be facing north. The high clouds will be coming from your left, and the odds are that the weather will worsen. At point B, you will see the cloud layers moving in opposite directions, a sign that you can expect more of the same weather. At C, if you stand with your back to the wind, you will be facing south and will see the high clouds coming from your right—a sign that the weather may soon improve. At D, high and low clouds would be moving in the same direction, meaning more of the same weather. In summary, back to the wind, watch the high cloud; from left is bad, from right is good; forward or backward means no change. Not all low-altitude winds are depression winds, of course, so wind direction alone is not enough to form the basis of your forecast. To an observer at point C, a north wind is good news, but not all north winds in the Northern Hemisphere portend good weather.

In the Southern Hemisphere, where low-pressure systems circulate clockwise instead of counterclockwise, the same prediction rules apply, but observations must be made while facing into the wind instead of away from it. Thus, at Point E, an observer facing north into the wind would find the high cloud coming from his or her left—an indication of worsening weather. At F, the high and low clouds would be moving in the same direction, meaning more of the same weather. At G, facing south into the wind, an observer would find the high clouds coming in from his or her right, auguring well. At Point H, the high and low clouds would seem to be moving in opposite directions, and it would be reasonable to expect no immediate change in the weather.

BAROMETER

After your radio, a barometer is probably the most useful aid to weather prediction you can carry. But the barometer offers no easy answers to weather forecasting. It tells only the present pressure. It's up to you to make an informed guess based on past pressure and apparent trends. Certainly there is a well-established link between low pressure and bad weather, and the patterns of pressure change can make your prediction better than a wild guess. But even with the knowledge provided by hundreds of barometric pressures over a wide area, the weather services of the world can't claim to have it tabbed—so don't expect too much from your single-location readings. Seen in the context of all the other changes going on around you, however, including your wind orientation observations, the behaviour of your barometer should give some meaningful clues.

In the tropics, where the only fluctuation you may get for weeks is the pulse of day and night, a sudden plummeting of pressure is sure indication that you are in for a severe storm. On the coast of northern British Columbia, Norway, southwestern New Zealand or Patagonian Chile—the lands of the eternal lows—a low barometric pressure may be much less significant, and you will make your decision to paddle or not to paddle according to the wind and wave conditions on the shoreline you hope to travel.

In the temperate zone, where most kayaking is done, there are certain pressure patterns whose predictability makes them worthy of comment. A long, steady rise from 980 millibars to above 1020 millibars is a good indication of a stable period of fine weather. Sudden rises seldom lead to long fine periods. A steady fall indicates a more general deterioration. But such rules of thumb should be only one factor in many on which to base your predictions of future weather.

Animals seem to know when bad weather is approaching. If we humans have lost this sense (though I am by no means sure we have), we can at least keep an eye on other creatures and pay heed to their warnings.

Birds become nervous and more twittery than normal when a big storm is pending. Gulls huddle together on shore, sometimes flying well inland, where they squat nervously in the fields or crowd the beaches on little islands.

Sandflies go on an orgy of feeding, and their increased presence is most definitely noticeable.

Mosquitoes tend to be thickest after a storm, but if you are in a badly infested area, their prestorm enthusiam is also noticeable.

Porpoises have the remarkable trick of leaping clear of the water and then slapping down on the surface with a report like a rifle shot when a storm is imminent. Seeing this, mariners on the west coast of New Zealand reckon a storm will break within twenty-four hours. I have observed the apparent connection there and also in Chile.

Frogs—ah yes, frogs. Such sensitive little creatures. No serious sea kayaker should be without one. Have you ever noticed how excitement and croaking runs high in the frog pond when the weather is about to break? If you don't have a frog pond near your campsite, why not take a frog along in a mason jar and seek its advice on the weather every morning. It might prove considerably more reliable than some of the other forecasts you will be listening to.

TROPICAL WEATHER

The tropics, regardless of what the tourist brochures may say, are loaded with unsettled, wild weather. Much of this can be anticipated from a study of the weather patterns and an understanding of the basic causes of tropical weather formation; here are a few generalities.

The tropics are an area of prevailing easterlies, usually in the form of the southeast or northeast trades, and you would do well to go with them if possible. In Southeast Asia and the western Pacific and Indian Oceans, monsoons have a profound effect. The January monsoon, for example, will provide fresh northeasterly winds until as late as March. A period of southwesterly winds takes over between April and October. Unfortunately, these monsoons don't always follow the textbooks. I have encountered weeks of near gale-force northeasterlies along the coast of Java during August.

In Southeast Asia and Indonesia, typhoons strike most frequently from October to December, as the July monsoon weakens.

In the Caribbean, December through May is the period of strongest trade wind activity. June through October is the hurricane season, and though the storms are terrible when they strike, they are mercifully rare and the intervening weather usually has long periods of calm.

Severe squalls (known as waves) may cause prolonged unsettled weather in the tropics. Visually these resemble the low-pressure bad weather of the temperate regions, though there is minimal barometric variation.

Let's hope that as a sea kayaker you are not going to be caught out by a hurricane. Unless it forms right over you (in which case you will know about it as soon as the weather satellite), your radio should give you at least a day's warning of its arrival—but don't count on it; keep your eyes peeled for natural signs. If you are in a populated area, you will certainly get the message even if you miss the radio broadcasts. Birds have nothing on people when it comes to flapping! A storm warning of square red flags with black square centres hoisted one above the other at the port entrance (or, at night, a white light between two red lights) is customary, and warnings will usually also be broadcast on a public address system. The sky itself will also be plastered with warnings, and the tension will be considerable.

Nature's hurricane warnings:

1 Unusually high swells coming from the direction of the hurricane
2 Dramatic cirrus displays
3 A spectacular drop in the barometric pressure
4 An ominous calm period
5 Darkening skies that gain a coppery hue
6 Waterspouts or tornadoes on the right front quadrant six to twelve hours before the arrival of the big winds
7 Panic among the seabirds
8 Rapidly increasing wind as the storm approaches
9 Your weather frog's voice becoming tremulous

The hurricane is a circular storm (spiralling inward counterclockwise in the Northern Hemisphere, clockwise in the Southern Hemisphere) with winds that may exceed 320 kilometres (200 miles) per hour. The devastation is staggering. The sea level may rise by more than 3.5 metres (12 feet), and waves are very destructive. Kayakers will have their work cut out surviving on land. Pity help you if you are caught by one at sea, but if you are, you will not be the first. Franz Romer died at sea in a large hurricane in 1928. He had just crossed the Atlantic by kayak and had survived two other hurricanes in the course of his crossing.

WEATHER IN THE SUBPOLAR & COOLER TEMPERATE ZONES

Some of the finest kayaking routes are found in the colder latitudes. After all, the kayak is originally a cold weather craft. It seals around your waist, encasing the lower part of your body in still air, which acts as an insulator. (Open the spray skirt, however, and the chill factor increases dramatically.)

Western Canada, Alaska and the eastern Arctic, Labrador, Greenland, Scandinavia and Scotland all provide fine cold weather kayaking. So do Patagonia, the Falkland Islands and the southwest coast of New Zealand. These areas have in common a vulnerability to polar air masses, with most of their weather coming off the sea. All were once heavily glaciated, so their coastlines now offer excellent protection and great interest for kayakers in a maze of fjords and rocky islands. These areas are subject to constant storms, and a kayaker must be prepared to paddle in all but the very windiest of weather or risk waiting weeks for it to clear. Such latitudes are the breeding grounds of the low-pressure systems that invade temperate regions. They can produce snow showers in midsummer, when the sun hovers in the sky for twenty hours a day and the nights don't really get dark at all, whereas in winter you have barely six hours of dim light in which to paddle and the routine of making and breaking camp is done in freezing darkness. One would normally try to avoid paddling during these winter months, but if you are well prepared, there is no reason why you cannot do so.

Patagonian weather, like Alaskan weather, comes mostly from the west, but north and south, of course, are reversed in their significance. Storm winds blast Patagonia from the northwest, and bitter polar air masses occasionally sweep in from the south. The southerly wind following the passing of a low-pressure system foretells fine weather. Wet westerly winds drop hundreds of inches of rain a year on the tangled mossy forests of the mountain valleys and feed the great Patagonian icecap with an endless supply of snow. The needle of your barometer will mostly oscillate between 980 millibars and 1000 millibars, with only the occasional high taking over for a day or two. You mustn't be disconcerted, though, if the bottom drops out of the glass. Patagonian paddling is so protected that you can almost always find a calm side of a fjord to travel—and as that veteran of Patagonian exploration, the late Eric Shipton, once remarked, "If you wait for good weather in Patagonia, you'll never do anything."

Williwaws may result from the deflection of high winds by steep landmasses. They occur most frequently off headlands that are backed by high mountains or on the fringes of the lee of a high island. These are hardly unique to Patagonia, though the name originates from the region. *Williwaw* is the Yahgan word for the wind squalls of the Strait of Magellan. Some of the healthiest specimens may be found frolicking off Cabo Froward. A williwaw manifests itself as a blast of wind, sometimes twisting, sometimes falling out of the sky as a downdraft and rushing across the sea in a wall of spray over 60 metres (200 feet) high.

As it travels it collects water from the wave tops and appears as a white cloud. You can hear williwaws coming; at night the noise is all you have to judge their approach. When they hit, lie low, leaning well into them and holding your paddle so that it is not caught by the wind. In an unstable boat, a low-profile paddle brace to windward will improve stability. In a stable one, hold your paddle hard against the deck or, if it is feathered, in the water alongside, on the windward side of the boat. These positions reduce the chances of having the paddle blown out of your hands.

Katabatic winds, or bora, are the result of the drainage of cold air from high ground under the influence of gravity. A vast reservoir of cold air gathers over the icy interior and is tripped by a light offshore wind. It gathers momentum as it avalanches towards the sea. Katabatic winds are common in Greenland, Alaska, Norway, the Antarctic and the Adriatic.

Such a wind once struck our camp on the shores of the Strait of Magellan. It was a still, moonlit night, and the only warning we had was an eerie howl that brought us out of our tents. The wind almost blew our camp inside out on the first blast. For two hours it slammed into us; then, as suddenly as it had started, it stopped and there was silence. It is unlikely that vessels at anchor with an eye to protection from the west would have survived that devastation from the east.

TEMPERATE WEATHER

The temperate zone, lying as it does between the perennial lows of the subpolar latitudes and the tropical high-pressure systems, is the area of greatest unpredictability. It is also, however, the area where you are most likely to get skilled assistance with your weather forecasting, since it is home to the world's most technological civilizations. Here your most important piece of weather forecasting equipment definitely will be your radio or telephone line to the weather office, but you should take care to stay in tune with the signs of nature yourself, since sometimes the edge your guess may have over the weatherforecaster's is that you looked at the sky that morning.

By the way, don't underestimate Mediterranean weather. The summer winds can be fickle and devastating, making long crossings more hazardous than in areas where the wind remains steady. Summer is surely the best time to paddle in the Mediterranean, though I have kayaked there myself only during the winter. It was excellent training for Patagonia—katabatic winds and all.

For weather buffs I recommend David Burch's Starpath Weather Trainer computer program, complete with a certification option (if such things tickle your fancy).

CHAPTER SIX

READING
the SEA

Almost everything a kayaker needs to know about the sea is written there in a code of colours, swirls, patterns, shapes and sizes that reflects the weather of the moment and may indicate weather to come. This code can tell you the character of the sea bottom and how far beneath the surface it lies. It can tell you about currents and tides. It can even tell you something about the nearby land. Foremost among the messengers of the sea are the waves—complex pulses of energy that move relentlessly through the oceans. Waves originate chiefly from the action of wind passing over the water but can also be formed by water flowing over an obstruction or by earthquakes and landslides (tsunami waves). Their energy is ultimately lost through dissipation as heat—either gradually, as a result of viscosity, or abruptly, as the wave breaks. The longer they are, the faster they move.

Remember, though, that for all but current-generated waves, what moves is the wave, not the water. The passage of a wave through water does not result in any net movement of the particles of water except where the wave is breaking—and there is little movement even then, as the crest tumbles and carries a small surface flow after it. Only the wave energy crosses the seas; the particles within the wave move in a circle, returning more or less to their original position when the wave has passed.

The waves you will encounter on the open sea will seldom be simple and uniform even when they all appear to be travelling in the same direction. Some waves are obviously larger than others, and there are moments when the sea almost seems to flatten out. That is because waves of different sizes, and therefore different speeds, alternately complement each other and cancel each other out. These waves probably have different origins, and their interaction is highly significant for the kayaker trying to get through a line of breakers. Sometimes a pattern of big and small waves can be discerned, enabling you to anticipate the arrival of the next set of big ones and sneak through before they hit. Frequently, however, no reliable pattern emerges. It is chaos out there.

Let's have a look at the more common types of wave and how they affect a sea kayaker.

OCEAN SWELLS, WINDBLOWN WAVES & CHOP

Ocean swells are raised by the wind, but their stormy origin may be hundreds of miles distant. They may exceed 450 metres (1500 feet) in length, from crest to crest, and travel at speeds in excess of 30 knots. As they approach the shallows near land, these great waves steepen and slow. When their height reaches roughly one-seventh of their length, the crests topple and the waves crash ashore as surf.

On the open sea, these waves normally pose little problem to a kayaker. They just slip by, occasionally obscuring the land and other paddlers. They become a problem if you happen to be where they are forming in the midst of a storm; then they can reach their critical height at sea and their crests go plunging down their 15-metre (50-foot) slopes, enveloping all in their path.

Swells also cease to be slumbering giants when they run against a strong current. Under such conditions, the leading face of the swell is undercut and steepens, and the crest crashes over as a plunging breaker or ocean roller. Such waves form in the shallows off harbour entrances when there is an outflowing tide and can occur in the currents of the Gulf Stream and off the east coast of Africa and Japan. This situation is certainly to be avoided, since it is extremely difficult to judge the size of the rollers without getting too close. Other places to watch for them include shallow banks fringing deep ocean and in the estuaries of large-volume rivers that flow into open sea. If you cannot avoid these waves, you must handle them as you would surf: head-on if you are going against them, broached-to on a paddle brace or even with a pre-emptive roll (to reduce their destructive impact) if they are abeam.

Windblown waves differ from swells only in that they are smaller and formed locally. They build and die relatively quickly in the open sea, being readily cancelled or altered by a change of wind. They are of shorter wave length than the ocean swells and move correspondingly more slowly.

Their size depends on the wind speed, fetch and length of time the wind has been blowing as well as on the composition of the water, which in some of the most interesting ocean-kayaking areas is anything but constant. In places, the sea may contain hundreds of square miles of fresh surface water, which will cause waves to form more readily and more steeply into the sort of chop one might expect to find on freshwater lakes.

A chop forms where the fetch of the wind is short and equilibrium has not been reached. Such conditions occur in a harbour on a windy day. Chop offers little serious threat to a well-found kayak, though it can be most unpleasant. Steep 1-metre (3-foot) waves are just big enough to throw a bucket of cold water into your face every five seconds when you are paddling into them.

INTERFERENCE WAVES: RIPS, OVERFALLS & CLAPOTIS

A current setting over a shallow, irregular bottom, or two currents intersecting each other, will often cause a patch of chaotic water called a rip. Since the currents responsible for these rips are often tidal currents, the rips are often called tide rips—not to be confused with the so-called riptides, better called rip currents, which are found on beaches. Tide rips and their attendant eddies and whirlpools are notoriously common among the archipelagoes of British Columbia and Alaska, where some but not all of them will be marked on your charts.

Rips are composed largely of standing waves. These are waves that "jog in place," moving up and down while the current flows through them. Standing waves are normally more sharply peaked than travelling waves, and the water in them is for the most part moving up and down and side to side instead of rolling in stationary circles. When these waves break, either from wind action or from the force of the current flowing through them, the result is called an overfall. These are regularly encountered in Alaska's Alexander Archipelago.

When a wave strikes a steep cliff, either obliquely or directly, it is reflected as if from a mirror. The rebound waves may pass right through the incoming waves, if their crests and troughs do not coincide, but the confused sea that results can make for hair-raising paddling. When the crests of such contradictory waves do coincide, however, their amplitudes combine, creating huge standing waves, again much steeper than travelling waves. This phenomenon is called clapotis. (The same word is used on French charts to mark tide rips.)

Off the northern tip of New Zealand, where major wave patterns collide in deep water, clapotis is regularly seen. The pinnacling waves formed here have so much vertical power that they can throw a laden kayak clear out of the water. In the Grenadines, between Isle Ronde and Carriacou, is an 8-mile crossing known, for good reason, as Kick'um Jenny. Here the waves often enter both from the Atlantic to the northeast and the Caribbean to the northwest. They strike the steep cliffs at Diamond Head and rebound into a four-way chaos of pinnacling waves for miles out to sea. A current setting side-on at 2 to 3 knots complicates matters still further. The resulting illegible confusion can be very rough going in a kayak.

When the current is running hard against normal ocean waves, the wave length shortens and the faces of the waves steepen, causing the crests to tumble. This phenomenon is another form of overfall, and it too can be very unpleasant for a kayaker. In milder form, however, such conditions usefully betray the movement of the current. Even out of sight of land you can detect a change in the tidal flow from the altered angle and length of the waves. In a kayak during dark night crossings, if the wave patterns are not too confused, you may even hear or feel this change through the seat of your pants.

When the waves become smoother and more rounded than you would expect from a certain wind strength, it is reasonable to expect that they are running with the current, though this is more difficult to identify. When the wind blows across the current, the wave length is normal, but the crests are twisted slightly as they break, with a tendency to form toppling pyramids.

A wind blowing against the waves is usually a temporary situation, since waves are normally a product of the wind. When a sudden wind change occurs, however, there can be a period of chaotic seas as the new pattern establishes itself. This situation is not normally a threat to a kayaker, though it is nice to be prepared for the change when it occurs. Local wind blowing against heavy swells has little effect on the direction or size of the swells. Instead, smaller waves will travel on top of the long swells regardless of their direction. Mostly the chaos caused by wind against waves should be taken as a warning that something unsettling is happening to the weather.

BREAKERS

The way a wave reacts on reaching land depends on the depth of the off-shore waters, the nature of the land and the angle at which the wave strikes it.

Plunging breakers, or dumpers, form where there is a steeply shelving drop-off to open water. There is little shortening of wave length as the wave approaches the shore, and typically there is only one row of breakers that curls and bursts directly onto the foreshore from which the spillage of the previous wave is rapidly receding. From seaward the ferocity of these waves can be gauged by the explosive quality of the break as the air trapped within the plunging crest is compressed and then expands, throwing sand and gravel up with the water. Perhaps the most danger-ous plunging breaker is the one that forms on shoals or coral reefs.

Spilling breakers form where the offshore gradient is gentle and their energy is dissipated gradually. On the north coast of Java, the gradient is so gentle that the waves reach their critical depth miles offshore, and getting out through the surf in the morning can mean a one-hour battle against breakers. Spilling breakers are probably the most manageable for a kayaker, since they lack the explosive quality of dumpers. They also allow you to judge the water depth, since their height declines shoreward in fixed pro-portion to the depth of the water. (The effect of the tide can be important when planning your landing or departure through these breakers. Where the tidal range is great, you may have plunging breakers on the beach at high water and spilling breakers for a quarter of a mile when the tide is out.)

On occasion you will encounter a third type of breaking wave, which occurs when the beach slope just exceeds the steepness of the wave. Then, instead of plunging, the wave surges up the beach, breaking as it climbs.

The distinctions between plunging, spilling and surging breakers are frequently blurred, however, and more than one type of breaker can often be seen on the same beach.

When waves reach land and their energy is not dissipated as breakers, they are variously affected according to the nature of the land and the angle at which they strike. A small island, for example, causes the waves to change direction and bend around the landmass, spreading their

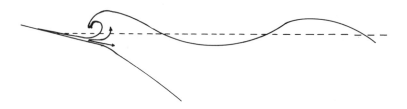

Plunging breakers, or dumpers, are recognizable from seaward by their violence. They occur where the beach drops off steeply. Avoid them if possible. If you must land in dumpers, try to sprint in on the back of them and scramble out of the danger zone.

Spilling breakers can usually be identified from seaward by their long sweep towards shore. The gently sloping bottom against which they form may be visible on your chart.

energy as they do so. Standing waves sometimes form behind and somewhat beyond the island, at a distance about equal to the diameter of the island. Here, if the water is shallow and the bottom sandy, a bar will form. When you are paddling inside such an island, choose a course in close to the island. Inside this "wave shadow" is usually the most desirable place to make a landing. The approach from behind the wave shadow, of course, should be avoided, since converging wave patterns are likely to create a difficult, breaking sea.

BOOMERS

On exposed coasts, barely submerged rocks can be spotted by the heavy swells that break on them. But suppose the rock is 3 metres (10 feet) beneath the surface and is not quite uncovered by the average passing swell. A wave larger than usual comes through, the top of the rock is exposed, and the crest folds over and virtually explodes on the rock. This type of wave is known as a boomer, and it is a common danger for kayakers

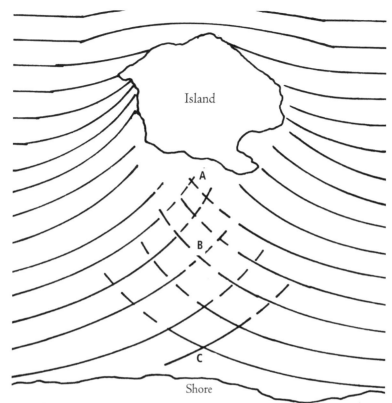

The water is calmest at A. B is a zone of clapotis and chaotic seas. At C, the converging wave patterns focus energy on the shore, creating difficult surf.

paddling a rocky lee shore exposed to open ocean. Watch at least a mile ahead to locate boomers. Eventually you will make an automatic mental note of any breaks in the wave pattern, just as a hiker will note obstructions on the path. Deeply submerged rocks may catch only one wave in twenty—but if you are on that wave, you will be in for quite a surprise.

Some basic rules for avoiding boomers are as follows:

1 Check the chart and tides well in advance and know when currents are likely to push you onto an infested area.
2 If you are paddling through shoal waters, keep a keen eye for and remember the position of all isolated breakers near your course.
3 Avoid patches of kelp, which at higher latitudes probably conceal rock.
4 If you see rock beneath you, sprint clear.

5 Watch out for waves peaking unusually sharply. They could be "feeling bottom" on a submerged rock. Spume with no obvious cause may also point to a boomer.

In the tropics, isolated coral heads can produce boomers. Their position can sometimes be seen from a darkened patch in the sea. Because kayaks frequently travel where no other craft would go, you may find yourself in incompletely charted waters. Besides, coral grows, and charts based on fifty-year-old surveys cannot be relied on to show inshore coral patterns.

WAVES & WIND SPEED

Waves are the principal telltales of the weather at sea and are used to categorize weather conditions. Waveforms and wind speed as ranked on the Beaufort scale appear on the following page.

The table assumes a steady wind on the open sea. In coastal waters with onshore winds, the condition of the waves will be very different, and a kayaker unassisted by technology will have to estimate the wind strength from the appearance of the water surface and the effect on trees, if trees are visible. Gusts are more frequent close to steep land, and their velocity is especially difficult to estimate.

TIDES & TIDAL CURRENTS

Since there is no shortage of manuals on compass and chart work, so there is no shortage of books and now computer programs on tides and tidal current prediction. I assume on the reader's part some knowledge of the theory of tides and an ability to use tide and current tables. It is one of the pleasures of kayaking, however, to go where no other boat can go, and this sometimes means going where no tide and current table is available. At the same time, the kayak, with a cruising speed on the order of 3 knots and a top speed of perhaps 5 or 6, is highly susceptible to the effects of tidal currents. (As a boat that frequently spends the night on a beach, it, like its paddler and sleeping bag, can also be vulnerable to the tides.) Current and tide predictions of some sort are indispensable to coastal kayaking, especially in the higher latitudes. This all adds up to the fact that the sea kayaker must develop the primitive sailor's wary and attentive eye for what the water and the moon are doing.

If you are paddling under an opaque Alaskan overcast, your lunar

Beaufort Force	Wind	Sea	Wave Pattern & Paddleability
0	0–1 knot	Calm	Monotonous kayaking, risk of hyperthermia in the tropics, old wave patterns only, smooth surface.
1	1–3 knots	Light air	Slight relief from heat unless the movement is from astern; scale-like ripples.
2	4–6 knots	Light breeze	Comfortable kayaking. Small wavelets.
3	7–10 knots	Moderate breeze	Large wavelets; crests start to form and break with clear foam. Good kayaking weather.
4	11–16 knots	Good wind	Small waves becoming longer. Whitecaps. The comfortable limit for novice kayaking.
5	17–21 knots	Strong wind	Large waves form; whitecaps are numerous. Weather for experienced kayakers.
6	22–27 knots	Very strong wind	Breaking waves begin to streak; williwaws near headlands. Try to avoid this weather.
7	28–33 knots	Near gale	Moderately high waves with streaks and spray flying from their crests. Definitely outside the realm of normal kayaking.
8	34–40 knots	Gale	High waves, dense streaking and flying spray. This is the practical limit for kayaking (no progress into it).
9	41–47 knots	Strong gale	High waves start to tumble, dense streaking; the paddler is blown backwards.
10	48–55 knots	Storm	Very high waves; long overhanging crests tumbling. Survival situation running or lying to a drogue.
11	56–63 knots	Violent	The sea is white with spray; huge waves. The kayak is running before the wind or lying to a drogue.
12	64–71 knots	Hurricane	The air is filled with foam and spray. Visibility from a kayak is near zero. Running with warps astern is probably your only practical option.

sightings may be few, but if the moon can be seen at all it will tell you much about the state of the tide. Spring tides come with the new and the full moon. Neap tides occur when the moon is neatly cut in two, at the first and third quarters. The moon's effect increases at perigee (when it is nearest the earth) and decreases at apogee (when it is farthest away). When the perigee coincides with a new or full moon, an event that occurs at least twice a year, the tidal range will be greatest: the high waters will be especially high and the adjacent low waters especially low—perhaps several feet lower than the lows shown on your charts.

High water can be expected a couple of hours after the moon crosses the meridian. At new and full moon, high water occurs somewhat after noon and midnight. At the quarter moon, when the tides are smaller, high water occurs somewhat before noon and midnight. Successive high and low waters are likely to be about equal when the moon is riding the equator. In the Pacific and Indian Oceans, the tides tend to be wildly unequal when the moon is "in the tropics"—that is, when its orbit runs to the Tropic of Cancer or Capricorn. The visible declination of the moon will depend on where you are when you're looking, but the changes of declination are easily seen, and your tide table should include a lunar calendar that will help you get the hang of it. In thick weather, this calendar alone will give you much of the information you need for seat-of-the-pants tide prediction.

When you have the luxury of using the tables themselves, remember that the predicted heights and times can be drastically altered by high winds. Prolonged or severe barometric drops are generally accompanied by an increase in the tidal range, and a sudden or sustained rise in atmospheric pressure will usually reduce the range. These factors too will cause the tides to depart from the tabulated heights and times.

When you have to negotiate a long passage in which the sea is peaceable only at high or low slack, keep an eye on the tables for a standing tide. This phenomenon occurs when a relatively low high water is followed by a high low water, usually followed again by a low high tide. For hours in such a case the tide may scarcely budge.

Standing tides are common at the quarter moon on the Pacific coast of North America. In other areas, such as the Gulf of California and the South China Sea, the tidal cycle routinely runs at half speed, with only one high and one low water per day, all month long.

Often the item of real concern to a kayaker is not the tide itself but the

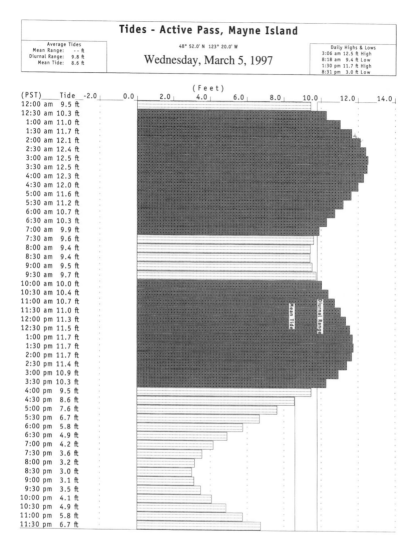

Tides - Active Pass, Mayne Island

Average Tides	48° 52.0' N 123° 20.0' W	Daily Highs & Lows
Mean Range: - - ft		3:06 am 12.5 ft High
Diurnal Range: 9.8 ft	Wednesday, March 5, 1997	8:18 am 9.4 ft Low
Mean Tide: 8.6 ft		1:30 pm 11.7 ft High
		8:31 pm 3.0 ft Low

(Feet)

(PST)	Tide
12:00 am	9.5 ft
12:30 am	10.3 ft
1:00 am	11.0 ft
1:30 am	11.7 ft
2:00 am	12.1 ft
2:30 am	12.4 ft
3:00 am	12.5 ft
3:30 am	12.5 ft
4:00 am	12.3 ft
4:30 am	12.0 ft
5:00 am	11.6 ft
5:30 am	11.2 ft
6:00 am	10.7 ft
6:30 am	10.3 ft
7:00 am	9.9 ft
7:30 am	9.6 ft
8:00 am	9.4 ft
8:30 am	9.4 ft
9:00 am	9.5 ft
9:30 am	9.7 ft
10:00 am	10.0 ft
10:30 am	10.4 ft
11:00 am	10.7 ft
11:30 am	11.0 ft
12:00 pm	11.3 ft
12:30 pm	11.5 ft
1:00 pm	11.7 ft
1:30 pm	11.7 ft
2:00 pm	11.7 ft
2:30 pm	11.4 ft
3:00 pm	10.9 ft
3:30 pm	10.3 ft
4:00 pm	9.5 ft
4:30 pm	8.6 ft
5:00 pm	7.6 ft
5:30 pm	6.7 ft
6:00 pm	5.8 ft
6:30 pm	4.9 ft
7:00 pm	4.2 ft
7:30 pm	3.6 ft
8:00 pm	3.2 ft
8:30 pm	3.0 ft
9:00 pm	3.1 ft
9:30 pm	3.5 ft
10:00 pm	4.1 ft
10:30 pm	4.9 ft
11:00 pm	5.8 ft
11:30 pm	6.7 ft

tidal current. In many narrows and passages along the coast of British Columbia, for example, tidal currents reach 10 to 15 knots. The tide and current tables give accurate current predictions for many of these channels, but the fjords and passages most tempting to the sea kayaker are often precisely those for which no predictions are published. A copy of the relevant *U.S. Coast Pilot, British Admiralty Pilot Guide* or *Canadian Coastal Sailing Directions* will often give you a general idea of what to expect. Remember, though, that the coast pilots and pilot guides are not written with kayaks in mind.

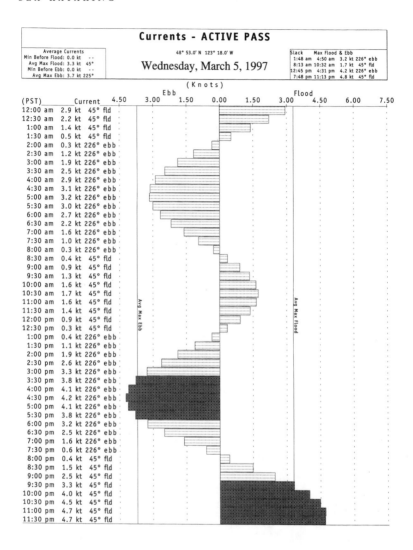

Currents - ACTIVE PASS		
Average Currents Min Before Flood: 0.0 kt -- Avg Max Flood: 3.3 kt 45° Min Before Ebb: 0.0 kt -- Avg Max Ebb: 3.7 kt 225°	48° 53.0' N 123° 18.0' W **Wednesday, March 5, 1997**	**Slack Max Flood & Ebb** 1:48 am 4:50 am 3.2 kt 226° ebb 8:13 am 10:32 am 1.7 kt 45° fld 12:45 pm 4:31 pm 4.2 kt 226° ebb 7:48 pm 11:13 pm 4.8 kt 45° fld

(Knots)

(PST)	Current	Ebb 4.50 3.00 1.50	0.00	Flood 1.50 3.00 4.50 6.00 7.50
12:00 am	2.9 kt 45° fld			
12:30 am	2.2 kt 45° fld			
1:00 am	1.4 kt 45° fld			
1:30 am	0.5 kt 45° fld			
2:00 am	0.3 kt 226° ebb			
2:30 am	1.2 kt 226° ebb			
3:00 am	1.9 kt 226° ebb			
3:30 am	2.5 kt 226° ebb			
4:00 am	2.9 kt 226° ebb			
4:30 am	3.1 kt 226° ebb			
5:00 am	3.2 kt 226° ebb			
5:30 am	3.0 kt 226° ebb			
6:00 am	2.7 kt 226° ebb			
6:30 am	2.2 kt 226° ebb			
7:00 am	1.6 kt 226° ebb			
7:30 am	1.0 kt 226° ebb			
8:00 am	0.3 kt 226° ebb			
8:30 am	0.4 kt 45° fld			
9:00 am	0.9 kt 45° fld			
9:30 am	1.3 kt 45° fld			
10:00 am	1.6 kt 45° fld			
10:30 am	1.7 kt 45° fld			
11:00 am	1.6 kt 45° fld			
11:30 am	1.4 kt 45° fld			
12:00 pm	0.9 kt 45° fld			
12:30 pm	0.3 kt 45° fld			
1:00 pm	0.4 kt 226° ebb			
1:30 pm	1.1 kt 226° ebb			
2:00 pm	1.9 kt 226° ebb			
2:30 pm	2.6 kt 226° ebb			
3:00 pm	3.3 kt 226° ebb			
3:30 pm	3.8 kt 226° ebb			
4:00 pm	4.1 kt 226° ebb			
4:30 pm	4.2 kt 226° ebb			
5:00 pm	4.1 kt 226° ebb			
5:30 pm	3.8 kt 226° ebb			
6:00 pm	3.2 kt 226° ebb			
6:30 pm	2.5 kt 226° ebb			
7:00 pm	1.6 kt 226° ebb			
7:30 pm	0.6 kt 226° ebb			
8:00 pm	0.4 kt 45° fld			
8:30 pm	1.5 kt 45° fld			
9:00 pm	2.5 kt 45° fld			
9:30 pm	3.3 kt 45° fld			
10:00 pm	4.0 kt 45° fld			
10:30 pm	4.5 kt 45° fld			
11:00 pm	4.7 kt 45° fld			
11:30 pm	4.7 kt 45° fld			

Whatever your sources—a modern computer printout, a coast pilot, published predictions, advice from locals or the results of reading chicken entrails—it is useful to have an advance notion of the set (direction) of flood and ebb currents, their maximum velocity and the approximate times of slack water. The current may peak anywhere from two to five hours after the turn, but an interval of a little over three hours from slack to peak is most common. The zero current, at the turn, may last only a moment, but for some time before and after the turn, the current will be negligible. How long this slack period will last depends on how fast the current is running when it peaks. At neap tides the current may not be running anywhere near its maximum spring-tide velocity, and the duration of slack water may be much increased. As a general rule, if the current peaks at 2 knots, there will be a period of about sixty minutes at slack water when the current runs at no more than half a knot. If the peak rate is 4 knots, the half-knot slack period is likely to last only about thirty minutes. For a 6-knot current, the half-knot slack may last about twenty minutes, for an 8-knot current, fifteen minutes; and for a 10-knot current, only ten minutes.

In the archipelagoes of Alaska, British Columbia and southern Chile, the intricacies of tidal currents are such that, with careful planning, a kayaker can paddle around an island on the flood current to a point at which the tidal currents diverge and, arriving there at high slack, can continue the journey at once, riding the ebb.

With a few significant exceptions, the current will run fastest where the water is deepest. When you are forced to buck the current, therefore, you will usually find it easiest to do so by paddling close ashore. Where shoals or a shallow bar obstructs the main flow, however, the shallow-water current will be faster, not slower, than the deep-water flow. Tide rips and overfalls frequently form in such circumstances, and the current can push you mercilessly through a forest of jagged standing waves. Headlands protruding into the flow will also accelerate the current, creating patches of very swift water called tide races. If you are obliged to cross a tidal current, the narrowest part of the channel may therefore be a poor choice. Up-current from a headland or shoal the flow is likely to be less hazardous.

Tide entering a shallow channel may break into a steep-fronted wave called a tidal bore, whose speed is dependent on its height and the water depth ahead of it. Tidal bores may form on expansive mud flats and in tidal rivers. They occur on the coasts of Britain and France, and large ones regularly form in some of the major river entrances of India, Asia and North and South America. A bore 7.5 metres (25 feet) high advances up the Amazon during spring tides at speeds sometimes exceeding 12 knots. Where bores exist at all, they are usually regular features and will be mentioned in your coast pilot. The large ones can be very dangerous, though smaller ones may provide excellent surfing.

OCEAN CURRENTS

The ocean currents are like great eddies between the continents. They rotate clockwise in the Northern Hemisphere and counterclockwise in the Southern Hemisphere, driven by the spin of the earth and the force of the winds. They have a profound effect not only on tidal flow but also on climate and weather. The relative warmth of the Japan Current, for example, is responsible for the mildness of the sea-level temperatures in southeastern Alaska. Currents such as the Gulf Stream off Florida or the Kuroshio off Japan may exceed 4 knots, throwing up dangerous seas when opposed by a strong wind. In the West Indies, the North Equatorial Current sieves through the narrow channels of the Windward and Leeward Islands and into the Caribbean, sometimes running in excess of 3 knots and creating a major navigational problem for craft as limited in speed as a kayak.

In the Mediterranean, a current of quite different origin exists. Rapid evaporation of surface water increases salinity, and the denser solution sinks, setting up a deep flow into the Atlantic through the Strait of Gibraltar. The inflow from rivers is not sufficient to compensate for this outflow, and as a result, a steady surface flow of Atlantic water runs eastward over the top of the deep westward outflow, sweeping the coasts of North Africa and Southern Europe. The entire Mediterranean is said to be flushed through in this manner every seventy-five years.

CHAPTER SEVEN

HAZARDS

Books such as this one usually seem to be full of dire warnings of doom. So as not to disappoint you, here is a whole section of doom; but remember, such hazards are only a small, albeit crucial, part of this game, without which sea kayaking would probably interest a very different sort of person. Sitting at home reading lurid descriptions of freak seas can be intimidating, but it somewhat resembles the panic you feel on waking suddenly in a car that has braked heavily before a corner: you are confronted by the hazard without the reassurance of the approach, in which you make automatic calculations that indicate that you are not approaching too fast. Most sea kayaking is plain paddling, sprinkled with more than its share of euphoric moments.

SURF

Surf is probably the most serious hazard for sea kayakers, who must frequently land and launch on exposed coasts. Surf kayaking can be great fun and is good for building confidence, but it is usually the aim of a cruising kayaker to spend as little time in surf as possible, since the boat is often loaded with expensive equipment and not really suited for riding breakers. True surf kayaking is a different sport, with different boats, different rules and often different people, but some of its tricks are useful to the sea kayaker. The most important thing the surfies can teach the sea kayaker is how to judge a wave from seaward—a skill that would otherwise have to be learned through painful, expensive trial and error.

The three main types of surf—plunging, spilling and (rarely) surging breakers—are discussed in Chapter 6. Dumpers, or plunging breakers, are worst and should be avoided where possible, since they can smash your boat to pieces against the sand. If you cannot avoid surf, spilling breakers are your best choice, particularly if there is no explosive quality to the wave as it first breaks. The ideal wave has a crest that collapses well out from the beach, gradually spilling its energy on its way to the land.

Beware of areas where the dissipation of the soup is abruptly completed before the wave reaches land. This smooth area may indicate the presence of a rock or coral shelf with a very shallow layer of water over it. If you come surfing merrily in, you may rip the bottom out of your boat.

Surf seldom breaks evenly on a beach. There will usually be a quieter spot at one or both of the ends of a crescent-shaped bay as a result of the refraction of waves hitting the beach obliquely. If there is kelp or a reef off the beach, the waves will be broken in the lee of this and you can probably sneak in behind it.

Out Through It

Assessing surf from shore is relatively easy. If you decide the waves are marginal for the experience of your group, you can sometimes improve your chances by timing them and counting the sets of big ones. There may be three big waves and then two small ones, followed by five medium ones—or some similar pattern that will enable you to judge your break for open sea—though I confess to having poor success at predicting slack periods. You may also be able to take advantage of a rip current—discussed in more detail a few pages on—to get a fast ride out through the danger zone. Any relative novices in your group should follow the example of a more experienced paddler, but leave a veteran ashore until last to help them out if things go wrong in the danger zone. If you only have two boats, send the less experienced kayaker or team of kayakers first so that these people will have assistance getting off the beach and someone ashore to rescue them if necessary.

Assume you are travelling in a group and your kayak is chosen to go first. Make yourself snug and secure the spray skirt while someone from another boat holds your bow into the incoming soup. When the timing is judged to be right, the person holding the bow pulls your boat past himself or herself, giving it a mighty push into the breakers while, at the same time, you begin to paddle as hard as you can, gaining enough momentum to punch through the wave. Continue to paddle with a strong, steady rhythm until you are well beyond the line of surf. From there you can watch the performance on shore and wait for the party to regroup.

If you are travelling solo or when yours is the last boat, the manoeuvre is a little trickier. Place the kayak at the edge of the surf where it can be reached by the larger waves that sweep up the beach. If you have a double, No. 2 holds the bow while No. 1 (the forward paddler) gets seated and zipped up. No. 2 then quickly slips into the boat and, if time allows, makes the spray skirt fast. If the receding wave is already carrying the boat out to sea, the arrangement is necessarily a hasty one, since both of you must immediately paddle hard directly into the surf. More often than not you will find yourself sitting in your boat on the wet sand and feeling a little foolish with the sea still 6 metres (20 feet) away. Stay put and arrange your spray skirt snugly. When the next wave reaches you, push off with the paddles or bare hands (not easy with a loaded boat!). Watch where you put your hands, since cuts can be bad news. It is also easy to break a paddle when launching in this manner. Sometimes, particularly with singles, the dissipating wave slues and then strands you sideways, exposing your beam to the next wave. A trick that sometimes works is to rock the kayak onto its side and then, still in your boat, spin it on the sand so that the bow is facing the next wave.

In Through It

Forward is usually the easiest way to come in through surf, but not necessarily the safest when you have a heavily loaded kayak. Going forward involves considerable commitment—perhaps, in view of the difficulty of assessing an unfamiliar beach from seaward, a reckless commitment. The great virtue of this method is that it is quick, thus minimizing the time spent in the danger zone. It is a method for heavy surf where you want to get through fast and the beach is clear of obstructions. Let me quote Paul Caffyn (whose first major challenge was the formidable west coast of New Zealand) on how he gets through.

> When waves are over 4 feet, I wait offshore and count the sets of big ones going in (usually 3). I wait till a big set is on its way then hammer in behind the last one—casting occasional glances over my shoulder to watch the next set building. This usually gets me past where they are breaking because I'm doing sprint speed of 6 knots or

more. When I hear and see the leading breaker of the following set, I let it get within 20 yards, then I do a right rudder and go into a broach position parallel to the breakers, then lift my paddle into a high brace and lean into the breaker as it hits. It carries the kayak in front, sometimes high up the face, but more often on the smooth water immediately in front of the breaker. On two occasions, I got in through 15-foot surf using this method. By going in at 90 degrees to the beach on steep waves, the bow digs in just as the wave caps, and the boat executes a graceful loop.

When entering sideways through surf, it is essential to lean seaward. Leaning into the land inevitably results in capsize.

Method number two is to go in backwards. This technique is useful for unknown or marginal beaches, since you are pointed the right way to get out of it fast if you have to. I don't recommend this method for crests in excess of 2 metres (6 feet) or for dumping breakers. Once you have chosen an apparently clear path of entry, turn the bow to the oncoming waves. Cock the rudder or skeg clear of the water and then paddle in backwards. When the cresting wave approaches, paddle hard into the wave so that the boat gathers enough momentum to prevent its being swept backwards at great speed. As soon as the wave passes, back-paddle quickly again until the next wave is almost upon you and then repeat. Although this method offers greater control over your entry, it leaves you in the danger zone longer and you can take quite a hammering. As you are going in, you should look over your shoulder frequently to judge distance to obstacles and the beach. In a double, the No. 2 paddler should take this job while No. 1 watches the waves. If you do see a hazard astern, you can usually manoeuvre sideways within the line of surf by ferry-gliding across the flow of the soup.

Method number three is to swim. This is a last-ditch technique for when you must get through exceptionally heavy surf with your equipment dry and intact. It entails getting out of the kayak seaward from the surf and then swimming it ashore through the breakers. This method is only suitable for beaches that are definitely clear of obstructions, and for strong swimmers. Put on either your life jacket and helmet or your mask and fins, whichever you prefer, and then go over the side. Collapse the paddles and stow them inside the boat along with rudder and cables, if

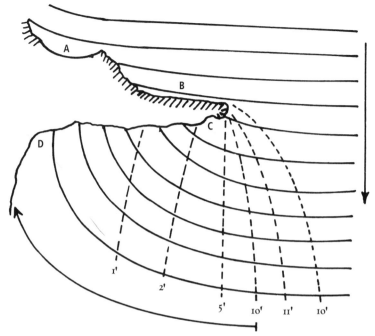

You can often predict a safe landing site from your chart once wave direction is known. Site A has 3-metre (10-foot) surf on the beach and should be avoided. At site B, steep cliffs make landing impossible and will cause chaotic waves offshore. Site C would offer adequate protection for most parties, with waves usually of 1 metre (3 feet) or less. At site D, wave strength would be dissipated still further.

applicable, and then seal the cockpit by tying off the entrance to the spray skirt. Even if the boat capsizes, it will take in little water. In a double, swim the boat stern first towards the beach with one person pushing the bow and the other holding a loop at the end of the bow painter. (Do not put the loop around your wrist or a wave may carry the boat away with you tied to it.) If you keep the boat going stern first, it should hold into the waves, thus minimizing the drag on the anchor person. A good swimmer will find it an advantage to reduce buoyancy in the life jacket during this operation, so as to duck below most of the turbulence. The person steadying the boat should take care never to get "downhill" of the kayak, a position that can be lethal in the grip of a big wave. If you are a solo paddler and find yourself swimming in surf, simply push the boat ahead as you swim for shore.

The way to land in heavy surf on a rocky shore is, don't. Stay at least two wave lengths away from the breakline as a precautionary measure while you hunt for a spot where the waves are truly benign or the land is less forbiddingly constructed. Derek Hutchinson has suggested a daring technique for surf-landing on rock, which he calls "seal landing." It involves riding up onto the shore on a breaker (assuming that you have managed to stay at the front of the wave), holding your position as far up the rock as possible and then scrambling out quickly and dragging the boat clear of the next wave. This may work for an unloaded boat under surge conditions on smooth rock shelves, but it should not tempt a well-loaded kayaker confronted by real surf and a jagged landscape.

A method I have used for landing on sheer, rocky shores is to search the coast for a protected location. (If you can't find such a place, don't land! You can anchor or paddle on all night if you have to.) Preferably, the shore should be vertical, with a shelf you can reach and no underwater ledges, which could catch the approaching kayak and topple it as the wave recedes. Once alongside the shelf, before you can lift the kayak up onto it, you have to get rid of most of the weight. In doubles, one way is for No. 1 to squat in the cockpit while No. 2 edges the kayak close enough to the rocks to scramble ashore. (Check to make sure you can pitch your tent there above high tide before unloading all your worldly belongings.) No. 2 then takes out the bags and balances them on the deck or sits them just inside the forward cockpit and then returns with the boat, riding in on a surge to where No. 1 can snatch the bags. The boat is eased clear again as the wave recedes. When the boat is light enough to be handled (it must, of course, be thoroughly bailed), No. 2 scrambles out on a surge and, with a paddle, holds the boat off the rock while at the same time keeping a hold on the bow painter. The boat can then be brought in on the next suitable surge and pulled higher as the wave recedes. This method is quite out of the question unless the direct force of the waves is already spent. It will also be much trickier with a single. And don't forget: after a very long crossing, your legs may have trouble supporting your body weight. They're unlikely to enable you to leap nimbly over the rocks with your boat.

If you are paddling near beds of bull kelp, you have the makings for a fine natural anchor should night catch you on an inhospitable shore. Kelp tends to take the sting out of breaking waves, and if you get in behind a dense mat of it, you will find the waters subdued. Drag the kelp into bunches and lash it firmly with the painter. Sit the boat back on the line and then haul more long fronds over the decks so that the boat is held fast.

RIP CURRENTS, TIDE RIPS, WIND RIPS & WHIRLPOOLS

As surf piles up on the beach, countercurrents form to return the excess water to the sea. If, as sometimes happens, the breakers have built a beachfront sandbar, these counterflows may take the form of rip currents or beach rips—often called riptides, though since they have nothing to do with tides, this seems a poor name for them. The neck of the rip current is a narrow outflow from the beach, gouging through the sandbar, splitting the breakers and dissipating into the sea beyond them. Its velocity will rarely exceed 2 or 3 knots. Water is supplied to the neck by shallow feeder currents running across the beach and into the neck. In a big surf, the feeder currents can be forceful enough to complicate the task of exiting onto unsteady legs from a kayak. The neck of the current, being deeper and stronger, can provide a quick route out to sea from the beach—as unwary swimmers have so often discovered.

Tidal currents and tide rips can pose other, greater problems. As suggested in Chapter 6, swift tidal currents and tide races can so alter the game that in dealing with them, river experience may be more valuable to you than knowledge of the open sea. Remember to lean your boat away from the current as you enter it, and always brace on the down-current side. A bracing stroke to the up-current side will only capsize you into it. Large tide rips are best dealt with by staying in the middle of the main flow of water if you are going with them or very close to shore if you are obliged to fight them. If you have to cross a major tide rip area, wait for slack water. For the smaller ones, it is simply a matter of muddling through, watching your balance and, again, leaning your boat away from each new band of current you come across. Wind rips, which occur when the wind runs counter to the current, at least have the advantage that the current is more or less uniform, though the chop can become very steep and unpleasant, readily forming overfalls.

Converging and diverging tidal currents create other hazards as well—eddies, or, in their larger, more frightening form, whirlpools.

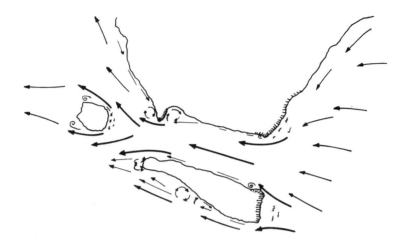

**Where water flows between masses of land, eddies and backflows form
complex patterns, which may assist as well as hinder a kayaker,
who must be able to read and anticipate their flow.**

These may be encountered off points and behind islands even where the
surrounding sea appears quite calm, but the small ones are unlikely to
do you any harm, and of the large ones you are likely to have forewarn-
ing. Big whirls will probably appear on your chart and be mentioned in
your coast pilot. They are also likely to be a part of local folklore, usually in an exaggerated form. It is often worth examining island channels
from a cliff top before paddling them or, as the case may be, paddling
around them.

CORAL

Coral thrives in the warm, clean waters between 30 degrees north latitude
and 30 degrees south latitude. It forms as long fringe reefs on exposed lee
shores and as scattered outcrops on the more sheltered coasts. Each reef
is a mass of spiky, jagged calcium formations, often quite close to the
surface. It is hard to imagine a more deadly snare for kayaks. Atolls are
coral reefs that have formed in shallow water, usually in a circle with calm
water in their centre.

Coral reefs can sometimes be crossed by a kayak at high tide when
almost no other craft could make it, but this is a dangerous game to play.
More often, lines of breakers crash onto the shallows and cream in over

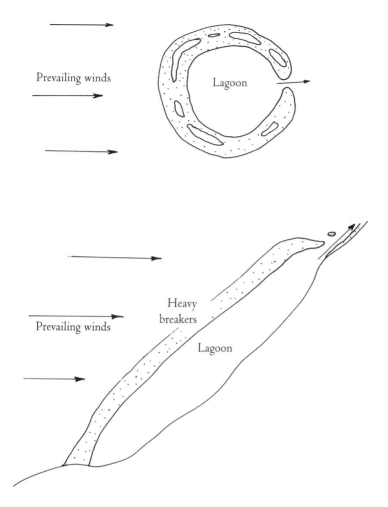

What goes onto a coral reef must come off. There will be a runoff channel somewhere—
usually on the side opposite the prevailing winds. The rip current in this channel may be
strong, but it is far better to buck the current than to try to surf over the coral.

the coral pools to the lagoon, making landing out of the question. Never attempt to run heavy surf on coral. The water that breaks over a coral reef must come off, and a runoff channel can usually be found away from the direct force of the prevailing winds. Scattered offshore reefs frequently offer a sheltered lee, and finding the entrance may be just a matter of reading your chart carefully, if it has been recently surveyed, or simply taking advantage of openings as they appear. Try to get the very latest charts available.

RIVER ENTRANCES

When large rivers pour into rough seas, very dangerous waves may form. There is frequently a shallow bar off the entrance where plunging breakers dump hard. This danger zone can usually be avoided by either closely following the coast or, if you are crossing rather than entering the mouth, by staying well out from shore. Which alternative you choose might depend on the weather and how far offshore the waves are breaking. If you intend to enter the river, it is usually best to sneak in via the shallow water on each side of the entrance. Unless the wind is blowing straight upstream, one side of the mouth will receive some shelter from the killing effect the strong current has on waves. Use this wave shadow if the water is clear of obstructions.

Rivers in flood carry trees and other debris down to the sea. These obstructions are often deposited in the muddy shallows near the mouth and may lie just below the surface. Keep a careful lookout. It can be most embarrassing if the top of a snag appears through the bottom of your kayak when you are half a mile offshore.

LIVE HAZARDS

Whales, Dolphins & Porpoises

Whale watching from kayaks has become quite the rage in North America over the past few years, and dozens of tour companies offer the opportunity for a close look at gray and humpback whales. Novices can also be assured of a heart-pounding encounter—frequently at very close quarters—with killer whales in the Robson Bight region of Johnstone Strait in British Columbia.

Because of a kayak's stealth, it is probable that these boats unnerve dozing whales more than power boats. There have been several reports of whale-watching kayakers being attacked by Pacific grays breeding in the lagoons of Magdalena Bay in Baja, Mexico. Kayaks have been upset and smashed by great flukes, and news of a paddler's death would not be surprising.

Gray whales were known among the old whalers as devil-fish because they sometimes reacted to abuse by smashing boats and drowning their crews. On the recent occasions when kayakers were attacked, the whales had been harassed on previous days by motorboat loads of tourists, and a couple of times a kayaker had ventured very close to a calf, causing the mother to take action.

Once in the Caribbean our kayaks were shadowed for two hours by a shy, apparently amorous humpback. Our first indication of its presence was a piercing, pinging squeak, which was much like that of a misbehaving rudder but which seemed to be coming from everywhere at once. Only when the great tail rose in the air several hundred yards ahead were our suspicions confirmed. It is very exciting to be sharing the sea with such creatures; still, their great size demands caution.

Porpoises will often come to investigate a kayak. They are fine company and will not normally harm or upset you, though when playing they may come close enough to clip your hull with their fins. I have personally experienced the delight of being escorted into harbour by porpoises after one particularly arduous night crossing in the Caribbean. Lindemann, however, reports being almost capsized by large porpoises in mid-Atlantic and would no doubt advocate giving them a wide berth.

Sharks

It is said that where you have porpoises, you won't get sharks, but don't count on it. Once, off the coast of New Zealand, only a couple of hundred yards from a school of porpoises, I surfed down a wave almost onto the back of a very surprised 12-foot hammerhead.

Sharks do not normally bother a kayaker, but they are a bit like people; there are good ones and bad ones. A kayak is an unfamiliar object to them, and it is rare indeed for one to attack without checking you out pretty carefully first. This checking-out process at worst involves a dummy-run bump with the snout, at best a casual glide by. Your instinct will probably be to clout the shark with your paddle, and that is no doubt the best thing you can do under most circumstances. Aim for its snout or eye. But don't splash excessively with your paddle, since this may be interpreted as distress and have an effect opposite to that intended. The only reliable exception to this comfortable rule is the great white, who, so the story goes, checks you out with a bite. I believe I have had one encounter with one of these. It came at us without warning in the

Tongue of the Ocean, a deep-water trench near the Great Bahama Bank, and it was pure chance that my paddle entered the water forcefully just as its snout was speeding towards the middle of our kayak. It seems that the unexpected blow with the paddle put the shark off its aim enough to miss the first pass; then the commotion we kicked up as I fumbled for the shells for our bang stick checked its confidence and cast doubts on our edibility. The shark turned off at the last moment in making the next few passes, clipping the hull with its dorsal fin while circling beneath us in frustration.

Wade Doak, well-known New Zealand diver and researcher, found that sharks would not come near a diver wearing a zebra-striped suit. As soon as the striped diver left the water, the sharks were back again. Maybe there is an idea there for the hulls of sea kayaks. An interesting conclusion of U.S. Navy research into sharks is that the most effective protection for a swimmer to use is a black survival bag. The navy's experiments with the sharks' reaction to colour revealed that the beasts were liable to attack brightly coloured objects, such as orange or yellow life jackets. Indeed, one shade of yellow popular with life jacket manufacturers was dubbed by the researchers "yum-yum yellow" because sharks attacked it so readily.

Discourage sharks by being quietly aggressive with them whenever they come within reach. The greatest risk occurs during a capsize, when one is obliged to remain swimming beside the kayak while a difficult pump and re-entry job is performed. In these circumstances have a diving mask, snorkel and fins close at hand—and carry a bang stick or shark stick (a 4-foot stick with a nail in the end) at all times while paddling tropical waters. It is, of course, important that the person entrusted with fending off sharks in this manner be a competent free diver, and if this is not the case, one may be better off pumping the boat dry from the protection of a black survival bag.

Seals, Sea Lions, Walruses & Renegade Sea Otters
Seals and sea lions can usually be relied on not to attack unless provoked, though what constitutes provocation is open to their interpretation, especially that of the larger bulls. Large bulls get particularly annoyed with paddlers venturing too close to their colonies, so bring binoculars if you wish to observe the mammals undisturbed. If you are on a wilder-

ness expedition that requires hunting seals or sea lions for food, avoid shooting them from the kayak. A wounded seal or sea lion will attack, and one that is shot dead sinks like stone, explaining why eastern Arctic and Greenland kayak hunters relied on harpoons connected to air bladders as floats.

Encounters with walruses must be strenuously avoided, as these animals do have a reputation for apparently unprovoked attack, and their size makes them doubly threatening. A smaller mammal not normally associated with sea kayaking hazards is the sea otter, which finds its way into this paragraph merely because one very deliberately nipped me on the elbow and threatened to claw its way into my cockpit as I paddled the waters of British Columbia's Bunsby Islands some years ago. The 90-pound critter, it turned out, had befriended the crew of a marine research vessel used during the 1969 transplant of Alaskan sea otters to the depleted B.C. coast. Amazingly, my playful attacker followed me ashore and curled up on my seat as soon as I vacated it.

Sea Snakes

Sea snakes may be encountered in the South China Sea, Java Sea and Indian Ocean, sometimes far out of sight of land. They are usually yellowish brown and are seldom more than 4 feet long, and they can be seen lolling lazily on the surface. The main risk for a kayaker is accidentally picking one up on the paddle so that it falls aboard, or having one washed onto the boat by a breaking sea. Sea snakes are nonaggressive creatures but very venomous. Their bite is fatal in 25 per cent of cases and is unusual in that the effects are not felt for as long as two hours after the bite, when paralysis and spasms finally occur. Survivors reportedly recover completely, with no aftereffects.

Portuguese Man-of-War

The man-of-war is a variety of jellyfish found throughout tropical and temperate zones. It possesses a blue flotation bladder supporting a mass of stinging tentacles, which can extend 12 to 18 metres (40 to 60 feet) down or, during windy days, may lie along the surface of the sea. The sting is painful and is dangerous to some people, especially if it covers a large area. Normally you will only be caught by the occasional filament swept over the arms and face by breaking waves. The effect does not appear to be more serious than that of stinging nettle. Some relief can be gained with a topical application of an antihistamine cream or a weak solution of ammonia (or, simply, urine, which is universally available). Should the stinging be extensive and in a dangerous place, such as the throat, the best treatment is with antihistamine tablets, which should be carried in a handy place for just such an emergency. In badly infested waters, it is advisable to wear a long-sleeved, high-necked shirt and gloves and tie a bandanna over your nose as a preventive measure. Australian lifeguards, who are exposed to regular encounters with stinging jellyfish, use a protective suit made of stretch nylon stocking material.

Sea Urchins

There are many varieties of sea urchins along the world's shorelines. All of them should be treated with respect by the lightly shod paddler. Sea urchins affect primarily those obliged to wade ashore across reefs or to launch in shallows. The tropical varieties with long, slender spines and remarkable powers of penetration are especially unpleasant. They are found on all sorts of shores except soft mud and are particularly common on coral reefs. Some tropical varieties contain toxin in the shorter spines.

If you are unfortunate enough to get sea urchin spines in your feet or legs, you will doubtless be flooded with earnest advice about dripping candle wax, lemon juice and goat semen as curatives. Speak politely to all free advisers and then leave the spines alone for a couple of days, disinfect the foot and coax the blighters out one by one with a needle. Very deep spines will work their way towards the surface over a couple of weeks. A few years ago my paddling partner and I acquired a total of 128 spines in our feet after a capsize on a coral reef. Some spines went right through our feet. None became infected, however, and the deepest emerged almost a month after the accident.

Note: You must not attempt to remove the spines with tweezers, since the pressure from the metal jaws will only crush the end of the brittle spine shaft.

Stingrays

Stingrays and stone fish can be a problem for tropical paddlers wading in the shallows. These creatures often lie half covered with sand and will slash or spike the unwary foot that lands on their backs. If you must wade the shallows, prod the ground ahead with a paddle to warn them of your approach. Sturdy shoes will be your best protection. Always wear shoes around coral shores.

Jumping & Flying Fish

It is not uncommon to be assailed by dozens of herring or mullet as you paddle through a school of them, usually in shallow water. The shape of the passing kayak panics them into bouncing all over you, and the air is heavy with the smell of fish.

Flying fish aboard are a rarer occurrence, though my wife has had the dubious privilege of being slapped in the face by one during a night crossing. As a rule they will fly away from the kayak but, like garfish, they can fly away from one boat and into the next, or away from a hungry dorado and into you. Flying fish weigh as much as a kilogram (2 pounds), so they can give you a nasty surprise. Garfish have substantial swords on their snouts, and there are occasional reports of a venturesome mariner having his cheek pierced by one.

SHIPS & OTHER MONSTERS

Don't expect to be seen by ships as you sit in your kayak on the sea. As I pointed out earlier, you won't even show up on radar unless you have a radar reflector aloft. It is you who must move.

When a ship appears to be coming straight for you, you may find it difficult to decide which side to move to get out of the way. It is worth a few seconds' pause to get it right. Resist the common reaction to scuttle across in front of her; instead, watch the line-up of the bow and the mast closely to see if she is likely to pass in front of you or astern. Then paddle away from the line of her course, taking care to watch the vessel until it is past—just in case it alters course. Don't use flares unless it appears that you truly cannot avoid the ship's course. If you do put a flare up in front of the ship, it won't alter course, but at least the crew will likely check to see that you are not wrapped around the bows. You don't usually need to worry about the wake of a big ship capsizing a kayak. A supertanker at full speed just sends out something like an ocean swell, which hardly affects existing wave patterns. Tugboats are more of a menace but seldom so bad as to seriously threaten a competent kayaker.

Naval vessels under power are a different matter: their wakes can be very steep.

Powerboats

These are the bane of the poetic paddler's life. Near marinas they can be as thick as hornets, and many is the time I have wished my Schermuly flare gun was a bazooka. Some powerboat operators seem to think that if an object is lower than their bows, they will bounce over it if they are going fast enough. Unlike those moving monoliths the merchant ships, small powerboats have the nasty habit of zigzagging and bouncing about so that it is almost impossible to anticipate their course if they are heading your way. You never know if they have seen you or not, and there persists to the last instant the fear that the operator will suddenly see one kayak and swerve into another.

Flares are not the answer. Leaving a major port on a weekend may produce close encounters with a score or more powerboats, and you can't go firing off flares every time a boat points your way. Instead, carry a big black or orange garbage bag. Keep it handy, and when you see the frothing upraised bows headed your way, stuff the bag over your paddle and wave it in the air as high as you can reach. At the same time, turn on your rudder so your boat faces the menace. If it is determined to hit you, at least it will be a glancing blow which will tend to push you aside rather than ride over you. Should a broadside collision be unavoidable, don't hesitate, roll the kayak away from the speedboat and push with your feet against the inside of the kayak so you are projected well below those propellers (not so easy if you are wearing a life jacket). Don't surface until the crashing stops. In some parts of the world (such as Miami), powerboats are the greatest single hazard to sea kayakers. As we approached Miami Beach at the end of a twenty-hour crossing of the Gulf Stream, there were speedboats everywhere, and our two kayaks were almost run down by what looked like a brace of giant fibreglass shoes thundering along at 70 miles per hour; we had unwittingly entered the unmarked lanes of an ocean powerboat race. With boats screaming by within 45 metres (50 yards) of us, one of our group fired parachute flares over them, but without effect. We did the only thing we could, which was to paddle on through, consoling ourselves with the thought that at 70 miles per hour any race pilot not looking out for obstacles would be courting suicide.

Encounters in Fog

When vision is drastically reduced by fog, you must rely on your compass and ears. When you hear shipping in the fog, paddle gently towards the sound so that you have steerage, following the engine noise until it passes. Then resume your course. By keeping your bow towards the source of the sound, you reduce the chances of a dangerous collision. If the source of the sound moves in relation to your compass setting, you are probably safe. If it stays in the same position and is getting louder, you are not. Sounding a whistle is not likely to help you much unless the boat has a very silent engine and an alert watch, though I suppose a fog horn or trumpet might do the trick. Your best defence against shipping in fog is to raise a radar reflector on a fishing pole or some other similar makeshift mast.

One nasty little story on this subject is told by Hilary Collins, who was in a cross-channel party that was almost run down in heavy fog by the Dover to Calais Hovercraft.

ICEBERGS, BERGY BITS & GROWLERS

Most of the ice encountered on a summer or autumn trip outside the extreme polar latitudes will be of glacial origin. Icebergs are calved into the sea by hundreds of tidewater glaciers in Greenland, Alaska, Baffin Island, the Svalbard Archipelago and elsewhere in the Arctic, and by several such glaciers in Patagonian Chile. These bergs split and melt into smaller pieces affectionately known as bergy bits (on the order of 500 to 1000 tonnes), which split and melt into yet smaller pieces called growlers. Since 80 to 90 per cent of an iceberg is normally below waterline, a bergy bit that looks to be the size of a house may in reality be the size of an apartment block, and a growler that really is the size of a house may be awash in moderate seas.

For a kayaker, the principal danger inherent in icebergs and bergy bits is that they may calve unexpectedly from a glacier, producing enormous swells, or that anywhere, anytime, they may roll. Icebergs are sometimes beautiful and compelling pieces of sculpture, but anyone who has spent a few days among them must have seen the unpredictable somersaults they perform.

In 1932 the kayak belonging to the flamboyant young British adventurer Gino Watkins was found bobbing in the waves off the coast of

Neil Gregory-Eaves

Glacial ice on the B.C. coast.

Greenland. Watkins himself was not found. It is assumed that he boarded an appealing iceberg just before it rolled.

A domed iceberg has probably rolled already, and you should expect it to roll again at any time. A berg with two distinct horns—a so-called drydock iceberg—probably has not rolled. It may still be stable, but there is no guarantee. Tabular icebergs, which are calved from shelf ice rather than glaciers, are far less likely to roll than the randomly shaped glacial bergs, but tabular bergs are rarely encountered outside the Antarctic Ocean. Floebergs—floes disengaged from the pack ice and drifting along—are also quite stable as a rule, but they are still not to be trusted, because they may calve growlers or floebits (baby floebergs) at any time.

The truly small pieces of ice rubble sometimes found around the faces of tidewater glaciers (or in leads through pack ice) are called brash. Remember when paddling among brash ice that just as with bergs, there is up to ten times as much ice below the surface as there is above it. The pieces are larger than they look, and if you jostle them with your paddle they may jostle you heavily in return.

SEA ICE

In winter and spring, you may well encounter another form of ice: sea ice. During a normal winter, the sea freezes as far south as the coasts of Nova Scotia and Hokkaido, whereas waters at far higher latitudes, irrigated by warmer ocean currents, remain ice-free. During very cold winters, ice may form in the North Sea and even in the Adriatic.

The freezing point of seawater depends on its salinity, but as a rule it will be in the vicinity of $-2°c$ ($28°F$). When this temperature is reached and sustained on the ocean's surface, sea ice forms in the following stages:

1 Frazil—Minute crystals that give the sea an oily sheen.
2 Grease ice—A thin layer of coagulating frazil, more viscous and with a dull or matte surface.
3 Shuga—Small, woolly white lumps in the grease ice.
4 Nilas—An elastic crust several inches thick. It flexes with the waves but has a definite calming effect on the sea. Thin nilas is dark like the water beneath it, but as it thickens it becomes a light grey and looks something like a mixture of ground glass and paper pulp.
5 Ice rind—A thin but brittle crust. As the rind begins to form, it enforces an angular shape on the waves. Under certain conditions, ice rind may form directly from grease ice and shuga, without the intermediary nilas stage.

The first four of these stages are varieties of soft ice. Frazil, grease ice, shuga and dark nilas can all be paddled through—though they will definitely slow you down. Kayakers who continue under these conditions, however, may well find themselves beset in ice that is too stiff to paddle through but far too weak to walk on. New sea ice is notoriously weak in comparison with freshwater ice, because it is honeycombed with brine. A thick ice rind may well prevent passage of your kayak across the surface and yet do nothing much to prevent your falling through the surface. New sea ice as much as a foot thick may be quite inadequate to bear the weight of a man.

As sea ice ages and thickens, the salt gravitates out of it and the ice becomes considerably stronger. Early in this strengthening process, the crust is often broken by wave action into relatively small slabs, which rub each other round like two-dimensional pebbles. The result is called pancake ice. The discs thus formed freeze back together with renewed vigour, and in a few weeks the ice may be sturdy enough to bear enormous loads.

Once sea ice passes the dark nilas stage, it is navigable by kayak only through leads and polynyas. (A polynya is an area of open water in the midst of the icepack.) During the colder months, leads and polynyas may begin to freeze over soon after they are formed and so grease ice, shuga and nilas may be encountered deep in the pack ice in mid-winter or early spring. A kayaker travelling in such conditions should be extremely well prepared—not only for sudden immersion in icy waters but also for camping out on the ice and for an extended walk across rough ice, pulling the kayak as a sled. The most insidious danger, however, is that leads can close just as suddenly as they open. Particularly during the spring or summer breakup, small leads may grind shut as icefloes or broken bergs are shifted by current or tide.

If you are serious about kayaking in areas subject to sea ice, you may want to equip your kayak with a sled such as those once used by the King Islanders in the Bering Sea, and by Fridtjof Nansen during his 1893 attempt to reach the north pole. A light sled can be carried on the afterdeck while the boat is in the water and strapped beneath the hull for travel across the pack or shelf ice.

SEA KAYAKING SOLO

To say that a kayaker should not go to sea alone is a bit like saying that someone should not walk in the mountains alone; it is prudent advice, but the reality of sea kayaking is that many of its most dedicated adherents prefer going out alone. The risk is increased, but so, arguably, are the rewards. Indeed, I believe that the appreciation and level of awareness of one's environment is diminished by a factor of the number of people in one's party. It is in the nature of some people to take their own risks and gamble their skill against the sea with their lives as the chips, depending on no one to assist them. Travelling solo is the most direct sea kayaking experience, and because of the greater risk, there is considerable social resistance to it—a resistance not dissimilar to that at first afforded to solo sailors and alpine climbers. I wish neither to discourage anyone from taking to the sea alone nor to encourage them either. Those who truly have the solo kayaking inclination will not be stopped by anything I could say and do not stand in need of my blessing. I do want to point out the dangers, suggest some precautions and techniques, and make it quite clear that the danger is greater. The sea will more readily kill you for your mistakes if you are alone. Above all, a solo paddler must be capable of quick and efficient self-rescue if he or she is to survive.

Solo kayaking demands the commitment and serious intent of a high wire walker or solo rock climber. Once you are out there, you are very definitely on your own. As a young single man, I always prepared for my solo trips by telling nobody I was going—so that nobody expected me back and no one would think to bother the coast guard. Irresponsible in a social (and personal) sense, perhaps, but in another sense of the word, totally responsible.

Here are some special tips to help improve your odds. Think safety. Run through "what if?" scenarios so as to be prepared for all possible mishaps. Have the right equipment ready to use and know how to use it. In addition, follow these guidelines:

1 Choose a kayak with good stability or carry a buoyancy aid such as inflatable pontoons for solo paddling. You may need that extra margin of safety if you become incapacitated on the water.
2 Maximize your buoyancy and backup buoyancy systems.
3 Check the condition and effectiveness of your spray skirt and keep a spare handy.
4 Develop your skills, particularly your bracing, roll and paddle turns in wind and waves.
5 Match your level of fitness with the type of trip.
6 Develop one or more solid backup self-rescue systems that leave you in a more stable position after the capsize than you were before it.
7 Dress for the occasion; in cold water, dress for immersion.
8 Carry a wide range of attention getters: flares, EPIRB, VHF radio, strobe light, flashlight, and so on.
9 Carry a waterproof shore survival kit and tie up your kayak ashore.
10 Avoid taking any unnecessary risk.

Running before a tropical squall. Note that the paddles are unfeathered to prevent the wind from spinning them, the boat is running between 30 degrees and 45 degrees off the direction of the wind, and the paddlers are ready to brace on the windward side if required. PFDs, essential in cool waters, are often carried but not used in tropical kayaking—instead, fins and mask/snorkle are kept at hand.

CHAPTER EIGHT

STORM & OTHER EMERGENCY PROCEDURES

It makes sense to think about what could go wrong at sea and what you are going to do if it does.

Storms may be the most common fear of sea kayakers—particularly those attempting difficult passages with many miles of open sea. What do you do if you are caught in a storm? The answers will depend largely on where you are in relation to land and what kind of boat you are using, since the best tactic is usually to get ashore. If the land is within your grasp, you may be able to run with the wind to a safe harbour; if the wind is blowing athwart, your best course would be to ferry-glide across the storm.

In a severe storm, fighting upwind is out of the question as a means for reaching land. You should avoid wasting energy fighting it unless the storm is expected to be a small one and battling it is seen only as a holding action until the wind drops enough for you to make headway. In such a situation, you simply maintain your course as best you can.

Sometimes you will not be able to make land either because the land to leeward is too dangerous or because the only available landfall lies into the wind. If you have been caught by a major blow and the wind is too strong for you to lift your paddle, or if there is a complicating factor such as a current that will hinder your return to shore, you will have to ride it out. The decision to do so is a critical one and should be acted on as soon as it becomes clear that this is your best choice, since the object of passively riding out a storm is conservation of strength. The moment you realize you cannot escape a storm, check the following:

1 All bags and equipment are secure inside the boat.
2 Foot, hand or electric pump is working.
3 The drogue is rigged and ready to go.
4 Food is handy, and, in the tropics, that mask, fins and snorkel are readily available.
5 Your emergency locator beacon, if you have one, is at hand.

Then do the following:
6 Tie your paddle to the bowline or paddle leash. In a double, tie off both paddles, one to the bowline, the other to the stern.
7 Take in all sail and unstep the mast if you were sailing.
8 Put on any protective clothing you are not already wearing.
9 Secure your life jacket.
10 Eat a meal of energy food, drink a little water from each bottle (so they won't sink), relieve yourself and then put a little food in your anorak pocket, together with your flares and a flashlight.
11 Prepare some warps ready for trailing. A 45-metre (150-foot) climb-ing rope will do nicely, if you happen to be carrying one. Your anchor warp, chain included, would also serve well enough; alternatively, use a shorter length of line with something (like clothing) tied to it to increase the drag.

When you decide to ride out the storm on the open sea, you are again faced with a choice: you can run before the wind or you can lie to a drogue. Your choice will depend on what lies to leeward, how strong the wind is, how large the waves are and what your plan is when the storm is over. It will also depend on what sort of boat you are in and on your previous experience with the different methods.

RUNNING BEFORE A STORM
This is a method suitable for situations where you have a great distance available to leeward or you are running with the wind to a safe harbour. In this circumstance you will appreciate using an unfeathered paddle and having a rudder. Turn the boat and steer a course about 45 degrees off the direction of wind and waves. Vary this angle according to your relative comfort or lack of it with the size of the waves. Try to avoid surfing directly down the wave face. You may decide to trail your pre-

pared warps at this stage. Have your paddle ready to brace into any heavily breaking crests. Normally, the paddle should be held across the coaming, with the blades tilted forward so that the wind pressure holds it down, but you may prefer to trail it on the windward side, thus reducing windage and placing you in a position of constant support.

As the wind increases, lean forward or snuggle lower in the boat to reduce windage and lower your centre of gravity. If you do capsize, your paddle will be attached to the kayak; you need only hold on to one to be assured of still having the other.

LYING TO A DROGUE

Lying to a drogue is useful in the open sea or when you plan to return to windward after the storm or where it is important to reduce wind drift because of a dangerous lee shore. There is considerable disagreement among bar-stool sailors about the use of drogues during a storm. It is generally conceded that they are fine for reducing drift under average conditions, but their use in a severe storm is hotly debated. So be it with kayaks.

In theory, a well-set drogue off the bow of a kayak will hold the boat's head into the weather. This may work with a sea-chute, or the commercially available DriftStopper (manufactured by Boulter of Earth in Toronto), but with a standard sea anchor of traditional dimensions, my experience is that the boat yaws badly in its backward drift unless fitted with a counterforce off the stern. Another kayak can serve as such a force, as we discovered while rigged in series for sleeping one night during a fresh wind. The boat at the end of the series yawed wildly as usual, while the kayak to whose stern it was attached held steady in the waves.

It is important to lift the rudder or skeg clear of the water when you are lying to a standard drogue, since you will still be going backward quite fast. Hold the paddle so that it won't be blown out of your hands, or lash it firmly along the deck.

During a gale, far more spray hits a kayaker than would hit a yachter. (The yachter, no matter how small his or her vessel, sits higher out of the water.) With the drogue off the bow, you will be facing the wind and run the risk of being blinded by spray. A diving mask will protect your eyes, and you can draw breath inside your parka lip. This arrangement can also be of assistance when you near the limit of paddleable

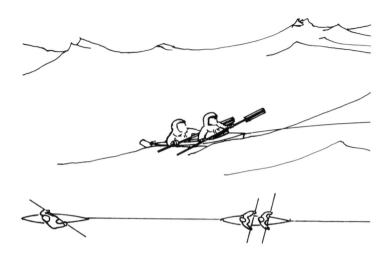

A drogue off the bow will hold the bow into the wind and reduce drift. If a sea-chute is used, a float should be attached to prevent the chute from sinking too low.

conditions or where an imminent lee shore demands that you claw your way along the coast by ferry-gliding against the wind to a place where you can land. To increase your stability and reduce wind resistance, snuggle low into your boat so that only your shoulders, arms and head are above the coaming. Keep the bilges pumped dry. Lindemann, on his Atlantic crossing, trailed his drogue off the stern, wrecked his rudder assembly and capsized twice. He might have done better with a larger drogue off the bow, though it would have put the spray in his face.

If you trail warps, possibly your best option for downwind control, they should run from cleats beside the cockpit and out through a loop near the towing point. Warps often have the bonus value of "tripping" a breaker astern of you rather than having it dump on your rear deck.

RAFTING UP

Rafting up is often taught as a storm procedure, but I do not advise relying on it in really severe conditions. It can, however, be a useful manoeuvre for stabilizing a party when some emergency occurs or if you just want everyone to come together for a snack or a discussion of route during moderate conditions. The two most common ways of doing it are to raft the boats cockpit to cockpit or bow to cockpit like sardines. In both cases it is necessary to hold the boats apart at arm's length in choppy

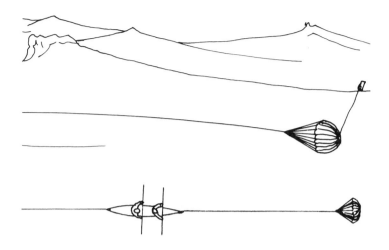

A drogue that allows significant drift will cause the boat to yaw unless a counterforce—such as a second kayak—is tethered astern.

water to stop them from crunching together and riding up one on the other. Rafting up can stabilize a capsized kayak during re-entry, and it can provide enough stability for sleeping in slender singles during calm weather. It is dangerous, however, to put too much faith in rafting up for stability in heavy weather. Rafting up tends to be the optimist's answer to any emergency, but it can be very strenuous keeping your raft together in high seas, and it turns into an awful mess when you are swatted by an ocean creamer. There can be broken paddles, crushed fingers and bleeding people wearing kayaks in strange places all over the sea. It is equally dangerous to count on rafting up when you cannot stay awake any longer.

Let me repeat what I have said in discussing self-rescue. I believe that to be safe in a sea kayak, you must be capable of surviving alone. The rhyme "less than three shall never be," though helpful for the lower level of emergency, deceptively lulls the inexperienced into believing that their ultimate safety lies in clutching onto two companions—but things are just not like that in heavy weather. Then, any boat close enough to touch you is an extreme hazard. A loaded rigid kayak carried into you by a breaking wave can cause serious injuries, including concussion and fractured bones. One kayak can be driven right through another—and how do you brace into a breaking wave if there is another kayak on top of yours? By all means paddle with two companions—it

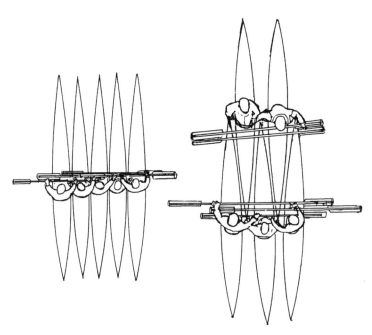

Rafting up cannot be relied on for security in really rough water; under normal cruising conditions, however, it can provide a secure platform. Of the two methods, bow-to-cockpit is the most secure. Side-by-side rafting is useful for rescue aid or to provide stability for some unusual operation.

is certainly safer, assuming they are not fools—but don't base your philosophy of survival on them.

THE ULTIMATE STORMS

Hurricanes—or typhoons, as they are known in Asia and the Pacific—are the ultimate storms: circular monsters anywhere from 60 to 1000 miles across. They, together with their less ferocious cousins, the tropical storms, lurk like wolves in the backs of the minds of sailors (and tropical kayakers).

Your first thought must always be to get yourself and your boat to high ground as fast as possible. Chances are you will have plenty of warning of the approach of such storms (see Chapter 5). The danger of low ground is that a hurricane may cause the level of the sea to rise 4.5 metres (15 feet) or more. Combine this rise with giant waves, and you have a sea that will sweep right over the lower atolls and coastal plains. Ideally, you want something like a bomb shelter on a mountaintop to weather it out. Certainly you want some form of substantial protection against wind-blown objects.

I am thankful never to have been caught in a full-fledged hurricane, but when I am in vulnerable areas my plan and priorities have always been carefully thought out. I frequently cast about me when camped at a new island and think, "Where is the best hurricane shelter around here?" Generally I have decided, if no hurricane-proof dwelling was handy, that I would carry the boat inland to some natural protection such as a rocky outcrop or a thicket of small trees and tie it down. (Larger trees might fall on the boat and smash it.) If my boat was of the folding variety, I would dismantle it and bury it on high ground.

As the eye of the storm passes over an area, there will be a lull in the wind and then it will start again from the opposite side. When you choose your protection, remember that it must serve from both sides.

SLEEPING IN A KAYAK

The ability and willingness to sleep in the kayak offer flexibility on long journeys. Sleeping in the boat is also a necessity for surviving bouts of illness or incapacitation at sea.

The kayak becomes extraordinarily stable when the centre of gravity is lowered, and the lower you can go the better. George Dyson has built kayaks into which he can retreat fully, closing a watertight perspex dome over the cockpit; but it is possible to wriggle down into almost any high-volume kayak if there is no forward bulkhead and if the bow is not laden with too much gear.

Many a kayaker seeking a better mousetrap has dreamed up a system of inner tubes and paddles to stabilize the craft, but this is not usually necessary. A beamy kayak with the weight kept low is inherently extremely stable. It will slide when hit by a wave. Lindemann used an inner tube outrigger on his Atlantic crossing and capsized twice *because* of it. His boat would slide until the outrigger dived, at which point the kayak would trip on the outrigger. Ed Gillet was more successful with two inflatable sponsons each side of the cockpit of his double on his trans-Pacific crossing.

I have slept slouched down in a kayak on many occasions and have ridden through gales while asleep. This is not the greatest way to spend a night, but neither is it the worst.

SEPARATION AT SEA

Once you have agreed that you are going to travel as a group, no one should leave that group unless everybody knows about it and an arrangement is made to link up again. During bad weather, it is important not to spread the party too thin. Not only will you be slow to give assistance if needed, but you may lose sight of a member who pauses to make repairs or adjust gear. In a party with three boats or more, leave a strong paddler to take up the rear if there is doubt that any of the members can handle the conditions. It is the lead boat's responsibility to see that no one is left behind. This is because a delay up front automatically draws the group together, while one astern spreads the party.

Surprisingly, it is often fine, calm weather that causes separations at sea. Everyone is relaxed and confident that nothing could possibly go wrong on such a fine day—"So let's not wait for those turkeys in the other boat. We'll go on and wait on the island." Then, of course, there is a misunderstanding about which island, or the following boat gets into some sort of unforeseeable trouble and is delayed or obliged to alter course. Once our kayak, which was travelling second on an 8-mile crossing of the Strait of Magellan under miraculously calm conditions, was attacked by a wounded sea lion. The animal bit through the rubberized hull in eleven places, and we scurried for a rock a couple of miles distant while the other boat continued, its occupants never suspecting that anything could possibly have gone wrong. It was two weeks before we were again able to make contact. There was, naturally, a misunderstanding as to the rendezvous point, and it is no simple matter to locate a solitary kayak in the midst of a peppering of wilderness islands with no radio contact.

Separations at sea can usually be avoided by following these guidelines:

1 Make it clearly the responsibility of the lead boat to see that everyone stays within communicating distance. (It is easier for someone to wait than for the others to catch up.)

2 Everyone in the group must hold the same course as the lead boat and nobody is to strike off alone. If you disagree with the course set by the lead boat, discuss it. If you can't agree, establish a rendezvous point.

3 Establish a rendezvous point each day. Normally this will be your lunch stop or the spot where you expect to camp that night. As an extra safeguard, you might also agree on a more distant, backup rendezvous point, or on the emergency principle of a return to the last camp at which you were all together. The first option is preferable, since it won't involve backtracking.

It can be very difficult to hunt for a kayak on a rough sea, even from a cliff top with binoculars. If you are carrying VHF radios, then your chances of prolonged separation are greatly reduced—but only if you have an agreed-upon listening time. This might be, for instance, five minutes before and after the hour.

TOWING

In an emergency, such as illness, exhaustion, accident or hypothermia, the best solution may be to tow the incapacitated boat. Towing is also an emergency measure to keep together two boats in which one individual or a crew is paddling more weakly than the other.

The towing point of most singles is about a foot astern the cockpit; that of a double kayak is immediately behind the rear cockpit. A bridle attached to cleats each side of the cockpit, or looped around the lip of the coaming if you have a rigid boat with a small cockpit, will provide secure attachment.

In doubles, a simple system is to pass the rigged drogue from the boat about to be towed across to the towing boat. It is delivered to the No. 2 paddler, who ties it off to the cleats each side of the coaming and tucks the canopy away under the deck rigging. This arrangement will often place the drogue swivel neatly over the towing point. It is handy to have a resilient support such as a short whip aerial just above the rudder to prevent fouling of the rudder assembly. Just put a clove hitch in the towline and drop it over the aerial.

Unfortunately, kayaks don't usually tow very well. They tend to yaw badly and must be steered carefully in the wake of the towing boat. This tendency can prove a problem in a single if the kayaker is incapacitated. If the victim is in one of the less stable boats, a third kayak will be needed to prop him or her up, so the formula is complicated even more—your one strong boat will be towing two kayaks.

A stronger system is to lay the injured or hypothermic paddler as low as possible in the kayak and then link up the two remaining paddlers in series (or in a double) to pull the crippled boat. Ideally, you should have at least one double kayak or better still a three-seater in every party so that you can transfer a sick person into the forward or middle cockpit. The triple offers the option of using the middle space to carry an inert passenger or a third paddler for extra towing power. A strong paddler can paddle a double alone and still average two knots under neutral conditions. Once when I was injured, my petite wife paddled a fully loaded two-seater 10 miles in four hours with me as an inert lump in the passenger seat.

CHAPTER NINE

CAMPING, FOOD GATHERING & *the* ENVIRONMENT

THE LOW-IMPACT PADDLER

Sea kayaking is generally an environmentally friendly activity, though as the number of paddlers increases, the way we treat the places we visit becomes more important. Preserving these places makes sense not only from a practical point of view but also, for me, in a personal, spiritual sense, since despoiling a pristine space diminishes one's own sense of self.

Following are some guidelines for environmentally friendly camping:

- Avoid trampling the intertidal life when you come ashore.
- Avoid camping in critical wildlife habitats and on fragile terrain.
- Do not cut trees or branches.
- Avoid digging drainage trenches around tents—instead, choose well-drained ground where your tent will leave no signs (for example, areas covered with pine needles or sand).
- Seek permission and follow guidance for camping on private land.
- Do not camp at Native cultural sites.
- Camp at least 50 metres (55 yards) from sources of fresh water.
- Leave no trace that you have been at the site.
- Where possible, camp at established sites where your stay will cause no additional damage.
- Use established trails, if they exist, to avoid trampling vegetation.
- Light fires in such a way that they will not scar rocks, soil or vegetation.
- Use existing fire rings if possible; otherwise light fires on sand below the monthly high tide mark.
- Burn only driftwood and allow the fire to burn down to ash.

- Disperse any remaining charcoal on the sea.
- When gathering food, such as shellfish, remember that some areas cannot sustain heavy harvesting and would be better left untouched.
- Return all shells and entrails to where you got them.
- Where outhouses have been provided, use them.
- Feces and urine degrade more rapidly in salt water than on land, so select a secluded site in the intertidal zone, make your deposit and then place a rock on it (imagine the surprise you will give some crab!).
- Wash yourself with sea water rather than using toilet paper—half the world's population follows this practice and it need not be unhygienic.
- If you must use toilet paper, burn it along with other indigestible delights, such as tampons and sanitary pads.
- In the tropics, a discreet crap may be taken by swimming out a distance, relying on the passing current to deposit your contribution somewhere suitable (if you stay at the same site long enough to develop a routine, you may find yourself encouraged by the gentle nipping of expectant sergeant fish).
- Waste water from cooking should be drained into the ocean, not onto the ground, where it will kill earthbound critters and provide a tantalizing attraction for wildlife.
- Keep soaps and detergents clear of freshwater sources and estuaries, and if you can get it, use biodegradable seawater soap.
- Pack out all garbage. On long trips, sinking burned cans and bottles in *deep* water is probably a reasonable option. As a diver, I find it dismaying to encounter garbage off popular campsites.
- Leave no unused food around an abandoned campsite, since it will attract scavengers.

SPECIAL EQUIPMENT

Some folks carry all sorts of imaginative gadgetry to make camping easier, but the wilderness has a healthy knack of trimming these extras so that by the end of the second or third week, you will be reduced to the most basic equipment. Chances are that by the end of a long wilderness trip, if the weather has been tolerable, you will not have used your primus for ages, having realized that you could light a fire almost as quickly and that the fire was a lot more friendly (although a gas stove will be preferable in high-use areas where firewood may be hard to find).

Probably your pressure cooker will have become an ordinary cooking pot, since you won't have to worry about fuel shortages once you begin to use firewood. And as for cooking time, what does fifteen minutes matter away from the hustle of city life? Your knife, fork, spoon, cup and plates will probably be reduced to a spoon, a bowl and a jackknife. The dinky little hatchet you started out with will have been traded for a 1.5-kilogram (3-pound), long-handled axe. Who knows, if the mosquitoes are not too bad, you might abandon the tent altogether and carry only a waterproof fly and groundsheet, as Native hunters do.

CAMPING IN THE LAND OF STORMS

Selecting the best campsite from the sea is an important first step. (In British Columbia or Patagonia you know you are doing it right when you start finding the remains of old Native camps, such as middens or the stumps of ancient lodgepoles, as you clear the ground for your tent.) Your chart will often give a good indication of the most favourable sort of place for a landing. According to preference, you might select a sheltered cove or fjord close to the jumping-off point for the next day or go in behind a headland that offers a better view of the seas outside. The head of a larger bay will usually have a stream, better shelter and easier landing. Streams large enough to appear on your chart may also offer a protected path to shore and of course a supply of fresh water. If you plan to camp for a day or two at the one site, choose a location with plenty of firewood. In Patagonia, this means looking for stands of tepu or dead cypress. Tepu is a feathery-leafed shrub common along the shores. A mature stand contains previous generations of dead wood, which is so resinous that it will burn wet or even green. Cypress too is excellent. On one occasion I pulled a pole of cypress from a bog where it may well have lain for fifty years. Once it was split it burned fiercely. In Alaska or British Columbia look for a windfall cedar or a beach piled high with driftwood.

If you are travelling by double or in a group, you will soon develop a routine. Try to make it a good one. For instance, as soon as you land, one person can take the tent, stove and pot to the selected site and put on water for a brew and then pitch the tent and loft the sleeping bags while another person unloads and cares for the boats. Whether you use a fire or a stove, it pays to get it going quickly, since if someone is cold, the warm drink is cheering and the activity of making a fire and a meal is good for morale. The first fifteen minutes after you clamber out of the kayak on a miserable day is the easiest time to get chilled.

If firewood is plentiful, I usually build a fire about a metre (2 to 3 feet) across. The initial blaze will boil the water quickly and the resulting coals can then be scraped into a pile and used to cook the main meal. If you also collect driftwood and dead timber, you can pile it nearby, ready to throw on as soon as the meal is done. During bad weather, a light-weight canvas fly erected well above the fire protects it from rain. Nylon is no good for this purpose, since sparks quickly ventilate it.

Starting a fire in the rain has probably occupied more pages of Boy Scout manuals than anything else. My own solution is to carry an old rubber inner tube. A few square inches of this or a wax candle can easily be lit and set in the midst of small twigs—gathered from the underside of some fallen tree or split from the centre of a dry log. The flaming molten rubber quickly establishes the heart of the fire if you have selected a site sheltered from the wind.

Contrary to popular belief, a kayaker can usually find a sheltered campsite on stormy coasts. Although you can expect to need a storm tent (and occasionally you will be glad of it), you can get by with a waterproof 3-metre by 3.5-metre (10-foot by 12-foot) tarpaulin pitched well into the trees and a sheet of plastic on the ground. Nylon or PVC is good for the fly, but make sure it is set well away from the fire.

Unfortunately, many North American rivers are contaminated with *Giardia*, which causes beaver fever. The problem is that you can never be sure that the water is safe to drink unless you are drawing it directly from the fountainhead of the spring itself. Questionable water should be boiled, chemically tested or pumped through one of the many water-purifying pumps available on the market today.

Mice and rats are occasionally a problem. Sometimes islands are overrun with them, and if you camp in old dwellings, you are bound to meet resident rodents or raccoons. In Chile I once had fifteen holes eaten in the buoyancy tubing of my boat; it seems the rats there fancied plastic.

In British Columbia and Alaska, bears too can pose a problem for camping kayakers. Camping at river mouths in August when the salmon are running is a particularly reliable way of getting into trouble. Woe betide the hapless kayakers who pitch their tents by a happy bear's exclusive fishing hole or beach their boats on the bear's buried food supply. Climb a tree if you must; it's probably better than running or sitting on the ground. Otherwise, turn to Plan B, below. (Grizzlies, unlike blacks, are restricted to the ground—though some are reported to be ignoring this rule.)

If you are venturing into bear country, it pays to give serious thought to some special equipment. For a start you have to decide if you are going to go armed and if so what sort of weaponry you should take. I would certainly carry an effective rifle (Plan B) (not lighter than a 30.06) or shotgun; to me, having the option to use or not to use it makes more sense than going unarmed and then needing to protect myself or my companions without having the means to do so. If I were travelling with children, I would not consider going unarmed.

For those who have no confidence in their ability to use a firearm or who disagree in principle with the idea of intruding into a bear's territory and then killing it because it challenges your presence (a principle that I agree with but am not prepared to die for!), there is now a magnum aerosol cayenne pepper dispenser that has proven extremely effective at repelling bear attacks, including charges by both grizzly and polar bears. As for me, I issue the kids with cayenne, but I have a rifle just in case.

Apparently there have been no reports of grizzly attacks on groups of six or more people. Ken Leghorn, who runs commercial kayak tours in Alaskan bear country, is convinced that small groups are more prone to encounters with bears than larger, noisier groups and that solo campers place themselves at a significantly higher risk.

A great deal of risk can also be eliminated by carefully choosing and taking care of a campsite. A good site is a fairly open and unrestricted area at least a hundred yards from a stream so that a curious bear, or one on its regular path to a favourite stream, is not obliged to walk close to your camp. Another problem with streams is that they mask the sounds of man and beast, making both vulnerable to surprise encounters. When you get ashore, look for the wide, flattened bear paths and make sure you don't camp close to one of these. Give the bear plenty of room to circle you at an unthreatening distance.

Part of the strategy for avoiding bear trouble is to take meticulous care to keep the camp clear of food smells and scraps from plates. Fish in particular should be cleaned well away from camp. Greasy plates should be washed thoroughly and stored a hundred yards or more from the tents, preferably in a tree, or wrapped and cached clear of all bear trails. Human waste, as previously stated, is best disposed of below the high tide level and the toilet paper burned.

Hungry bears are more difficult to avoid than full ones. Black bears raided the camp of the Washington Kayak Club when their members were on a summer expedition. They found the bears were far better at climbing trees than they were and that the trees were too close together to rig a safe food cache. Eventually they anchored a kayak offshore with their food supply in it and drove the bears off with much yelling and stone throwing. (The same trick tried by a group of inland kayakers on B.C.'s Bowron Lakes was less successful. The bears swam out to the boats, wrecking kayaks, cameras and other gear as they helped themselves to the tastier items in the cache.)

Jim Allan, a Canadian tour guide, uses a different technique. He carries a piece of ripe pepperoni sausage and ties it tantalizingly out of reach of the bears, well away from camp. "They'll fart around that all night," he says. On his tours to the North, however, Jim takes a gun, and on one of his ecotours a guide was accused of shooting five polar bears!

To avoid surprising a bear—or worse, surprising a mother with her cubs—travel with a noisemaker: a clanking tin cup or a chatterbox companion. If you do meet a bear, back off carefully; don't run. If you are attacked, your last resort is to curl up in a tight ball to protect your face and belly. Play dead and hope the fantasy doesn't come true.

CAMPING IN THE SUN

Life is supposed to be easier in the tropics, but camping has its own special problems. Shade is a priority, and you have to consider insects (especially if you are near a swamp), breeze and water supply. Tropical rivers are more contaminated than those in cold climates, and you must regard pools of water with great suspicion. All but rainwater should be boiled or treated with purifying tablets or filtered through purifying pumps. (More on this in Chapter 11.)

Coconut plantations make great campsites, but watch out for falling coconuts—and that is no joke: a 5-kilogram (10-pound) coconut falling

6 or 9 metres (20 or 30 feet) is quite capable of killing you. Your cooking fire and tent should be well clear of delicately poised coconuts and loosely hanging fronds. If you must camp beneath a coconut palm, first pull off all dead fronds and knock down threatening coconuts. Of course, you may have some trouble convincing the plantation owners that the coconut threatened you first, so it is well to befriend them beforehand.

Coconut plantations also provide an abundance of old dried coconuts for campfires, and the dried flowerstalks and fronds burn very well. If the plantation has been frequently worked, there may be piles of discarded dry husks left by the copra gatherers. These make excellent fuel. The young coconuts yield an abundance of sweet water compared with the mature nuts prized for their white flesh. You may find a population of large, edible crabs—either the tree-climbing variety or the burrowing land crabs—sharing your swaying garden of palms. Unfortunately, coconut plantations are also host to mosquitoes and a variety of sandflies, which may breed in the old coconut husks and down the burrows of land crabs. A tent with a fine-meshed netted entrance is well worth carrying, as is insect repellant. *Warning*: Land crabs are notorious for stealing things. We once retrieved a fine fountain pen from one of their burrows, along with an impressive collection of cups, forks and spoons from our own stock.

The problem with camping in a mangrove swamp is that the tide usually floods your campsite twice a day. Assuming there is no high ground, this leaves you two choices: sleep in the trees or sleep in the boat.

The best way to sleep in the trees is with a hammock. A good one is the military jungle hammock with sewn-in roof and mosquito netting. Take care to sleep on a layer of blanket as well as covering yourself, since mosquitoes are quite capable of biting into your back through the tight fabric.

If the mangroves are too tight or small for a hammock, you will have to turn your boat into a bed, and your comfort is going to depend to a large extent on the type of craft you have. If you come in to the swamp at high tide, be sure that you have not moored your kayak above a stake or submerged branch. Hang your gear in the upper branches to give you space and then inflate your air mattress and rig a mosquito net from the thinnest nearby branches. (These will flex when the tide drops.) Mosquitoes can be particularly bad in mangrove swamps near river or stream entrances.

SECURITY

When camping in populated areas where you fear malicious behaviour or theft from the locals, you must give some thought to security. The following points should be considered for protection against sneak thieves:

1　Pitch the tents within easy earshot and with the entrances facing each other.
2　Put the boats in the midst of the camp so that they are visible from every tent. You might also make the tents fast to a deck cleat.
3　Take valuables into the tents and store them between the occupants or under your pillows. Put the remainder of your gear inside the boats with the spray skirts tied off.
4　If you must, stretch a fishing line tight around camp at a height of four inches. Attach it to a precariously balanced pot of cutlery, which will crash down when the line is tripped. (Dogs are especially vulnerable to this trick.)
5　Keep a pack of miniflares and a powerful flashlight handy. A dazzling light can be most intimidating, as can a flare fired aloft. Miniflares are dangerous firearms and should not be pointed at prowlers unless life is threatened. (Cayenne pepper spray, however, incapacitates with a low risk of causing injury.)
6　Don't leave axes, machetes, spear guns or knives lying around camp at night; slip them under your tent or boat so that you know where they are and an opportunistic prowler does not.

FOOD

There has been a great deal written about food and diet on expeditions, and a kayak trip is little different from any other strenuous journey. You can expect to burn up a tremendous number of calories. It is most important to maintain this energy supply. No matter what you eat, you will feel great lethargy and weariness during the early days of constant paddling, but an inadequate diet will make things a lot worse. In cold climates, the problem of energy supply becomes even more serious, since so many calories are burned up just keeping warm.

The critical point in making the adaptation from the easy life most people lead to that demanded by a kayak trip of some duration is the availability of energy from the food. A body that is accustomed to extracting its energy from a readily available source such as sugar or starch will become starved as it struggles to cope with a protein diet. When it can no longer get its energy from one source, it moves on to the next, but the breaking down of protein into energy is so slow that at first the body cannot keep up.

During the first three weeks of our Patagonian trip, my companions and I developed an insatiable craving for carbohydrates. The hunting was excellent, and we could eat lean steamer ducks to the tune of 2 kilograms (5 pounds) of meat each day and still feel hungry. It was not until we were able to purchase forty-eight cans of sweetened condensed milk, which we quaffed at the rate of one can per person per day, that we began to recover from this strange form of starvation. Sweets and plenty of sweet drinks are not luxuries; they are necessities for most people under these circumstances. The right food, and time to let your body consume it, is necessary if you are not going to burn yourself up on a long trip. The ideal is to eat as you did at home—three hearty meals a day—and then sleep for eight hours every night, but more likely you will end up paddling twelve hours or more on a handful of raisins and a couple of buns with bully beef. You may do a lot worse than that, gradually drawing ever more heavily on your body's reserves. My suggestion for long wilderness trips is to carry only fats, milk powder, sugar, spices and carbohydrates (rice, flour, and so on) and rely on nature for the protein and greens. You should always, however, carry a small supply of emergency freeze-dried protein.

The best food for paddling is something with little bulk and high energy content. Raisins are good, as are almonds or walnuts. Peanuts and cashews are usually more difficult to digest. Sweetened condensed milk, granola bars and chocolate are great to keep you going until the next round of buns with bully beef, though it should be stated here that strenuous paddling discourages large meals, since hard-working stomach muscles just don't cope well with a full belly. Leave your main meals until you get ashore. Interestingly, Lindemann, who is a physician as well as a German, carried one can of beer for each day of his trans-Atlantic crossing.

HUNTING, FISHING &
DIVING FROM A KAYAK

The kayak was originally developed by the Inuit for hunting seal, walrus, caribou and even whales. It is silent, unobtrusive and swift, and you may hunt from it using a rifle, shotgun, spear or bow and arrow. In New Zealand the boats have even been used for small-scale commercial hunting. It is, however, difficult to shoot accurately while seated in a kayak if there is any wave action at all, and on the sea, of course, there usually is. One technique is to swing the rifle freely across the target, squeezing the trigger in brief anticipation of lining up. Plenty of practice with an air rifle is desirable before you start shooting for real.

Probably the best all-purpose survival rifle for a kayak expedition is the AR-7 .22 semi-automatic, which folds away inside its own butt, floats, resists corrosion and is quite accurate. You can carry a thousand rounds of ammunition in the same volume as fifty shotgun shells. For paddling in the Arctic, however, a heavier-calibre rifle is desirable because of the risk from polar bear or walrus.

The normal cruising speed of a kayak is just about right for successful trolling, though it may be a little slow for some species of fish. If you use a sturdy hand line—say about 80-pound-test monofilament with a stainless steel leader of 35-pound-test—you will have a line you can manage, yet one that will let off anything too big for you to handle. In barracuda country, this means losing a lot of lures, but you don't really want to share your kayak with a barracuda capable of breaking a 35-pound leader. A hand reel or a rod can be worked well from a kayak, giving you control of the line without cutting your fingers. A short-handled gaff with a wrist thong may also prove useful to bring your catch aboard if you plan to do a lot of fishing. Keep a cloth sack handy for carrying fish on deck.

A kayak is not the ideal craft from which to dive, but kayaking and diving nevertheless frequently go together. Besides, as we have seen, basic diving equipment can prove very handy during an emergency involving kayaks. Two divers can operate from a double kayak, but it is usually best for only one to be in the water at a time, the other waiting in the boat, ready to receive a fish off the spear or to give assistance. A good free diver can fish comfortably in 40 feet of water and with practice can go more than twice that deep. If you happen to have access to SCUBA, the tanks can be carried to the dive site on the afterdeck of your two-seater (in a calm sea) and put on either while you are sitting on the rear of the cockpit or as soon as you are in the water, where they can be held by slings. You should avoid carrying speared fish in the hand when there may be sharks in the vicinity; instead, thread fish at the end of a few metres of rope. When diving on the drop-off of a large coral reef, use the kayak to cross the wide, sandy shallows, which can often go a kilometre (half a mile) or more. It can then be tied off to a coral head inside the calm while you swim out through cuts in the reef to deeper water.

Feeling somewhat under the weather, the author is paddled
to hospital in Haiti by a companion.

CHAPTER TEN

FIRST AID

This chapter, like the chapter on navigation and the section on tides, is intended to supplement knowledge that you may already have or that you can and should gain from other sources. In this case, I assume that you will have some practical knowledge of standard first-aid skills. Basic instructions such as the treatment of wounds, fractures and burns, mouth-to-mouth resuscitation, external cardiac massage and treatment of shock are therefore omitted from the following discussion.

Ideally, you should include someone with practical medical experience in your party. Expeditions, however, may require ordinary members to administer treatment beyond the limits of normal first aid, and it is advisable to carry with you an advanced manual of medical emergency practice. A good choice is *Medicine for Mountaineering and Other Wilderness Activities*, edited by James A. Wilkerson, M.D.

The following is an outline of some special medical problems a kayak expedition is likely to meet.

TENOSYNOVITIS
This is a painful inflammation of the tendons in the wrist and arm. It is most common in the wrist and arm that twist the feathered paddle, usually with heavy boats, head winds, poor technique or all of the above.

PREVENTION: Use unfeathered paddles and/or narrow blades. Work up gradually to distance paddling. Do not grasp the paddle shaft too tightly. Keep the wrist in the same plane as the forearm as you paddle. Control the angle of the blade with the lower hand.

TREATMENT: Some relief may be gained from firm bandaging and a course of anti-inflammatory drugs, but the surest cure is rest. Acupuncture can also be a very effective remedy against tenosynovitis.

KAYAKER'S ARM (Carpal Tunnel Syndrome)

This may be just a more advanced form of tenosynovitis. A creeping numbness begins in the fingers and sometimes works its way up the hand, wrist and arm to the shoulders. In chronic cases the kayaker will not be able to hold the paddle. It is probably a result of long-term damage from the use of feathered paddles, since it is usually only the arm that twists the paddle that is affected. The damage appears to be long lasting and may require surgery to relieve pressure on the median nerve or to separate tendons from sheaths.

PREVENTION: As for tenosynovitis.

TREATMENT: Anti-inflammatory medication and splints may stall the problem and prevent the need for surgery. For mild cases, cortisone shots may do the trick. Once when I developed carpal tunnel syndrome building a cabin, I received advice from my doctor that the only course was to operate to separate the tendons, together with the glum warning that I would not be able to use the arm that summer. Four acupuncture treatments over a period of two weeks completely cleared the problem, and I worked the rest of the summer building.

KAYAKER'S ELBOW

This is tennis elbow by another name: a painful swelling that occurs on an elbow strained by too much paddling. It is similar to "water on the knee" and requires a week of rest with the arm out of action. The elbow and nearby tissue become very sensitive, and the healing of wounds or infection in the area is inhibited because of the impaired blood supply through the fluid-bloated tissue. This affliction is painful and demands to be treated as the serious injury that it is.

DISLOCATIONS

Shoulder dislocation is possibly the most common injury to kayakers after back damage from incorrect lifting. The problem occurs when pressure is applied to the arm at a position that is both behind and above the shoulder approximately in the position adopted for throwing a rock. The shoulder is usually dislocated anteriorily. Such a situation frequently occurs in surf or when one is rolling the kayak awkwardly.

PREVENTION: Begin by gingerly feeling out the zone of vulnerability by rolling your shoulder back with your arm up in the throwing position—then take every step you can to avoid that position while kayaking. Keep the elbows in close to your sides, particularly during a high brace in turbulent water.

TREATMENT: There are a number of nerve endings and blood vessels around the shoulder joint, so a dislocation should be treated as a serious injury (you can be sure the patient will be taking it pretty seriously), especially if this is a first occurrence. If at all possible, professional medical help should be sought to re-locate the arm. If you are on a remote shoreline, however, you may have no choice but to do the job yourself. A modified Hippocratic method is usually preferred, and this should be performed within an hour or so of the dislocation, before muscle spasm complicates treatment.

1 The injured kayaker lies on his or her back with the injured arm held at 45 degrees from the chest wall by one of the rescuers.
2 A T-shirt is folded and wrapped around the torso to be gently pulled away from the injured arm by one rescuer.
3 While the body is being so held, the arm is pulled from the wrist along its axis by a second rescuer using a gentle, sustained pull. The traction should be very slow, with a gradual increase in the amount of force being applied. This process may take several minutes; it must not be hurried.
4 The arm will be felt to slip back into position, at which time it should be laid across the body, supported in a sling and, ideally, taped to the body.

CHAFING & SALTWATER RASHES
Usually a problem of warm weather, rashes mostly occur under the arms and where the body touches the coaming, spray skirt or backrest,

or rubs against clothing. Aggravated by saltwater, rashes may be very painful and on long crossings may develop to the point of bleeding. When leaving the beach through surf, wave splashes can also carry sand up your trouser legs. This sand can be badly irritating if you then have to sit on it all day.

PREVENTION: Rub susceptible places with coconut oil before departure. A liberal coat over the whole upper torso provides effective protection for eight hours or so. Wash the sand out of your pants if necessary after launching through surf. Wear comfortable cotton garments.

TREATMENT: Rest ashore with frequent freshwater washes. Avoid sweating or swimming in the sea. Clean tape and bandages will ease discomfort until land is reached.

BLISTERS

These amount to friction burns and are usually worst near the start of the trip. It is better to tape your hands well before setting off than to patch the blisters at mid-day. Paddling in hot, humid weather causes more blisters than kayaking in cold weather. If a fluid-filled blister develops, avoid breaking the skin, if possible. Do not attempt to pop blisters with a needle.

BOILS, CARBUNCLES
& PRESSURE SORES

Lindemann was badly affected by these during his Atlantic crossing of 1956, and the problem has afflicted many sea kayakers with whom I have corresponded or paddled. Some people react to the salt, the chafing, the pressure of continuous sitting and the drastic change of diet and bodily routine that expeditions demand by developing these painful skin infections on arms, backs, buttocks and knees.

Boils can be treated either individually as they occur with a sulfur-based powder after being brought to a head with a poultice or, as a last resort when the infection looks as if it is becoming dangerous, with antibiotics, either by injection or in tablet form. Antibiotic cream can be very effective once the wound has been cleansed. Should the boil fail to respond to treatment and the infection become angrier, get the victim to a doctor quickly. More serious infection can readily set in, particularly in the tropics.

INFECTIONS

Sea kayaking journeys may force great changes on the body: new and strenuous exercises, irregular sleep routines, strange foods, different temperatures and a whole new variety of bacteria against which your body will have to develop fresh immunity. Add to this the stress factor from anxiety or interpersonal emotional stress, and it is not surprising that on kayak journeys the body appears to have less resistance to infection than normal. This is particularly so in the tropics, where your expedition medic can expect plenty of infected wounds, sores, bites, ears, eyes, and so on. Many will be manageable with ointments and creams, but you should be well stocked with a wide range of antibiotics in both tablet and injection form.

Kidney infections in particular are regrettably common on long-distance kayak trips. Doctors to whom I have spoken about this tend to agree that prolonged periods seated in a kayak combined with diminished water intake can retard the functioning of the kidneys and increase the likelihood of serious renal infection. Symptoms include painful and difficult urination, discharge in urine and fever. Should these symptoms occur when you are unable to reach a hospital, you should treat the condition with the appropriate course of antibiotics and take plenty of fluids.

Note: Antibiotics in your medical kit must match individual needs and tolerances. Check for allergies before stocking up.

SEASICKNESS

I have several times been badly seasick in a kayak and, as anyone who has suffered the problem knows, it is a grim experience. In a kayak, especially a solo kayak, there is little you can do except grit your teeth, so to speak, and keep paddling. Although no reliable treatment exists for the condition, there are several ways of preventing it.

The U.S. Coast Guard, having conducted exhaustive tests to find the best anti-seasickness remedy, has concluded that a combination of two prescription drugs, promethazine hydrochloride (an antihistamine with the trade name Phenergan) and the decongestant ephedrine sulfate is by far the most effective preventative available.

More recently an ancient drug, scopolamine, has acquired new respectability when used with a high-tech applicator known as the Transderm Scop. This is a small Band-Aid placed behind the user's ear that releases a steady quantity of the drug through the skin and into the bloodstream over a seventy-two-hour period. Four hours' lead time is needed to ensure effectiveness. Another scopolamine product, Triptone, can be taken orally with an even more impressive rate of effectiveness.

Anti-emetic suppositories can be used to prevent otherwise uncontrollable dry retching, though treatment after the fact is seldom successful. If possible, a period of rest should be taken, since the action of paddling aggravates an upset stomach. Try to eat bland, nonacidic foods and build up your water intake gradually. A bad case of seasickness must be treated seriously in the tropics where dehydration and the resulting hyperthermia endanger life.

SUNBURN

The potential for injury by this means on the open sea in a kayak is catastrophic because of the difficulty a kayaker has removing himself or herself from the source of the problem.

PREVENTION: In tropical regions, especially, begin with careful exposure to the hot sun. A wide-brimmed hat and long-sleeved cotton shirt can be removed occasionally to allow a gradual tanning, which will give you a degree of natural protection against sunburn, if not skin cancer. Many doctors may disagree with tanning on the grounds of an increased risk of skin cancer, but the tan can prove a survival asset in an emergency, and certainly makes living ashore in the tropics a good deal easier. For fair-skinned people, the protection required beyond the hat and shirt may include a bandit's mask to cover nose and lips, protective flaps or bandages for the backs of hands and wrists, and a zinc cream or waterproof sunblock for any areas that must be left exposed. If you have a choice between looking like an Egyptian mummy or a boiled lobster, take the mummy. Severe sunburn can occur even on overcast days in temperate climates.

TREATMENT: If serious sunburning does occur, the skin may blister and the victim dehydrate. Take the person to hospital if the burning is that extensive, but if this is not possible, you will have to camp and treat the burns yourself.

1 Be sure the victim drinks plenty of water.
2 Don't break any blisters, since they will be prone to infection.
3 Cool the patient with sponge baths of clean seawater.
4 Avoid the use of burn creams on open skin. An analgesic spray may provide relief.
5 Keep the patient well clear of the sun for several days after the burn has begun to recover.

PHOTOTOXICITY

Sudden overdoses of unaccustomed sunshine can cause distressing skin irritation often associated with sunburn. Symptoms include itching, a red flush and minute fluid-filled blisters. In some cases the situation may be triggered or exacerbated by some soaps or sunburn creams or from eating some types of food.

I know of no treatment other than keeping out of the sun until the symptoms abate, so prevention is the key. Cover the area with a dry, light cotton garment. Avoid soaps, creams and unusual spiced foods.

DEHYDRATION

The risk of dehydration is acute in the tropics, and water must be carried in quantity. Further, I suggest that any group that may face water supply problems during a long journey carry both a hand-operated desalination unit and the means to distill seawater using a fire on shore. Some people require considerably more water than others, and though one must obviously conserve water where it is scarce, it is important that everyone drink the amount he or she needs. Survival manuals usually suggest one pint per person per day as an absolute minimum, though this amount may be what some paddlers require every hour when it is hot. An indication of dehydration is abnormally dark urine, and here it should be noted that the subjective sense of thirst may not be enough to warn of a serious dehydration problem. A dehydrated person is more vulnerable to both hypothermia and hyperthermia.

EXHAUSTION & HALLUCINATIONS

Hallucinating as a result of fatigue and long hours of wakefulness is quite normal and should not be a cause for panic. You are not going mad; all you need is some sleep. Hallucinations occur more readily at night, sometimes after as little as twenty hours awake. They are just like dreams that intrude on your consciousness. Once you are visited by them, you can safely afford to continue paddling for only a short time, assuming you can still distinguish what is real from what isn't. If you begin hallucinating at 4:00 A.M., you will probably be able to continue paddling until dawn, when daylight greatly reduces the symptoms, but if you begin your fantastic visions early in the night, you will almost certainly have to get some sleep before you next see the sun. Strong coffee or caffeine tablets will help counter the effects. Common conscious dreams include out-of-body experiences and visions of land, trees, lights, farm implements and the like. Maintaining an accurate course becomes a hopeless task once you find numbers of these floating obstacles in your way. For the record, however, your exhaustion may eventually give way to the paddling equivalent of a runner's high.

HYPERTHERMIA

Hyperthermia, which is common in tropical paddling, is the overheating of the body, usually as a result of insufficient fluid intake combined with hot, still, humid conditions. It can also be the result of a high fever or being overdressed and overworked in hot climates. Symptoms beyond an excessively high body temperature and an inability to cool off are breathlessness, dry mouth, dizzy spells, affected vision, headaches and poor concentration, which may eventually lead to delirium, unconsciousness and death.

PREVENTION: Avoid paddling during the heat of day (mid-day) if it is reasonable to do so.

TREATMENT: Give the victim plenty of water. Keep clothing wet and give frequent cool sponge baths, particularly to the head, neck and wrists. At sea, wet the victim's hat often to cool the head, and have him or her wear a wet neck bandanna. Trail the victim's hands in the water frequently and, if the temperature won't come down, put him or her over the side for a swim.

Prolonged body temperatures in excess of 40°c (104°F) can damage almost every organ in the body and may result in both kidney and heart failure. Heat stroke, as it is commonly referred to in its more extreme form, calls for a trip to the hospital.

HYPOTHERMIA

Hypothermia, and its near cousin cold shock, are probably responsible, directly or indirectly, for more accidental kayaking deaths than all other factors combined. Although death by drowning may be the coroner's verdict, the cause of drowning is frequently hypothermia. Because it is the number one killer, it is vital that it be thoroughly understood and that appropriate precautions be taken when paddling in cold water.

Hypothermia is a drop in the body's core temperature below the critical level of 32°c to 33°c (90°F). Once body temperature reaches this level, unconsciousness usually supervenes. When the temperature reaches 30°c (85°F), a victim who has not already drowned through unconsciousness or loss of dexterity will usually die by means of heart failure.

Susceptibility to hypothermia depends not only on the conditions of exposure but also on body size. Children are considerably more susceptible than large adults, and thin people are more susceptible than the fat. The warning signs of hypothermia, in approximate sequence of severity, are as follows:

1 Erratic paddling and an inability to maintain course
2 Blurred vision and lack of coordination
3 Uncontrollable shivering and an apparent inability to warm up
4 Despondency
5 Ashen face and hands
6 Muscle rigidity, replacing previous shivering
7 Incoherence and collapse, weak breathing and pulse

Sometimes a person on the verge of hypothermia will recognize in himself or herself such early signs as uncontrollable shivering and blurred vision. If you find yourself in such a fix, you should immediately seek warmth and warn your companions of your condition. It is not safe, however, for members of a party to count on recognizing the onset of hypothermia in themselves. In cold conditions, always keep watch for the symptoms in other members as well as in yourself. Remember too that there is an established link between despair and hypothermia. People without hope are more prone to hypothermia, and those whose morale has sagged should be watched carefully for additional warning signs.

PREVENTION: If you are making a crossing involving wind and rain, wear your full protective regalia. Don't wait until you are already shivering to put on your windproofs. Try to maintain your warmth, rather than lose and regain it. Eat well before setting out on a cold crossing. After a day of hungry paddling, eat well and eat soon—especially if you are in for a cold, miserable night. Wear a hat in the cold. Guard against the possibility of an icy swim by wearing a dry suit with a hood or a wet suit with a hood.

If you do find yourself in cold water without the protection of an immersion garment or your boat, the outlook is grim. Thrashing around will bring your temperature down fast. Treading water will cool you into unconsciousness almost twice as fast as holding still. Swimming will only kill you unless the land is very close. Depending on the temperature of the water, you might be able to swim ten yards or you might get half a mile. If help is on the way, you can increase your chances by waiting for it quietly. Inflate your life jacket and hang in the fetal position. The so-called drownproofing technique, which involves hanging with your head under water between breaths, may be fine in a warm swimming pool, but in a cold sea it hastens hypothermia. It may be stating the obvious, but get out of the water and into the boat again as fast as you can!

TREATMENT: If someone in your party develops symptoms of hypothermia, deal with the problem at once. If it gets beyond the shivering stage and you have not yet reached land, the victim must be treated as a stretcher case. That means that he or she does no more paddling. The victim should be dressed as warmly as possible and should ride as a passenger in a double or be towed.

Ashore, carry the victim as gently as possible (preferably in the kayak) to shelter, and remove wet clothing so that heat—from whatever source is available—can reach the body more easily. The normal field procedure for concious victims of hypothermia is for one or two other members of the party to strip and join the victim in a dry sleeping bag to provide immediate warmth. In the meantime, a fire should be lit and water heated. The latest recommendation from the U.S. Coast Guard, based on research at the University of Victoria and elsewhere, is that pieces of clothing soaked in warm water should then be applied to the victim's head, neck, sides, chest and groin (or use chemical heat pads if you have them), and these warm compresses should be changed as often as required for continuing gentle warming.

Note: Stimulation of any kind—through physical exercise, jostling, rubbing of the limbs, immersion in hot water, or the administration of alcohol or hot drinks—should be avoided. Do not give the victim a warm drink until his or her body temperature has returned to near normal. A hot drink can apparently stimulate warm blood away from the vital organs, where it is most needed, and physical activity or heat applied to the overall body surface can bring cold, stagnant blood from the extremities to the body core, killing a victim who has already begun to recover.

It is useless to simply wrap an unconcious victim of hypothermia in a cold blanket or sleeping bag. Once the core temperature has dropped below the critical level, the person is no longer generating enough body heat to get warm of his or her own accord and will probably die unless treated professionally. Insulation alone will do no good; insulation and a focussed gentle source of heat are required. Evacuation is needed, but if it is not an option, you may be able to save a life by creatively using equipment on hand. You can, for example, put the victim inside a tent, inside a sleeping bag, and doing up the hood so that only the face is showing. This will not raise the person's temperature but will stabilize it and protect against unwanted stimulation. Next, create a sauna inside the tent by bringing in fire-heated rocks in a pot and generating steam by dribbling water over them. If the patient is breathing normally, his or her breath will provide a source of hot, moist air directly to the body core while protecting the body from a heat source that would otherwise trigger a shock-inducing rearrangement of the body's warm and cool blood. Monitor the pulse and be prepared to administer CPR.

COLD SHOCK

Sudden immersion in water below 10°C (50°F) may cause a series of involuntary reactions that greatly reduce the ability of an unwilling swimmer to survive. Practice in cold water can reduce some of these effects, but when the immersion is unintentional, the chance of a controlled response is not great. The first response to accidental immersion is an involuntary gasp, and if this occurs under water, it can be game over. Cold water suddenly rushing in through nasal passages and hitting the eardrum can also cause unconsciousness or confusion that makes rolling improbable. The gasp is followed by hyperventilation and a chest-gripping sense of breathlessness that can last several minutes and may leave you feeling dizzy and further confused. Your ability to hold your breath under water for your pool-practised re-entry and roll is greatly diminished by cold water, so you may end up inhaling some water and failing to complete the roll. This failure in turn leads to panic, increasing the risk that even a strong swimmer will drown. So what to do?

For a start, don't tip over. If you do, however, be prepared. That is not meant to be facetious advice, since it requires that you exercise good judgement (sound risk assessment) to avoid life-threatening events or at least prepare for them. If the previous paragraph puts you off sea kayaking, then maybe I've done you a favour. But I hope that this warning will strengthen your resolve to assess risk in a realistic manner. Sea kayaking is, after all, a risk activity, and the management of this risk is the essence of both the challenge and, for many, the appeal of kayaking. It does not call for paddling in a full quarter-inch wet suit with a nose clip and rolling every ten minutes to avoid hyperthermia, when the odds of your capsizing are small. Instead, it calls for understanding the conditions, knowing your ability and, when you go beyond it, dressing for immersion or at least being prepared for the results. (see Chapter 2 for discussion of protective clothing and Chapter 3 for rescue techniques.)

CHAPTER ELEVEN

SURVIVAL SITUATIONS

The key to survival at sea is to think survival long before the event. Like the Boy Scout, be prepared. If you become a castaway, thinking survival means wasting nothing; potentially useful equipment must always be kept, since it may contain a wire or a nail that will save your life. Thinking survival means always carrying essential articles in the pockets of your life jacket or anorak—waterproof matches, a knife, a space blanket, fishing line, hooks and a signalling mirror—so that if you make it to shore without your boat, you will have the means to improve your chances of survival. Thinking survival means taking precautions such as tying up your boat on windy days even if it is pulled clear of the water. I once watched a gust of wind pick up my partially loaded kayak and smash it down a hundred yards away. Such a wind could as well have carried it out to sea—with disastrous results if I had been on a wilderness island. Thinking survival means not throwing away your gumboots if you have to swim to shore; if you must take them off (your life jacket should keep you afloat), clutch them under your armpits. Filled with air they will provide buoyancy for your swim, and you will have boots to protect your feet from the rocks when you arrive. Cold weather survival preparation means having the right thermal equipment, but it also means getting your body ready for hardship by deliberately underdressing while in camp and frequently swimming in cold water. This may sound masochistic, but it will increase your resistance to cold.

The Ona Indians of Tierra del Fuego wore almost no clothes, even under snowy conditions. They were apparently no different from us

An improvised fire still.

physiologically, but they had developed extraordinary resistance to cold. Once upon a time they caught a zealous missionary and decided he was worth converting. The first stage demanded relieving him of his smelly clothes and plucking all his unsightly bodily hair. For six months that missionary lived naked on Tierra del Fuego before being rescued by a passing ship, and at the time of his rescue he was in excellent health. It is a good story to remember when you start to think about cold weather survival. The missionary would have had shelter, a fire and food—all of which no doubt contributed significantly to his survival—but most important, his body adapted to life in the cold.

You don't have to be on a major expedition to get yourself into a survival situation (though it certainly helps). You are in one of these crises as soon as you are in the water unable to get back into your boat. The main difference between being in the harbour and being in the middle of the ocean is your chance of getting outside help.

SURVIVAL AT SEA WITH NO BOAT

Your survival in the water is going to depend on how much warning you have of the emergency and what survival equipment is available to you.

If you have no special clothing to protect you, your chances of surviving in temperatures below 10°C (50°F) for longer than an hour are slim indeed. Your best chance is to be wearing a dry suit or an immersion suit with warm underclothing; second best is a wet suit (the more complete the better); third best is an exposure jacket (floater coat) with an inflatable cushion to keep you out of the water; and fourth best is rain gear with all the clothing you can get on, topped by a life jacket. The clothing will hold a considerable amount of body-warmed water. You should have a neoprene hood or woollen hat to cover your head and neck, since the body loses heat most rapidly from this region. The armpits and crotch are other areas of rapid heat loss. If you have only a life jacket, hunch your body into a tight ball and hang in the water, moving as little as possible. If there are several of you, form a huddle to share your warmth. (Huddling can double the time you survive.)

DRESSING FOR IMMERSION

In several parts of this book, I have alluded to the option of dressing for immersion rather than for air conditions. The problem with the former is that the paddler becomes too hot for comfort when, for example, the air is 24°C (75°F) and the water 4°C (40°F). The problem with the latter is that should a capsize occur, a person who is dressed for 24°C (75°F) will be in trouble in 4°C (40°F) water (see "Hypothermia" and "Cold Shock" in Chapter 10). Most kayaking fatalities are linked directly or indirectly to hypothermia and cold shock, so it is logical for the prudent teacher to advocate a cautious approach; right? That sounds fair enough, but it is a simplistic generalization that overlooks the encouragement that same teacher might give to sound judgement (risk assessment). Under moderate conditions, it is not reasonable to expect an experienced sea kayaker to endure the discomfort of overdressing, not to mention the risk of heat stroke, without questioning the risk. It would be like observing that most auto fatalities result from head injuries and concluding that we should all wear crash helmets when we travel on the highways. Wearing a helmet clearly makes sense in an auto race or (more contentiously) on a motorcycle, where there is a higher risk of crashing, but most of us will drive a quarter million miles without a serious accident. We use our experience to assess the risk and decline the unwanted precaution, contenting ourselves with defensive driving and seat belts and what we consider to be an acceptable level of risk. So it is with sea kayaking.

If you believe that there is a serious risk that you will end up in the water rather than on it—as, for example, on a cold surf shore like the west coast of North America—then it would be a bad call to dress other than for immersion. If, however, your trip does not involve marginal conditions, it would be an equally bad call to overdress. The risk should be assessed each day or each part of the day for each individual and a choice made whether to dress according to the air or water temperature. For high-risk groups such as children or beginners, tilt in favour of dressing for the water. Surfing cold water always calls for a dry suit or wet suit. An instructor of my acquaintance paddles the Gulf Stream in a full wet suit, complete with hood and a nose clip (because he has to roll every ten minutes to cool off). If I had to dress like that in order to paddle, I'd stick to backpacking.

SURVIVAL WITH A BOAT
Touring kayakers will normally have with them all they need to survive. The main danger is that they will squander equipment, strength and energy, abandoning mental resourcefulness through panicky behaviour.

As soon as you realize you are lost or unable to reach your destination, do the following:

1   Get out the chart and examine every possibility and factor affecting you and then decide on the best course of action and keep to it. Stay together.
2   Ration water and food immediately and see that everyone in the group fully understands your predicament.
3   In the tropics, paddle by night and conserve your strength during the heat of the day, when you can use a solar still or desalination pump to collect fresh water. Build a rainwater catchment system ready for instant use and keep it clear of sea salt. Rig a sail (tent fly) if this is consistent with your direction of travel. Do whatever you can to save effort.
4   If you require assistance, turn on your emergency locator beacon and watch for aircraft and ships. One person should always remain on watch when the group is sleeping, just in case a ship should appear.
5   If you are in cold conditions, dress warmly.
6   Start gathering seafood. A fishing line should be trolled and a spear kept at hand. In the tropics you may catch dorado, jacks, tuna or any of many varieties of school fish. In temperate climates, very small sharks may be caught or speared from the boat, but don't spear anything too big. Fish floats and other flotsam may yield edible barnacles, crabs and even small fish. The only bird a kayaker could hope to catch for food is probably the ever curious booby, which is naive enough to think people are harmless. Boobies will often come close to you, even attempting to land on the tips of paddles and attractive hats.

Dougal Robertson, author of *Survive the Savage Sea*, and of an excellent manual called *Sea Survival*, which should be mandatory reading for all sea kayakers, describes the capture and use of turtles for survival. Their blood can be drunk to quench thirst and their meat eaten raw.

"Survival-think" requires intense concentration on the problems involved with gathering water and food, protecting the group and keeping together. You must be prepared to spend the longest likely time on the sea and not develop a rescue-dependent mentality, which will only lead to despair when ships or land fails to appear. The morale of the group is most important during such a crisis. Those who fully understand the position should explain it clearly to those who doubt the course of action. A group whose morale is low, either because of navigational uncertainty or because they have given up hope of ever seeing land again, is a group that is more susceptible to mental collapse.

DRINKING WATER

After air and warmth, fresh water is your most valuable commodity. Preventing water loss and collecting fresh supplies therefore should become a priority as soon as it is obvious that you are lost at sea or due for a prolonged crossing. As we have seen, the continuation of bodily functions demands a minimum of one pint of water per person per day, but some people need much more than this.

To prevent water loss, especially in the tropics:

1 Rest during the heat of the day.
2 Wear a hat, and cool yourself off by frequently splashing seawater on your clothing.
3 Treat illnesses such as seasickness and diarrhea as soon as they appear; they waste valuable body fluids and hasten the onset of both hyperthermia and hypothermia.
4 Avoid filling water bottles completely. Always try to leave enough air in the container so that it will float should you drop it overboard.

The methods of water collection at sea, in the reverse order of technological sophistication, are these:

1 Rain storms can fill your water containers quickly. A tent fly spread wide on two paddles can do the trick. If wind accompanies the rain, however, you may have to devise a smaller catchment. Take care not to mix salt-contaminated water into existing freshwater supplies.
2 A survival still is ideal for carrying in a kayak during tropical trips. Depending on the size of the still and the strength of the sun, this little gadget may produce as much as a pint of fresh water an hour. It is fragile, however, and will repay rough handling with brackish water. Its greatest drawback may be that it requires the kayak to be stationary.

3   A reverse-osmosis hand-desalination pump will cost you almost as much as your kayak, but it could be equally important in keeping you alive. Recovery Engineering makes an excellent model, about the size of a large grease gun, which will produce fresh water at the rate of a gallon an hour. (Ed Gillet carried two desalination pumps on his Hawaiian crossing and found them extremely useful, as have some paddlers on the Baja coast.)

MAROONED

Stranded on an uninhabited island may sound like a junior accountant's dream, but it is not so far-fetched a possibility. You have only to misjudge the surf and break your boat in two, or leave your untied kayak within reach of the incoming tide, and you are marooned. A lot depends on your circumstances, of course. You may just be in for an uncomfortable night before you are missed and a search is mounted, or you may be on an Arctic or tropical island where mistakes could be fatal. Your chances will also depend on what you were able to salvage from your boat, on what protection you have from the elements and on the availability of fresh water.

Tropical Survival Ashore

On finding yourself marooned in the tropics, your priorities might be these:

1   See that your partner and other members are safely clear of the sea.
2   Treat any injuries that demand urgent attention.
3   Salvage the boats and any equipment that can be safely reached.
4   Find shelter and make an assessment of the damage, loss and prospects. Display a large sos on the beach.
5   See to your water needs. Start rationing water until you know you can get more.

You can survive for weeks without food, but in the tropics few people can survive three days without water. Ashore, as at sea, you must take care to prevent water loss by avoiding strenuous exercise during the heat of the day, by doing what you can to cool yourself off, and by treating conditions such as fever, vomiting and diarrhea without delay.

If you are on an island large enough to have streams, your water problems are solved. Swamps too can provide a regular source of water. Good water can be collected by digging a hole among the matted roots of plants near the edge of the swamp. Bail the hole continuously with a cup so that inflowing water is filtered through the ground. It is very important that water gained in this way, or from tropical streams, be boiled thoroughly. Failing that, purifying tablets or water purification pumps may do the trick.

On sandy atolls where there is greenery, you will be able to get fresh water by digging to sea level inside the vegetation zone. The water you will find has fallen on the island as rain and been segregated from the seawater by the sand. If the water is brackish, try further inland. One cheeky method is to use the burrows of large land crabs, which frequently reach fresh water. Lower a rubber hose with a cloth filter on the end, link the hose to your boat pump and suck out the water. You may have such a hose in the form of a spare elastic for your speargun.

Included in your regular survival equipment should be the makings for a fire still so that you can remove the salt from seawater. You need: the camp pressure cooker, 2 metres (6 feet) of rubber tubing (your spare speargun rubber), one aluminum tent pole, a 2.5-metre (8-foot) coil of quarter-inch copper tubing, some clear plastic surgical tubing, a large bucket (a rock pool will do) and plenty of water containers. The speargun rubber should fit snugly over the safety vent on top of the pressure cooker as well as over the end of the copper tubing. It should also fit inside the tent pole. The whole unit is assembled as shown in the photograph on page 208. You can use a waterproof bag or pool as a cooling tank. It will have to be constantly refilled with cool water from the sea, because the condenser heats it up quickly. Make sure you maintain the seawater level in the pressure cooker and scour the inside every four or five hours; otherwise, you may find some pretty acrid tastes contaminating your new water supply. This is a very reliable method for getting fresh water and, though it demands constant surveillance, it will produce a gallon of good water every two hours.

Once your supply of water is assured and you have shelter from sun, rain and wind, you will probably spend all your energy gathering and preparing food as well as perfecting your efforts to attract the attention of potential rescuers.

The sea is a vast larder for the wilderness paddler or the castaway. At low tide, shellfish can be gathered from rocks or coral reefs and an amazing variety of pool fish caught with a stick. Crayfish and crabs can often be nabbed in quite shallow water, and the pools may contain small octopus as well as shrimp, sea cucumbers and sea urchins. You may, however, encounter naturally contaminated sea creatures in many tropical areas, and throughout the world there can be occasional danger from red-tide poisoning. If in doubt, in the tropics it seems safest to stick to filter feeders (scallops, oysters, mussels and the like) and to small species of carnivorous fish; in temperate regions, where there is danger of red tide, it is best to avoid precisely these species.

Bottom fishing with a hand line is efficient if you can reach deep water without having to throw your line out over sharp rocks or coral. Fishing off steep rocks works well, or if you can get beyond the reef on a raft or a kayak, you can usually catch fish just beyond the drop-off. For bait you can use small, crushed sand crabs or shrimps, which you'll find in the coral pools.

If you have a good free diver in the group and a mask, snorkel and fins, you will be eating well indeed. A speargun is a great survival tool, but even without it the diver can collect crayfish and shellfish (such as conch) not available on the reef. Let me repeat here that divers in tropical waters run the risk of attracting sharks by carrying bleeding fish on their speargun or Hawaiian sling. To be safe, keep speared fish on a long string and get them ashore or into a boat as quickly as you can.

When the tide is out, you can hunt crabs, eels and snakes in the mud of tropical mangrove swamps—great fun! As the tide comes in, varieties of herring and mullet can be caught either by stunning them with a paddle or beating them with a spiked stick as they gulp on the surface. You can also fish using a light line baited with a bit of crushed crab. Oysters grow on the trunks of mangroves in some parts of the tropics and are easily knocked off with a diving knife. Many birds nest in the swamp too, and you may find a nest with eggs or young. Keep an eye out for larger creatures as well. Sharks often swim right into the mangroves to feed, sometimes in as little as a metre of water. If you fancy shark steak, it may even be possible to lure one into an enclosed piece of the swamp with carrion or fish heads and then close its only exit and wait for it to die when the tide recedes.

Remote islands are often the nesting grounds of seabirds whose eggs can be eaten raw. So can birds themselves if the castaway is hungry and stealthy enough. Day-feeding birds may be caught sleeping on their nests at night. Night feeders, often living in burrows, may be grabbed with a gloved hand and a long arm during the day. Land crabs, lizards, snakes and wild goats are widely distributed on remote tropical islands. Turtles too may provide an excellent omelet if you can locate a new nest—identifiable from the scratchings in the sand above the high-tide mark.

If you have coconuts on your island, you have a source of food and drink, as well as material for roofing a shelter and a source of fuel. Getting any variety of food from the jungle, however, requires specific knowledge of plants and trees. The roots of ferns, wild taro and yams, the young centres of palms, succulent shoots of creepers and grasses, fruit and nuts may all be found by those who know what they are looking for. If in doubt, use great caution and apply the following tests to any plant that you believe may be edible:

1 Are other animals (birds, pigs, insects) eating it?
2 Break it in your fingers and then sniff the juice. Be suspicious of pungent juices, such as those found in many lilies.
3 If the juice is not too repugnant to the nose, put a little on the tip of your tongue and leave it there for some minutes, testing it for a tingling or excessively bitter warning taste.
4 Should the plant appear safe, chew a small portion and then spit it out and wait to determine the effect it has on your mouth lining.
5 Should an abundant food supply prove unpalatable raw, boil it with salt and then repeat procedure 4. Many vegetable toxins are destroyed by heat.
6 No matter how tasty it seems, eat only small quantities of strange food at first.

This test is by no means infallible. Leeks, onion or garlic would probably fail, and it is possible that deadly nightshade would slip through. The best thing is obviously to know your jungle plants. Second best is to carry a manual on jungle survival to help you identify the plants you see.

Cold Weather Survival Ashore

If you have an accident, your priorities on reaching shore are these:

1 See to the needs of anyone suffering from exposure or serious injury.
2 Salvage the boat and all the equipment you can safely reach.
3 Find shelter from the elements.
4 Make a fire and dry your clothing.

If you managed to get your boat and equipment ashore, you will have the means to survive almost indefinitely provided you don't squander your resources.

First, build a permanent camp well protected from the wind.

Second, prepare a signal for attracting the attention of any passing vessel. A cairn with an orange survival bag over it may suit the terrain, or you can write an SOS in orange plastic on the rocks or snow so that it can be read by aircraft. Lay a smoke fire, ready to be ignited at the sight of a vessel, and keep it dry with a sheet of plastic.

Third, all around you is food. Wilderness survival techniques can become a way of life when you are kayaking in remote cool temperate or subarctic regions of the world, where it is usually both unnecessary and undesirable to carry masses of unpalatable freeze-dried mush. All varieties of seaweed are edible. There are hundreds of edible ground plants. In season, there are wild berries rich in vitamins. There will be fish, duck, goat, bear, deer. Water is seldom a problem in these latitudes, even on the most barren islands, since pools abound and rain is frequent.

Seals, common to most cold latitudes, can provide the castaway with meat, oil and skins. When a colony has been located, a hunter armed only with a club can be quite successful if he or she approaches carefully from downwind. (You will be in no doubt as to which is downwind of one of these colonies!) The quicker you regain your hunter's instinct, the better, when it comes to wilderness survival in hot or cold climates.

Inside the reef in Honduras.

CHAPTER TWELVE

PLANNING
an
EXPEDITION

The information in this chapter will help you plan a major kayak expedition either abroad or at home.

THE SCHEDULE

Most expedition schedules are governed by such considerations as the length of the favourable season and the date at which you have to be back home for work, but it may happen, if you take sea kayaking seriously enough, that you leave your job and put your savings into paddling some distant sea that has always fascinated you. At least I hope that is not too improbable a suggestion.

Even with no time limit at all, you still need an idea of how long your journey is going to take. You will still have to estimate costs, choose equipment, plan provisions. To do this you must estimate both the total and the average daily distance. When you divide one into the other to estimate trip time, add 20 per cent for the unexpected. Most sea kayakers can easily do 20 miles a day on a short trip in good weather. Many can do 30 miles a day under such conditions, and some, like Paul Caffyn, comfortably cover 40 miles a day, every day, so long as the sea is agreeable and the weather holds fair. On a long trip, however, you will not likely put water behind you at such speed. As a general rule, plan for an average of 10 to 15 miles a day. Ten miles would seem about right for a long wilderness trip, if you are surviving off the land. (If you are exposed to continual storm, as in the Aleutian Islands, your progress could be slower still.) Fifteen miles would likely constitute a comfortable pace for trips of less than 350 miles.

On an expedition, you should expect to paddle 30 or even 40 miles on some days, but if you plan to keep going for weeks or months, such efforts will have to be interspersed with rest days. After a 40-mile crossing, you may need three days of rest and good eating so that you can maintain your strength over the long term. During a six-month trip in Chile, we evolved a routine of two days on and one day off, followed by two days on and two days off. This schedule gave us one day for resting and two days for gathering food, hunting and preparing food for the four days of travel. This was a good arrangement, but it is only possible for straightforward coastal cruising; where you have open sea, such regular schedules have little meaning because you can't stop paddling until you reach land.

Some kayakers, eager to travel at a fast clip, organize land-based support teams. This plan requires a carload of friends willing and able to follow your progress along the coast and meet you most nights, as Paul Caffyn was able to arrange on his remarkable circumnavigations. Under these conditions, you should be able to make considerably better than 10 miles per day, since you will be able to travel more lightly. You may also eat better and will no doubt save precious hours by not having to set up a camp and prepare your own food. Paul averaged 21 miles a day over the two summers required for his New Zealand voyage, 26 miles a day on his well-supported voyage around the United Kingdom in the summer of 1980, the same mileage for his Australian circumnavigation (a year-long, 10,000-mile epic) and some 35 miles a day for Japan.

Often one of the most difficult tasks of the whole expedition is selecting who is to go, and it is a job that has to be done right. The safest thing, one would think, is to go with old friends—but you might be better off choosing competent strangers. Old friends taken out of the environment in which the friendship developed have a tendency to become strangers, and everyone seems to drag along unspoken preconditions and unrealistic expectations, which fester badly on a long or dangerous trip. In published accounts of kayak expeditions, conflict is often played down, but if you read carefully you will soon realize that conflict is the rule, not the exception. Aside from the insecurities of being away from home and the element of danger, the polarization between the leader and the led tends to invite trouble. In fact, my advice—given with sadness, not cynicism—is, if you really value your friendship with someone, don't take him or her on a long sea kayaking expedition unless the friendship was forged on a similar trip in the first place.

You should no doubt avoid taking moody and depressed people, who can affect group morale and may become a great liability under stress. People who are rigid in their ways or reluctant to chip in are no help either. (Have I just eliminated someone you know?) Be willing to judge and to trust your judgement. You will probably select the right balance of companions intuitively and do a better job than if you psychoanalyzed everyone. All too often, though, the final decision boils down to who has the funds and the time. If you really get stuck, a carefully worded advertisement in a newspaper can produce an amusing variety of applicants from which you may well be able to select a good companion.

Before everyone makes a commitment to the trip, get your heads together and sort out what you all expect from it. This is a very important step no matter what your trip involves. Even if yours is just a bunch of friends paddling up the coast for a week, you should clarify your hopes and expectations in advance. A casual chat over a beer in the local pub may be enough among friends, but if your trip has a $50,000 budget from a scientific foundation, forget the beer. You will have to work out in advance as much detail as you possibly can and get it down on paper— and you may also need a lawyer if the stakes are that high.

For most expeditions, however, a homemade written agreement is in order. What is needed is a statement of intent by people of good will so that in times of stress—and there are always plenty of them—the group can refer to established common goals. The exercise of writing this statement down will serve to make quite sure that you all have compatible aims and priorities, and it can help in clarifying the division of workload, responsibilities and privileges as well as the financial status of the enterprise. It is usually obvious who is the expedition leader, but it is sometimes a good idea to put this information in writing to eliminate needless indecision and jockeying for position.

Roles such as medic, treasurer, route researcher, secretary, photographer, transportation organizer, equipment and insurance organizer, fund raiser and press liaison should be assigned at this stage. If your expedition is this elaborate, the agreement should be also; and remember that it must be fair to everyone. Inequities will only fester until a more inconvenient time—such as the middle of the trip.

The agreement may cover details of finance, liabilities, distribution of profits from photograph or article sales, and ownership of equipment, and it may lay down procedures for resolving disputes. It should establish a policy for such occurrences as walkouts, accidents, illness and death. It can define an attitude to publicity, the acceptance of outside assistance, use of sails, hotels or tents. You should agree on a rate of travel and the relative priorities of science, filming, photography or other activities. Finally, the agreement should include a clause that spells out amendment procedures.

The Caribbean expedition I participated in from 1977 to 1978 was structured so that all four members had a single vote, with an additional tie-breaking vote available to the leader (myself). Since there was considerable discrepancy of experience, I was given an absolute veto on sea decisions. This provision, we hoped, might save us the pains of the democratic process in emergencies. I am pleased to say that at no time did I need to use either the tie-breaking vote or the veto, though we had our share of differences.

Disputes will arise. The very nature of the exercise seems to attract people with strong wills. The agreement and the will to stick to it can help to resolve many of the differences. If you can preserve the willingness to discuss problems, you will be able to handle most policy and personality disputes.

PRE-DEPARTURE WORK

As D-Day draws nigh, the organizing acquires a frantic quality. Equipment piles higher and higher in various rooms of the house, and mountains of letters are shuffled in and out. The garbage is full of crumpled envelopes, while the paperweight can hardly maintain its position on top of the ever growing pile of exotic cancelled stamps. There is hardly a clear space to put down a cup of coffee while you answer the telephone. People are visited by gut-flutters and second thoughts as they begin to realize what they have let themselves in for. Training is well under way, muscles ache, and there is a sore spot in the place where your back rubs the backrest. The medical kit is in order, and you have a memo to pick up the prohibited drugs at the airport. You have found an airline that is prepared to bend the rules and give you a discount on your air ticket and free freight in exchange for some sort of public acknowledgement if you succeed. Nobody has agreed to back your movie, but you are still working on that.

Amid this excitement, insurance may seem to be a strange priority—especially from someone who has pontificated on the virtues of self-reliance—but once you have decided to travel as a group, you are obliged to take extra precautions. If you have a sponsor, you have an additional duty to keep the odds in favour of success as great as possible. Most kayak trips are run on budgets so tight that having a member hospitalized overseas could spell financial disaster for the project. It is for this reason that you need adequate insurance. I would suggest at least $20,000 in medical insurance per person. Since your kayak is carrying valuable equipment, the loss of which you may not be able to absorb, you may need insurance on the goods as well. When you talk to the adjuster, it may be wise to designate your trip as simply "travel" rather than trying to explain your mode of travel more explicitly, since few insurance adjusters can distinguish between sea and whitewater kayaking. Look into insurance against the cost of calling a search—some search-and-rescue organizations expect you to pay for a search you call.

By this time, the area you are visiting will be taking shape in your mind. You will all have read up on local history, geography and politics. You'll already have had to put plastic over your charts, not to protect them from the water, but to keep them from wearing out as you paw and ponder their mysteries. Everyone on the expedition should be familiar with the charts and see the full route mapped out on them; the leader should have them virtually memorized. Coast pilots and sailing guides should be studied carefully and marked where relevant. Escape routes should be marked for difficult passages. Where your course follows a dangerous lee shore, estimated times to safe harbour should be jotted on the chart with chinagraph pencil. Check the history of past weather from as many sources as possible and be quite sure you understand how weather will affect your course. Don't hesitate to alter your plans radically as you learn more about the area you are visiting. Know what to expect from currents and winds, how frequently you can restock with food and what nature can do to supply you en route.

You won't find room on the charts to make notations about local history and geography. Put this information into a notebook instead, where you can review it day by day as your voyage proceeds. Even if your expedition is not obligated to bring back salable photographs or publishable accounts of the wonders you encounter, you'll want to remember for your own sake to paddle up that fjord where the big glacier is hiding, or to look into that cove to see what's left of the nineteenth-century whaling station. Preparatory historical research not only will give your expedition an added dimension of enjoyment but it will also put your effort in perspective.

If your journey takes you through the Caribbean, along Central America or even along some of the coasts of Europe, you may face a new country and a new set of laws every few days. Again and again you may be confronted by a platoon of officials whose job is to check you out and see that your papers are in order. They may request such wonders as deratting certificates, ship's doctor's report, quadruplicate lists of crew and cargo, as well as port clearance from the country you have just left.

Most authorities don't know how to handle the arrival of a kayak, and your presence will probably be the cause of great hilarity. This can be to your advantage. While they are laughing they are unlikely to make things too difficult for you—but don't count on it.

Part of your pre-expedition work should be to contact every customs authority along your route, providing an approximate arrival date and a list of the equipment that may be of interest to them. The letter should be addressed to the Chief Inspector of Customs and if possible should be written in the language of the country involved. Authorities will feel better disposed towards you if you ask in advance about restricted items such as fruit and firearms. Another letter to the local diplomatic representative of each country to be visited will clear up any conflicting rumours about the various visas needed. Check to see if there are any restrictions on coastal landings or the use of cinematic equipment.

The rules vary widely. For example, if you are going to the Dominican Republic you may need a special cruising permit even to approach the shore. In 1978, in order to cruise the remote north coast by kayak, we needed a letter from the vice admiral himself. (We really did need it, too. Without it we would have been explaining our position from behind bars on a number of occasions.) Often a letter from the minister of tourism will be useful as well, but in troubled areas nothing may help.

Charles Miller, an American kayaker who has paddled extensively in the Aegean and Greek Islands, tells of intensive interrogations by both Greek and Turkish authorities and reports that both Bulgarian and Rumanian shore patrols fired shots at him.

In more volatile countries, your embassy should be given your schedule and contacted as regularly as its representatives advise. If you present your passport to them on your day of arrival, you may have an easier time replacing it should it be lost. Where political unrest is extreme, notify all local authorities whenever you arrive in a town. (You may be required to do this anyway.) Remember that after a few days' paddling, a kayaker can look as wild and woolly as any guerrilla or desperado, and jumpy authorities may need a little reassurance. A good trick is to contact the local press as soon as you get to the country where you plan to paddle. You can give them a photograph and an outline of the trip and then keep several copies of the published article. When you are later faced with a suspicious police officer or a gibbering seventeen-year-old soldier with a machine gun, you can wave your press clipping at him; it is an impressive example of the power of the printed word.

My first Patagonian kayak trip began only three months after the overthrow of Allende, at a time when the military was still pulling communists out from under the beds. Near the end of the six-month trip, the police picked me up while I was taking photographs in the poor part of the town of Castro, on the island of Chiloe. I did look suspicious (though I was not under my bed). I was wearing a bushy beard and beret, and I had a military-looking pack full of fancy cameras. I had loose ammunition in my pockets and my visa had expired, yet none of this mattered once I produced the newspaper clippings with the story of our expedition. To my considerable relief, I was immediately treated as a bosom friend, and a special letter was provided to cover the expired visa, which could only be renewed in Santiago.

There is, of course, another way to do things if your party is really small and you make absolutely no contact with the press—and if the countries you visit are safe and peaceful. During my first paddle through the Caribbean, in 1967, I was so ignorant of procedure that I entered and left half a dozen countries without bothering to disturb the authorities at all. Nobody complained. I just paddled up to a white sandy beach, made my camp, caught my fish, bought my stores in the local town and moved on. People who saw me thought I had come from one of the cruise yachts or from the next town. Nobody suspected that I had paddled in from the faded blue island on the horizon. I do not seriously advocate this procedure, however, since it could get you into trouble and spoil your trip. There is usually little to be gained from it anyway, since most authorities are friendly to kayakers.

One of your most important pre-departure contacts is the coast guard. Write and tell them your plan before you get where you're going. Once you arrive, contact them personally and discuss with them, in as much detail as they can bear, the finer points of your journey through their jurisdiction. Give them an outline of your schedule—but with a reasonable delay factor, in case you are holed up on a beach during bad weather. You can do without the embarrassment of an unnecessary rescue. Let the coast guard know your storm procedure so that they can anticipate your thinking in case there is a need to search.

It can save time if you carry a printed list of expedition information useful to coast guard and other local authorities. As well as your route, it should contain a description of your boats and the names, addresses and next of kin of all members. List the safety equipment you carry, as well as your expected supply of water and food. If you carry a radar reflector, tell them that.

The attitudes of coast guards vary more from station to station than nation to nation. Generally, though, you will find them friendly, helpful and prone to underestimate kayaks. One blustery Easter day when we contacted the British coast guard at Dover to tell them we were paddling to Calais, they not only gave us detailed advice on currents and weather but also actually drove us about in search of some last-minute safety equipment we had been unable to pick up in London. The Miami coast guard were just the opposite. When we contacted them from the Bahamas to warn of our attempt at the 62-mile crossing of the Gulf Stream, they did not want to know. "If you aren't in trouble, we don't want to hear from you," their operator said curtly, and then hung up. They did not even record the frequency of our radio transmitter—a simple enough precaution that could have saved them a lot of effort, not to mention our lives, in the event of a search. (Miami is a busy shipping area, of course, but Dover Strait is busier.) Fortunately, the Miami experience is not typical. The U.S. Coast Guard in Puerto Rico was extremely helpful on that trip, and we were able to return the favour by assisting in the prosecution of an oil tanker we photographed pumping its bilges between the islands.

SPONSORS

Most sea kayaking expeditions are financed entirely by the members, but lengthy ones in foreign waters can be too expensive for ordinary folk. You somehow have to find enough money for boats, equipment, food, transport, freight, medical and equipment insurance, cameras, film, spending money and a 20 per cent contingency fund. When costs are high, finding a sponsor may be your only hope.

The important thing to remember when seeking sponsors is that they too will want something out of the deal. Begging letters only cause irritation and waste postage. Instead, think carefully about which manufacturer could use your trip to promote its product and then write the company a letter outlining the trip and the ways you would be prepared to assist with promotions in return for assistance. You should include a detailed outline of your track record—previous expeditions and any satisfied sponsors you may have had in the past—and a profile of each crew member. If your list does not look very impressive, you will have to produce a very good idea for the actual kayak trip and promote your cause personally. It can be a disheartening business. Even when you are sure a company could benefit from your trip, you may have no fun convincing their advertising manager of these benefits and will probably have the greatest difficulty just getting in to make your pitch. Make your plans at least a year in advance to avoid being told that "this year's advertising budget has been fully allocated."

Lay hands on all the newspapers of the area into which you plan to paddle (the country's embassy will have them) and read the advertisements. Find out who is spending money on newspaper advertising and what angle they are using and then tailor your proposal accordingly. But be warned: few advertising managers have the imagination or nerve to risk a break with tradition. You might point out to your potential backer—and to yourself—that Columbus, Magellan, Vasco da Gama and Marco Polo were all sponsored by commercial interests. Still, it is likely to be an uphill job, perhaps the toughest part of your journey.

If yours is a noteworthy adventure, you can get assistance from newspapers and magazines themselves, but make sure you don't give away more than they are paying for. Here you will need a very knowledgeable friend ashore, or a professional agent. But take care. Publicity, far more than commercial sponsorship and promotion, can seriously warp the adventure itself and may lead you to continuing beyond reasonable limits of safety.

PHYSICAL PREPARATION

Sea kayaking depends on stamina and efficiency more than strength, and stamina, apart from being a mental attitude, depends on training and being fit. Set your body a training schedule, including regular sessions in the boats and general fitness activities such as running, swimming and exercises for the back and arms.

An excellent specialized exercise, which can be done before going to bed each night, requires a 45-centimetre (18-inch) stick and a good hefty climbing boot. Tie the boot to the centre of the stick with a 1.5-metre (5-foot) bootlace. Hold the arms out horizontally and rotate the stick until the boot reaches it and then wind it steadily down again. Start with five of these exercises and then increase by one every night until you are doing thirty. This fine exercise for arms and shoulders will give you the chance to explore the subtle distinction between stoicism and masochism without even having to get wet. As for the kayaking side of the training, get out there and train hard in the boats at every opportunity. Most kayaking discomfort results from sitting in one position for long periods and from chafing. There seems to be no way to improve one's tolerance to these evils, but do take the trouble to rig yourself a comfortable seat. The only training for endurance is to endure—and that, I am afraid, is what sitting on your butt for twelve hours is all about.

If your expedition takes you to a new climatic zone, you will need to allow a period for adjustment to the new conditions. Two weeks at least will be needed when travelling to the tropics from a temperate climate. Ease up your training program a little when you get there and take care to drink plenty of water. Moving to colder climates, you will have to make a conscious effort to underdress. Where possible, cold swims will help with this adjustment.

Note: An alternative regime is to not train at all but simply to begin paddling gently each day, starting with 5 miles the first day and increasing this distance by a mile every day.

Participants in an Alaska Discovery guided trip.

CHAPTER THIRTEEN

TOURS, RENTALS & INSTRUCTION

For beginner paddlers, kayak tours, lessons, clubs and kayak rentals provide the opportunity to try paddling without significant financial commitment and with the presumed advantage of getting guidance from someone knowledgeable.

TOURS

Tour companies specializing in sea kayaking are springing up all over the North American continent. They offer a wide range of trips from local day cruises to exotic expeditions exploring Belize, Baja, Baffin Island and even Antarctica. Most tour companies are excellent and provide a sociable, safe introduction to kayaking. Some, however, may be less than adequate, with client-to-staff ratios that are far too high, poor equipment and/or poorly trained staff. As far as possible, check out the company you are considering. If you can't get a firsthand account of the sort of trip the company runs, be sure to ask the right questions before you sign up for a tour. Such questions include the following:

- How long has the company been in business?
- What is the client-to-staff ratio? (5:1 is acceptable.)
- What is the focus and philosophy of the company? Of the trip?
- Who is leading the trip you are considering? How many times has that person led that particular trip before? What are his or her qualifications?
- How far will trip participants be expected to paddle in a day?
- Does the company carry liability insurance?

- What does the price of the tour include? (When comparing prices, be sure you are comparing like products. For example, are the trips of equal duration, and do they offer comparable menus or services?)
- What type of boats and other equipment does the company use? How much safety equipment will be available to the group?
- Does the company run trips that adhere to the safety guidelines set out by its trade association?

To locate sea kayak tour operators, check the advertisements in the specialty kayak and outdoor magazines; in North America you can phone TASK (the Trade Association of Sea Kayaking). Or contact a specialty store and ask for a list of tour operators. As kayaking becomes a mainstream activity, more tour operators are registering with regular travel agencies, and you can be sure that such companies at least carry insurance.

If you are dissatisfied—or especially satisfied—with your trip, write and tell the operator; copies of your letter can be sent to relevant parties such as an appropriate consumer or trade magazine, TASK or the guides associations, and the place where you learned of the trip. You should register satisfaction or dissatisfaction regarding commercial courses or kayak outfitters as well.

Novice Tours with Teens—A Note for Organizers

Many community centres and schools have fine introductory ocean kayaking programs. These are frequently open to juveniles, and such programs require an entirely different approach from the one I have stressed thus far in this book. Where I have advocated self-reliance and acceptance of responsibility for one's actions, the organizer of a trip of juvenile novices must be a defensive thinker—defensive to the point of extreme caution.

For individuals in the 13-to-16 age group (a younger novice will likely be in a double with an experienced adult), you will need to take special precautions against hypothermia. Since children succumb to hypothermia much more quickly than adults, wet suits should be worn and warm, windproof clothing kept on hand when paddling in colder climates. Be prepared for the unexpected, such as a capsize in totally calm waters. Boats with good stability are an obvious advantage.

The organizer of juvenile groups should see to it personally that every boat has the required safety equipment and that everyone—including instructors—wears a life jacket.

If you decide to send young beginners to sea in kayaks, you are, in my view, obligated to provide massive supervision by experienced adults. Avoid novice parties that are too large. Open-sea kayak excursions for juveniles with an experienced-to-inexperienced ratio greater than 1:2 should include a safety boat. The question to ask yourself is, could you as leader handle an emergency if all the novices were in trouble at the same time? You cannot afford to run novice trips of juveniles if the answer to that question is no.

In the early seventies, I accompanied a group of Outward Bound boys on an ill-advised sea trip in New Zealand's Marlborough Sounds. Fourteen boys, 16 to 19 years old in slalom singles, were making a 2-mile crossing of a bay during rather rough weather. A sudden squall capsized nine of the boats in one blast. It immediately became so rough that any form of group rescue using the techniques the boys had been taught was out of the question, even though they were in unloaded kayaks. There were two instructors with the group as well as myself and another instructor shadowing them in a 7-metre (24-foot) jet rescue boat, watching through binoculars from a distance of half a mile. In less than twenty minutes we had picked up all nine paddlers and their boats. Without the rescue boat, we would have needed a 1:1 staff-to-pupil ratio to handle the emergency, and even then, the result would have been in doubt. My advice to anyone running an exposed novice trip, particularly involving children, is to take a safety boat whenever you have any doubts, and provide the youngsters with appropriate training beforehand.

RENTALS

Today both double and single sea kayaks can be rented from dozens of outfitters throughout North America and a small but increasing number of overseas locations. The singles are generally either one of the plastic single models or representative fibreglass designs intended to familiarize the renter with the lines sold by a particular retailer. No regulation of the trade exists other than standard coast guard requirements, but a set of guidelines issued by TASK currently sets out reasonable safety guidelines for its members.

Renting a kayak is definitely a case of renter beware; the ultimate responsibility for seeing that the equipment is sound and appropriate is placed firmly with the customer by means of a waiver. If you decide to rent, check the condition of the equipment and be sure it is suited to the area in which it will be used. Most outfitters rent stable, medium- to high-volume kayaks by the hour, day, or week. The rental price will usually include paddle(s), spare paddle, spray cover, pump, buoyancy, life jacket(s) and flares if needed. Wet suits, dry suits and emergency radio beacons are often available separately.

Don't be surprised by the type of questions the outfitter will want you to answer. You will be asked precisely where you intend to go and when you plan to be back. Very likely you will be asked for a description of your vehicle and where you intend to park it. There are good reasons for these questions. Should you be overdue, the coast guard will first call the local police to see if the vehicle is still parked at the put-in point. If it is, a water search will be initiated. If not, the authorities will assume that the kayakers are safely off the water. A conscientious outfitter will call the telephone numbers supplied by the customer within an hour of his or her failure to return from an hourly rental; if the renter has not been heard from, the outfitter will assume the worst and notify the authorities. It is obviously in everyone's interest to let the outfitter know of any changes or delays in your schedule.

At least one kayak rental company in California requires anyone renting a kayak to first complete their course on basic kayaking. This laudably responsible attitude is not universally followed because some legal counsel suggests that it could imply an endorsement of the paddler's competence, which could then be held against the outfitter in the event of a mishap. So today most rental kayaks come on the same basis as skis: you pay your money and are responsible for what you do with the equipment.

LESSONS & INSTRUCTION PROGRAMS

Kayak instruction has become an industry in itself these days, and although I have some reservations about a process that is usually not based on experiential learning, the myriad of schools that have sprung up in the past decade or so generally seem to be doing a pretty good job at easing would-be kayakers onto the water where the real lessons are to be learned.

INSTRUCTION SURVEY: To get a sense of current trends within the industry, I sent out a questionnaire to a rough sampling of about two dozen kayak schools. I received responses from twenty instructors representing eighteen organizations. There were three responses from the U.S. East Coast, four from California, three from Washington and Oregon, another three from British Columbia and one each from the Great Lakes, Mexico, Alaska and New Zealand. I have also taken into account the sea kayaking program taught by the nonprofit, Wyoming-based National Outdoor Leadership School (NOLS), with which I have become familiar as one of the school's trustees, and which runs sea kayaking programs in Mexico, Alaska, Patagonia and the Pacific Northwest.

Collectively, these organizations teach over twelve thousand students each year. The three largest operators in the survey accounted for more than half the students taught, with most facilities teaching between two hundred and eight hundred students each year.

Kayaking courses, both regionally developed and institutional, are available through kayak retailers, kayak clubs, schools, universities and community centres. They range from a two-hour basic introduction to paddling techniques for first-time renters to comprehensive nine-day instructor courses. In addition, there are specialized courses in rolling, bracing, surfing, navigating and weather forecasting as well as courses designed specially to develop leadership and sound judgement.

WHO TEACHES WHAT: One of the inherent problems with schools in general is that they tend to emphasize those subjects that can be most easily taught and measured, neglecting those that are difficult to verify. So it is with kayaking schools.

The quest for good instruction is very much a matter of buyer beware, and this situation may be interpreted either with alarm or as a sign that innovation and development are still flourishing in the sea kayaking culture of North America. Certainly the breadth of courses available varies widely and if there is a discernible trend, this is probably it. For example, one instructor, Penny Wells of California, teaches only a small number of students, but focusses on guide training for Environmental Traveling Companions (ETC), a nonprofit group that takes people with disabilities and specials needs sea kayaking, and has helped develop the course content for clinics that are tailored to the northern

California environment. Lynn Morrison, sea kayaking coordinator for NOLS, which was teaching sea kayaking in the 1970s, before it was even called sea kayaking, puts the emphasis on teaching safety, judgement, technique and group management skills all woven together with a message of minimum impact on the environment.

There has been a significant sharing of teaching methods and styles, as a result of teaching clinics and peer review classes at symposia sponsored by the likes of TASK, the Association of North Atlantic Kayakers (ANORAK) and a very active community of West Coast paddlers. Instructors get together over a long weekend and offer critiques of each other's teaching methods, taking home those ideas that work and suit their style, discarding those that fail. Through forums such as these, the best of all systems are incorporated. This fluid exchange of ideas is very healthy. I see it as a sign of the industry's vitality. Indeed, of the schools that responded, only one claimed to adhere strictly to the American Canoe Association (ACA) curriculum and only one to that of the British Canoe Union (BCU). The rest provided a composite of programs.

One of the crucial points with any sea kayak instruction is the student-to-staff ratio. Generally speaking, the lower the ratio, the better from the student's perspective, since greater individual attention can be expected. The higher the ratio, the better from the company accountant's point of view. The survey indicated a ratio of one instructor to six students for general courses is normal; 1:4 is favoured for more advanced courses and 1:2 for specialty rolling or surf courses. Another ratio of interest is the gender mix. Half the respondents reported an even male/female mix; the rest reported fewer women except for one that reported 60 per cent women.

There is no consensus about what is the most serious omission in sea kayak instruction today. For every person who thought there was not enough emphasis on rolling, there was another who thought there was too much. Twenty respondents offered almost as many gripes—not the stuff that helps make sense of trends, but the very lack of discernible consensus of malcontent makes the point that the instructional process is probably developing in a healthy manner.

Rather than burden the reader with pages of statistics, I have elected to include positive salient points within what I consider to be close to the ideal kayak class, combining a balance of experiential learning and direct instruction, with theory presented where it is most effective—in the field.

THE LEWIS/DAWSON PROGRAM

Dan Lewis and John Dawson are independent instructors who have developed their own curricula in close cooperation with the West Coast Kayaking community. They work together with various levels of students as well as training guides and other instructors. Both work as consultants, setting up sea kayak programs for private companies and colleges. Dan mostly teaches in Tofino, on Vancouver Island, where he has easy access to protected waters, tidal rapids, good surf beaches and exposed coast. John lives in Nanaimo and has set up a sea kayak program for Malaspina College. He ran the first government-sponsored training program for sea kayak guides (a six-month live-in program) and has worked with Dan on the development of a range of professional guide and instructor programs. This is their program, as Dan describes it.

The Two-Day Basic Course

The Two-Day Basic Course includes the following, in order of priority:

1 Safety (managing risk)
2 Seamanship
3 Chart reading
4 Equipment
5 Rescues
6 A four-hour trip
7 Strokes
8 A two-hour trip

The basic course is on a weekend and is a component of a five-day course called Basics and Beyond. By the end of the weekend, people know how to get in and out of the kayak, paddle around, check their equipment, think safety, read a chart and tide tables, and perform rescues. The "Beyond" part of this course is an opportunity to apply these basics during a three-day camping trip, which is completely geared towards experiential learning.

Basics and Beyond

The essence of this course begins immediately after the completion of the Two-Day Basic Course. The instructor demonstrates what to bring by unpacking his personal gear and then repacking it so that it is waterproof and compact. An emphasis is put on waterproofing the gear in case hatches or bulkheads fail, bringing enough gear for a margin for error but not too much and leaving cotton at home for B.C. coastal camping. Next, charts and tide tables are handed out and homework assigned; each person or couple is to look at various options for the three-day trip and choose a route or routes.

Monday morning, the group assembles early and packs the kayaks. The instructor has the group camping gear and food ready to go and once again demonstrates how to load the kayak by loading his first. Weight distribution is emphasized to achieve the right trim for the conditions; this is demonstrated by floating the boat briefly.

Once people are loaded and ready to go, the instructor discusses the route plans with an emphasis on balancing group strengths. The marathon racers have to go with the bird-watchers, and if they bully the bird-watchers into an overly ambitious plan, they likely will not be able to keep up. For the three days, they will be a team and must think and act as such. They emphasize that it is the little voices that think "No" to a plan that are more important to hear than the assertive, gung-ho voices saying, "Yeah! Piece of cake!"

The course has a student-to-staff ratio of 4:1. The instructor's role is to nudge the group into making decisions, not to make decisions for them, though the instructor retains a right of veto if he thinks the situation may prove dangerous. If no one will get hurt, it is better to let the group members make mistakes so that they can learn. It is better to make a mistake when an instructor is present than when students are on their own. The emphasis is on the need to pre-plan "what if?" scenarios. What if paddlers get tired? The wind picks up? They are slow and miss the tide?

This decision-making process occurs in the context of the observable conditions, combined with the information provided by charts, tide tables, weather forecasts and occasional hints by the instructor.

Once there is a plan that everyone feels happy with, the groups heads off. During the three days, each participant spends up to half a day being the route finder. That person paddles up front and makes decisions about where they are, what heading to take, how to monitor drift, what the weather and traffic are like and so on.

One instructor paddles beside the route finder and asks the kind of questions that people must learn to ask themselves: Where is such-and-such a point? When will such-and-such an island become visible? Where is this channel deepest? Which way is the current going? The other acts as sweep or may move back and forth through the group asking questions that keep the group monitoring the route finder's progress.

Once they have made a decision that is safe (right or wrong), the instructor communicates that to the group: "We're aiming for that white house with the big dock." If the route finder was wrong and wants to communicate that to the group, he or she does that through the instructor. This puts the instructor in a good position to monitor group response.

Dan and John try to provide an experience of what it is like to paddle into unknown territory, assessing all the variables and making decisions that work, as well as providing experiences of ways of reacting when they don't.

The route finder is not responsible for controlling the group on the water. That is the job of the instructors, who at the same time are able to ensure that everyone remains current with what is going on and understands that in a nonguided group, everyone needs to pay attention and share leadership responsibilities, in case the leader, designated or unspoken, makes mistakes. This is an important component of the course, since it is in effect a structured approach that gives everyone an equal opportunity to learn skills that are, in the normal classroom sense, unteachable. The idea is to let students make (monitored) mistakes, give it their best judgement and learn to react appropriately when things change or go wrong (not to the point of capsizing!).

Beyond that, students gain daily practice paddling, loading boats, setting up and breaking camp, cooking (the staff are instructors, not guides), planning meals, monitoring weather and radio reports, using charts and tide tables. Informal evening lectures cover "Past Casting"— an idea from NOLS, in which weather forecasts are regularly monitored and recorded and compared with the reality of the day; the level of reliability is then used to critically assess the forecast for the next day. The instructor calls the coast guard to verify the results. If there is no response, that too is a valid demonstration.

If there is a theme to the course in addition to safety, it is one of enhancing the environmental consciousness of the student so that a responsible environmental ethic is as much a part of sea kayaking as paddling skill.

Following is a summary of the contents of Basics and Beyond, in order of priority:

1   Route finding
2   Group decision making—recognizing and accepting group limits
3   Weather observation, monitoring and interpretation
4   Contingency planning/risk management
5   Camping skills
6   Compass skills

Intermediate Course
This course takes off where Basics and Beyond ends and follows a similar format: a two-day weekend course called Surf and Currents is immediately followed by a three-day course called Open Coastal Paddling.

The contents of Surf and Currents are as follows:
1   Intermediate Strokes
   a)   Leaning the boat
   b)   Bracing: low brace, high brace so as to keep the shoulder in its socket
   c)   Turning: leaning the boat while sweeping to turn around quickly in surf, low-brace eddy turn, stern rudder, carved turns
2   Rescue Revision and Skill Update
   Self-rescues are reviewed on day 1, to see that everyone wet-exits okay and can handle cold water before students go surfing. This gives the instructor an idea of who they need to pay special attention to.
3   Surfing (by priority)
   a)   The whole group climbs up on a big rock to identify the different zones: soup, impact, green and beyond. The instructor explains that they will be doing their learning in the soup zone,

where basic skills can be learned and where capsizing won't mean an epic swim. Often beginners get panicky and paddle too hard, going right out to the green, where the biggest wave of the day swamps them, and by the time they make it back to shore by swimming through the impact zone, they've sworn off surfing. While one instructor is talking, the other is demonstrating the two principal things the group will be doing that day.

b) Students point their kayaks straight out to sea, close to shore, and don't paddle. As a wave approaches, they take one stroke in front of it, punch through (or over) the wave to take the second stroke behind it and then quickly take one more (braking) stroke to prevent back-sliding. Then they stop paddling, relax and get used to the noise and commotion of the surf zone.

This exercise teaches two things: (1) how you can take a breather by pointing into the waves (much like sitting in an eddy in a river), and (2) how to punch through waves without getting back-surfed. Many people will gladly spend the whole day doing this, but they are encouraged to move on to the next exercise, which they should spend the bulk of their time doing.

c) Next students learn to turn the kayak parallel to the wave, lean into it and high-brace. They also learn to look towards shore when they are side-surfing.

d) After lunch the instructors take students out one-on-one and teach them how to punch through the surf zone to go touring and how to re-enter the beach without surfing. Once students have done this at least once with an instructor, and they feel comfortable, they are free to pair up with another student and repeat the exercise.

e) The lowest-priority surf skill is how to ride the waves like a surfer. It has two applications for sea kayakers:

i) It makes following seas into a boon, not a hindrance.

ii) It is fun to do when you're not touring or after camp is set up on the beach.

Note: When students are surfing, they are always buddied up. One partner is on the shore constantly watching his or her surfing partner. One instructor is on shore watching surfers and giving feedback when they swim in. The other instructor is out surfing, demonstrating and encouraging people.

4   Tidal Currents Training (This technique is fourth in priority, not time, and takes place on the morning of the first day after the strokes session.)

The group paddles to a small tidal rapid and practises two skills:

a) eddy turns

b) ferry glides

This is basic moving-water technique for canoes, which behave more like a sea kayak than does a whitewater kayak. These skills are handy when you are touring in areas with tidal currents. The ferry glides are a miniversion of a crossing on a mile-wide inlet in a 1-knot current. Transits are emphasized as a means of maintaining the ferry line.

Open Coastal Paddling

After supper on the Sunday of the Surf and Currents weekend, the instructor goes over packing and asks students to plan a trip as homework. The trip is done in a similar fashion to the one in Basics and Beyond but this time on the fully exposed west coast. During this trip, the instructors cover many of the same topics as in Basics and Beyond, including route finding, group dynamics, weather observations and contingency planning. More emphasis is put on compass use here, since sea fog is a constant threat.

Every time group members land on a beach, they do a full surf landing, even if there is a double with a couple wearing thongs, shorts and straw hats with a baby in their lap landing 45 metres (50 yards) away (this happened once!), for people learn by doing. Typically, one of the instructors goes in first and signals the other to send in the students one or two at a time, depending on surf conditions. When the group leaves the beach, the process is reversed, with one instructor on the beach and the other beyond the break where the group assembles and waits. Everybody always wear helmets at these times. They are carried strapped to the afterdeck at other times.

The instructors emphasize that swell size is random! Students are constantly reminded not to stack up side by side in swell, to keep a constant watch for the next incoming wave and to always keep an eye on what lies down-wave of them. The question on everyone's mind should be "What if a big wave came right now?"

On the last day, the group paddles a dead-reckoned course. The students agree on the compass bearing taken from the chart and then paddle on that course, wearing visors that enable them to look only at the compass until they arrive at land or are told they can stop. It is the instructors' job to keep an eye on traffic as they paddle from one kayak to the other, finding how the experience is going for them and encouraging them to trust the compass.

Usually most people make it more or less to the target. The instructor stops those who are well off the mark, and then they group up and have an on-the-spot debriefing. This process is important. The students are encouraged to discuss how the experience felt, what they learned, how they could do better and whether they would want to do that in fog. It is usually pointed out that if it didn't work in broad daylight, it won't work in fog either. They are encouraged to repeat the exercise frequently before they attempt real fog.

Leadership Course

This is a nine-day course for eight participants. The first three days include Basics (with the emphasis on *teaching* the basics) and Surf and Currents, where the emphasis is on increasing the student's skill level. The group then embarks on a six-day trip.

Before the trip, students are paired up. The instructors are the leaders on day 1, demonstrating how to plan a route, follow it, choose a campsite, set up camp and prepare all meals. Then each pair of students is put in charge for a day. As in other courses, an instructor paddles with the route finder, questioning and challenging decisions, but the students control the group on the water. The instructors meanwhile pretend they are not there, though occasionally they will create an "emergency" for the leader to deal with. For example, John capsizes, pretends to panic and, leaving his boat, strikes out for shore, which may be a mile distant. As soon as the first "rescue" boat comes close, he scrambles aboard, capsizing it, and then continues swimming towards shore while the stunned students grapple with the crisis. If anyone else is silly enough to come close, he capsizes them too and so on until the group wises up and devises a solution to the problem. (The solution to this problem is for two rafted kayakers to pull alongside the errant swimmer and slip him into a headlock until he stops struggling and can be manhandled into his boat and towed, rafted, to shore.) Apart from such managed emergencies, the instructors oversee safety and will intervene if a life-threatening situation develops. If the group is strong enough, the leader may be allowed to lead them into a capsize situation for the value of the learning experience.

The problem is that leadership students are usually skilled enough not to capsize in the kind of conditions that a prudent leader would take a group into. Care must be taken to make the scenario realistic and not too overdone.

Each day one or more scenarios are planned. These might include a capsize, a paddler leaving the group or someone missing on the beach at lunch. Often the scenarios are more subtle: a PFD is not tied properly, a hatch-cover is missing and so on.

Basically, a leadership course contains all the material of the other courses but with the emphasis on how to teach it. In addition, it emphasizes group management on the water, what to watch for to anticipate problems within a group and how to deal with crisis. It also shows how exhausting it can be to lead a group for a day.

On leadership courses, the next day's guides sit down with an instructor before dinner and look at how they are doing in the planned trip for the week. They look at how the day's events have set them up for their day tomorrow (Is the group exhausted? Is it late? Did they cover more or less distance than planned?). They then plan their day, thinking about distance, tides, currents, weather forecast and group energy. They see how their plans for tomorrow will fit into the bigger plan for the week and how their plan will set up the next leaders. Maybe the week's plan will have to be adapted.

After supper's evening talk and discussion topic, the group members speak uninterrupted about how they're feeling, how their day went, how the course could work better for them or how it's working well and what they learned that day. The day's guides start by reviewing and evaluating the day and their performance as leaders. Then they get other people's feedback. The instructors speak last. When the students have gone to bed, the instructors debrief the day and review the plan for the next day.

Dan and John would be the first people to admit that what they teach is seldom original but is the sum of information from a wide range of sources, including instructor exchanges, symposia, current literature and the feedback from their students. To a large extent, what they teach are the building blocks of good judgement. With every course, the program evolves further. But it is the balance of what they have chosen, combined with the way they present it, and above all, their openness to new ideas that I believe makes their program worth emulating.

CLUB COURSES

Many of the North American kayak clubs now in existence appeared in response to a vacuum in the supply of sea kayaking information during the eighties and are creating an excellent source of paddling companionship. Club-sponsored trips that run regularly also provide a nurturing environment for beginners—and a testing ground for aspiring leaders.

Club involvement is often an economical way to acquire basic skills and get open water experience with the attendant support of other paddlers. But keep in mind that the instruction of club volunteers is often more enthusiastic than professional and that ultimately you'll be the one responsible for the overall balance of your learning experience.

Calm water.

CHAPTER FOURTEEN

SEA KAYAKING *for* PEOPLE *with* DISABILITIES

Every year more than 220,000 people become disabled in the United States and Canada. For many people who become disabled, life in the outdoors may be the last thing on their minds. But for others, some of whom may have received their injuries as a result of extreme outdoor activity such as skiing or climbing, the loss of the freedom to move unimpeded in the wilderness has to be one of the cruelest blows. Sea kayaking offers some hope to these people—a chance to move as they once did, with the able-bodied.

Once when I was still in the kayak business, a wiry-looking middle-aged man rolled into my shop in his wheelchair and announced that he was planning to go kayaking up the coast; would I help him set up? At first I was tempted to try to dissuade him from what appeared to me to be a very risky venture for someone without the use of his legs—particularly as he was determined to travel solo. But the man had once been a solo sailor, and he was not one to be readily dissuaded.

We worked together to develop a system for anchoring and sleeping in the kayak using outriggers made from paddles and floats and devised a comfortable sleeping system with Therma-Rests and a deck table for his propane cooker. Toilet procedures were something he had the answers to already, and with the help of a VHF radio, a cellular phone and a carefully planned list of the phone numbers of grocery stores along his route, he solved the problem of re-supply. Most marinas had dockside water, and besides, any fishing boat or passing yacht could top up his water supply or sell him some food. In other words, so long as he did not need to come ashore, there was no obvious impediment to his kayaking the coast like any other paddler.

Recently, when I heard that a longtime friend of mine, Mercia Sixta, was teaching sea kayaking to people with disabilities, I decided to find out more. What I learned was that this was no ordinary kayaking class. For a start Mercia was very passionate about the program—not that she isn't passionate about kayaking generally—but this was something more. She had just completed a weekend workshop with nineteen students with disabilities, a weekend she described as the most fulfilling experience of her life.

True to form, she had rounded up fourteen volunteers, including physiotherapists, occupational therapists and kayak instructors. Using the manual *Canoeing and Kayaking for Persons with Disabilities*, by Anne Wortham Webre and Janet Zeller, as a base, they developed their own techniques and improvisations according to the different needs of each student.

Teaching the disabled to paddle is certainly not new; Environmental Traveling Companions has been doing it for almost twenty years in California (see Chapter 13), but it appears that no matter how much experience exists elsewhere, a great deal of experimentation, improvisation and personal development is required from new teachers and students.

Mercia says that "it takes a year to train a volunteer to the point where they are really useful. Just overcoming the common aversion to dealing physically with people who have major disabilities takes time—lots of time."

Another problem is that new assistants often tend to rush in with help when it is not needed. They become embarrassed by the awkwardness of the struggle they are witnessing and try to end it by heaving the person into the seat or dragging them out of the water. One of the first things Mercia had to learn was to slow down and respect the efforts of the individual. "Listening is the key," she says. "They are the world expert on their particular injury and your job is to assist as required, not to take over and run the show."

According to Mercia, the biggest problems the students encounter are psychological. The fear of being thrust into an alien environment, dependent entirely on others to avoid drowning, is a big one. To get some idea of what it is like, Mercia had her legs and arms taped, and then she capsized and learned to deal with the problems that would occur to someone who had lost or partially lost the use of those limbs. She discovered what it is like to be so maddeningly vulnerable. Fear of entrapment was abruptly very real. The experience went a long way towards helping her develop empathy with her students.

One of the other problems students have to deal with is a special vulnerability to cold. Because so many of them have circulatory problems associated with their largely immobile state, they are particularly vulnerable to hypothermia. Special care must be taken to ensure that students are dressed warmly. They are also prone to injury from sharp or protruding parts of the boat, and often they are not even aware they are being hurt because they have no sensation to give warning. Some boats must be stripped of internal sharp objects like foot pedals.

Getting into the kayak, which I thought would be the number one problem, turned out to be one of the easier ones to solve. Usually more people or special chairs or creative techniques need to be used for the more challenging tasks of re-entering and righting a capsized kayak.

Mercia claims that there is "no limit" to who can go sea kayaking. Even severely brain-damaged quadraplegics gain pleasure from the sensations of floating and feeling the salt breezes. People who cannot paddle strongly can travel with a "temporarily able-bodied" paddler in a double. Those who have the strength to paddle but not the lower-body control to maintain reliable balance may have their boat fitted with outriggers attached to the rear hatch. Usually these consist of a paddle with a couple of paddle floats attached. When the boat is sitting evenly on the water, the outriggers are well clear of the surface and only come into play when the craft tips.

Those who are unable to paddle yet wish to go in their own boat can use a specially rigged open double where the rudder assembly is replaced by a small electrically driven propeller and the "paddler" can control the boat with a joystick.

If you have a disability and want to kayak, you must develop a level of comfort with the water. Sometimes it can take six months or longer just to master such skills as rolling over in your life jacket so that your face is clear of the water, or blowing bubbles without gagging.

After you have mastered these skills, you must learn how to re-enter a capsized kayak. A common technique is "the scoop," in which you are floated into a kayak on its side and then flipped upright with the assistance of a sturdy paddler stabilized by a raft formation. Even this simple method, sometimes used for paddlers who are temporarily incapacitated, has its problems if you are disabled. You may find that your legs sink and require ankle floats to enable them to slide readily into a kayak in the scoop position. In short, you must develop an entirely new and creative way of thinking.

Seldom do two people have the same requirements, even when they apparently have the same disability. For example, everyone requires different padding, usually in the form of folded towels and sheets. Other helpful devices include inflatable bags and wine sacks, which can be arranged to stabilize an otherwise uncontrollable torso and legs. Special firm-grip straps of Velcro and nylon may be used to strengthen a weak grip on the paddle, or in other cases, the hands may be held in place with rubber bicycle tubing.

Plastic is the preferred material for kayaks, since it is less likely to have hard edges that could injure. Larger cockpits are an obvious advantage when the lower limbs are extremely stiff, though I once helped fit a wheelchair athlete into a normal sea kayak with a custom body-pod, complete with a restraining seatbelt so that he could roll.

Today you can be out on the open sea, paddling alongside someone and not even suspect that he or she has a disability until you get to shore and see the wheelchair waiting. That has to be one of the greatest sources of satisfaction for anyone who has been living with a disability in a society such as ours, which virtually deifies athletes and physical perfection.

TRANSOCEANIC
SOLOS

On the morning of August 1, 1928, Capt. Franz Romer was discovered fast asleep in his kayak in the harbour of St. Thomas, Virgin Islands. Romer had paddled and sailed nearly 4000 miles from Lisbon, Portugal, via Las Palmas in the Canary Islands. He had encountered two hurricanes—one between Lisbon and Las Palmas and the other between Las Palmas and St. Thomas—and on the last leg of his journey had been continuously at sea for two months. Between April and August the New York Times *carried several brief articles on Romer's voyage. A more extensive report appeared in the issue for Sunday, September 23, 1928—ten days after it was written. Here are some excerpts.*

SAN JUAN, PUERTO RICO, Sept. 13– . . . Captain Romer's visit here was unheralded. He put into port from St. Thomas after about twenty hours' sailing time. At St. Thomas he had had a rest of six weeks after 58 days of calm and storm from Las Palmas, Canary Islands, to the Virgin Islands. His experiences during that time can best be imagined, for he spoke little of them. He knew though, he said, that he was going to get all the way across the Atlantic, and he still had the greatest confidence in reaching the United States safely when he left here. From Florida he plans to make his way up the coast to New York City. If possible he will fly back to Germany. Neither the air nor the sea nor things above or beneath seem to have any terrors for him.

Other men have crossed the Atlantic alone in various kinds of boats, have gone around the world, in fact. But Captain Romer's craft is certainly the first of its kind to venture on such a journey and probably the tiniest.

The *Deutscher Sport* is a wooden frame craft of the sailing canoe type, covered with rubber and canvas. It is 21 feet long with [2.5] feet of beam, and a depth from canvas covered deck to rubber bottom of 18 inches. Frame and covering may be dismounted and rolled in a bundle a man might haul under his arm. It carries an 8-foot mast. The deck is not more than 6 inches above the water line. At most times it is awash. So close is Romer to the water all the time that he may drop his hands over the sides and dabble in the ocean. Water is kept out of the cockpit by means of rubber sheets which he fastens to a framework about the cockpit and then about himself. At night he may cover himself over completely with a combination helmet and cape of rubber which he fastens to the deck. He then breathes through a tube, gas-mask fashion. He puts this on instead of pajamas when he goes to bed—and going to bed is just the same as sitting up. His navigating instruments include a small compass, barometer, sextant and glasses. At St. Thomas, Captain Romer mounted a small out-board motor that was sent out from Germany. He said the motor might come in handy in the case he ran into hurricane weather. His fuel supply—five gallons—was lashed on deck just aft of the tiny cockpit.

The craft is Captain Romer's own design and he set sail in it from Lisbon, Portugal, on the last day of March. . . .

What happened during those first days of the lonely voyage only Captain Romer and his log know. Some day he may publish his log. He told little here. But he suggested enough to set the imagination to work. For instance, he said that the seas were so high at times that he did not even think whether he would ride them. When he anchored at Las Palmas he said he knew that his trip would be successful, that nothing any worse than the experiences of the first part of his journey could possibly befall him.

In those first days there were periods when he was wholly unconscious, he believes, and other times when he was only partly conscious. He managed to keep his course much of the time with rudder line tied to the boom so that it mattered little whether he was asleep or awake. But there were days and nights when he had no sleep. And during all this time he was steeling himself to the discomfort and soreness that came from the necessity to remain for hours in one position; the exposure to sun and wind and rain and spray; fair days and storm; nights of either stars or clouds. And day or night for companions he had the waves and the uncommunicative inhabitants of the sea. Sometimes he sang to all outdoors, or talked to himself.

Arriving at Las Palmas on April 17, it was not until June 2 that he got underway again. During that time he says he was ill and had a fever. If it was from exhaustion he neither admitted nor suggested it. But during that six weeks he got himself in shape to sail again, only to find that officials were so astounded at this daring that they refused him clearance papers for his ship. He slipped out of port at night.

If it may be said he had a little more room in his canoe after leaving Las Palmas, it is as much figure of speech as fact. At Lisbon he had stored in almost the entire hold of his craft sufficient supplies of food and water to last him across the Atlantic. The more food and water there was, the less room he had to stretch his legs. Gradually he ate himself into his own ship.

. . .

From Las Palmas Captain Romer set out again, little dreaming that it would take him 58 days to travel the 2,730 miles between Las Palmas and St. Thomas. At St. Thomas they gave him an official public reception and a medal. But this was after he had caught a few winks of sleep and visited the barber for the first time in two months and had had a chance to park his canoe in George Levi's store, where thousands viewed it with much awe and exclamation.

Between Las Palmas and St. Thomas there were days of dead calm, days of blistering heat, days and nights of storm. Sun and salt spray tortured Romer's hands and arms, and they were swollen and blistered and stiff. He lost his hat in a wind. Then his head and neck and back got more of the sun. He sat until he could sit no more. He stood until his feet and legs would bear his weight no longer. Then he sat some more. Three sharks took a curious fancy to his craft. They played about the canoe, swimming from side to side, at times darting under the boat and coming so close that he could feel the scrape of the fins through the flexible rubber bottom. Romer, lonely, talked to the sharks. They swam away.

His trip from St. Thomas to San Juan was probably the shortest leg of his whole trip to New York, unless he makes more stops up the coast than he seemed to have in mind here.

Romer is 29 and was born at Constance, in South Germany. . . . During the war he was in submarines, and before that he worked in the Zeppelin plant. After the war, for a time, he took up aviation and later went to sea.

Captain Romer said he did not swim. "What good would it do me?" he asked.

A few days after the foregoing piece was written and before it was published, Romer slipped out of San Juan harbour, missing the hurricane warning which apparently had just been posted. The addition of motor and fuel tank had ruined the trim of his kayak, but given the fierceness of the storm he unwittingly paddled into—surely the worst of the three he met on that voyage—it is hard to believe that he would have survived even in a perfectly balanced craft. As it is, no one ever saw Franz Romer or his boat again. Fifty-seven years after Romer's solo transatlantic voyage, American Ed Gillet made a successful transpacific crossing, from Monterey in California to Kahului Harbor, Maui, Hawaii, paddling sixty-three days to do so. The following are excerpts from a story which appeared in the Maui News *on August 28, 1987.*

The 35-year-old San Diego man set out from Monterey Bay on the central California coast June 25, hoping to become the first person to make the 2,400-mile transpac crossing in a kayak. He made it, but the voyage took longer than expected, and Gillet's tardiness made national headlines when his family pled with President Reagan to order a Coast Guard search for the overdue paddler. Gillet knew nothing about the furor ashore because he lost his communications system July 7. His last contact was with a Navy convoy. . . .

The 80-pound yellow kayak, which Gillet named "Bananafish," proved its seaworthiness by carrying its owner and 600 pounds of survival gear across the Eastern Pacific without capsizing or swamping. The only signs that it had made the crossing were clusters of barnacles growing along the rudder.

Gillet had planned to "kite surf" much of the way across by deploying a small colored parafoil that would catch the tradewinds like a sail and pull the kayak along at a smart clip. But light winds restricted the parafoil's use. . . .

Gillet lost 25 pounds on the crossing, much of that in the week before landfall, when his food ran low. At the same time, a northerly current coupled with unexpected Kona winds from the south made his parafoil useless and threatened to drive him past Hawaii altogether. "For the last 10 days or so I really didn't know whether I'd make the islands or not," he said. "One day I wrote out my will." . . .

Gillet ran out of food four days before he reached Maui, but twin "reverse osmosis" desalinization units provided enough water to keep him alive and paddling, if not altogether coherent. "I was in such a weird state of mind, not expecting to see land after all that time, that when I finally saw it I didn't realize what I'd seen. I was taking a sight and I thought 'Too bad that mountain's there blocking my horizon.' It was the Big Island."

Gillet had hoped to land in Hilo, but the current and Kona winds swept him northward. He . . . finally settled on Kahului Harbor as the safest bet. . . . "I was steering on the Pauwela light all night along," he said. "I had been without food for three days and without sleep for 40 hours, and I was getting a little bit lightheaded. I was looking at these lights (on Maui) and I thought: 'I could be dreaming all of this: I wonder if I am.' "

He finally entered Kahului Harbor just after dawn [August 27], paddled to the beach fronting Maui Beach, and walked for the first time in 63 days. "I just stumbled around the beach like a drunken fool," he laughed. Then he pulled "Bananafish" above the high water mark and wobbled into the hotel to find something to eat.

SEA KAYAKING PHOTOGRAPHY

Good sea kayaking photographs are not easy to get. They usually fall into two categories: impromptu and contrived. Impromptu pictures result from your being ready and willing with your equipment. In a kayak this means having a waterproof camera close at hand, preferably around your neck. On land it entails watching for the magic moment as kayaks cruise by and having the right equipment to record that fleeting shot.

In both cases the lens most likely to be required should be kept on the camera. For shots from a kayak this is usually a wide angle lens between 24mm and 35mm, either of which offers a depth of field allowing you to keep both the kayak and the middle distance in focus.

Some movement is almost always present when you are sitting in a kayak on the sea. Consequently, any use of long focus lenses usually results in fuzzy pictures unless you have a film fast enough (ASA 400 or more) for really fast shutter speeds. I try to avoid a lens with a greater focal length than 135mm if I am shooting from the kayak.

When using a 35mm lens, bear in mind that it is usually important to keep a strong image in the near to middle distance to avoid exaggerating the distances and the long thin line of the horizon. Ashore, I prefer to keep a zoom lens on the camera for ready use.

The set-up picture is frequently necessary because of the elusiveness of that "pure moment" in real life. In its loosest form it requires asking your companion to "paddle close to that rock where the wave is breaking." Or it can mean waiting hours for the right light then contriving a realistic scene in which the paddler is supposed to look natural. The best scenes are those in which the set may be contrived but the action and interaction of the paddlers are real. Someone who has been sitting in one place for half and hour as you tinker with your equipment is likely to be wearing a bored expression and the resulting photograph, though perfectly composed, will look lifeless.

The most dramatic light is found in the early morning and early evening, and it is wise to be in position for the picture ahead of time. Storm clouds building can provide a dynamic set for kayaking pictures. If you are waiting for the right light to get a series of kayaking pictures, remember to get both the shore-based long focus lens shots as well as wide, in-close angles. A very dramatic angle for the latter is from the perspective of a swimmer. Surf shots are particularly well suited to this position, though the swimmer runs the risk of becoming impaled by the speeding kayak. That situation, however, could lead to its own dramatic series—for those on the beach!

CAMERA CARE

Salt water and cameras don't mix unless the camera happens to be of the waterproof variety, of which there are an increasing number on the market today. Most paddlers, however, use the standard single lens reflex because it gives them access to a wide range of lenses and accessories. This type of camera, however, is vulnerable to the ravages of water. If you drop a single lens reflex into sea water, you may as well leave it there, for it will cost you more to repair than to buy a new one and its reliability will be in doubt from then on.

Pelican waterproof boxes are ideal containers for cameras. These polycarbonate plastic cases with their foam insert provide excellent shock protection and are air-tight enough to require a pressure release screw to compensate for changes in altitude. The problem with such boxes is that they are an awkward shape for storage inside a kayak so that getting to them at sea can be cumbersome. They are also expensive.

More pliable, but offering minimal protection against impact, is a series of waterproof bags made of PVC or proofed nylon that have been heat-sealed with radio waves. These less expensive options use a fold-down flap to seal against water. If you choose this option, wrap the camera and lenses in some bulky fabric, such as a towel, which will provide impact resistance as well as absorb any drips that might enter through an imperfectly closed seal.

From Europe comes the EWA camera bag, which has a 52mm lens built into one panel, an eye piece on the other panel and a surgical glove built into one side so that a standard SLR camera can be operated from outside the bag.

Keep your camera out of direct sunlight, particularly in the tropics. The heat has been known to melt the cement that holds some lens components in place. Film is another vulnerable item, not so much because of water damage since it comes in waterproof containers, but because of sun. Film can be ruined by leaving it in direct sunlight; the emulsion breaks down into blotchy patterns, and the reds and yellows become bluish. In the tropics, refrigerate your film in small quantities along your route if possible. Otherwise, carry it inside your kayak well wrapped or protected from the heat by a soft cooler or gear bag stuffed with clothes.

This list includes many but by no means all of the existing English-language publications about sea kayaks and sea kayaking, as well as a select few of the basic reference works useful to any expeditionary sea kayaker. Coast pilots, pilot guides and sailing directions for individual areas, though vitally important, are quite numerous and are therefore omitted from the list. Generally speaking, the most useful pilot guides and coast pilots are those published by the National Ocean Survey or the Defense Mapping Agency Hydrographic Center in the United States, and by the British Admiralty in the U.K. For Canadian waters, excellent sailing directions are published by the Canadian Department of Fisheries and Oceans. Several Scandinavian countries publish good pilot guides to their own coasts, and Danish government also publishes a pilot guide that is particularly useful for Greenland waters.

Adney, Edwin Tappan, and Howard Irving Chappelle. *The Bark Canoes and Skin Boats of North America.* Washington, DC: Smithsonian Institute, 1964. A classic piece with contributions on technique by John Heath.

Arima, Eugene Y. *Inuit Kayaks in Canada: A Review of Historical Records and Construction.* Ottawa: National Museums of Canada, 1987. [Illustrated monograph, 235 pp.] A respected academic work.

Brand, John. *The Little Kayak Book: Museum Kayaks—Five surveys with some details of equipment; History of each as far as it is known.* Colchester, England: John Brand, 1984.

Brower, Kenneth. *The Starship and the Canoe.* New York: Holt, Rinehart, and Winston, 1978.

Burch, David. *Fundamentals of Kayak Navigation,* 2nd ed. Old Saybrook, CT: Globe Pequot Press, 1993. This has to be the definitive work on kayak navigation.

Caffyn, Paul. *Cresting the Restless Waves: North Island Kayak Odyssey.* Wellington, New Zealand: New Zealand Kayaking Association and Paul Caffyn, 1987.

____. *Dark Side of the Wave: Stewart Island Kayak Odyssey.* Wellington, New Zealand: New Zealand Canoeing Association, 1987.

____. *Obscured by Waves: South Island Canoe Odyssey.* Dunedin, New Zealand: John McIndoe, 1979.

Courtney, G. B. *S.B.S. in World War Two: The Story of the Original Special Boat Section of the Army Commandos.* London: Grafton Books, 1985.

Diaz, Ralph. *The Complete Folding Kayaker.* Camden, ME: Ragged Mountain Press, 1994. This is a loving evangelical look at a kayaking tradition too often overlooked by mainstream paddlers.

Dutky, Paul. *The Bombproof Roll and Beyond!* Birmingham, AL: Menasha Ridge Press, 1993. For competent instruction in modern rolling techniques, this has to be the best.

Dyson, George. *Baidarka.* Edmonds, WA: Alaska Northwest Publishing Company, 1986. A historical and modern-day exploration of the baidarka.

Fenger, Frederic Abildgaard. Alone in the Caribbean. Belmont, MA: Wellington Books, 1958. An epic account of a lone kayaker's cruise through the Windward Islands in 1911.

Getchell, Annie. *The Essential Outdoor Gear Manual.* Camden, ME: Ragged Mountain Press, 1995. This book is full of tips for preserving and maintaining outdoor equipment.

Great Britain. *Admiralty Manual of Navigation.* London: H.M.S.O., 1973.

Great Britain. *Nautical Almanac.* London: H.M.S.O., annual.

Harrison, David. *Sea Kayaking Basics.* New York: Hearst Marine Books, 1993. An unpretentious little book written by a racing canoeist.

Lindemann, Hannes. "Alone at Sea." *In Great Voyages in Small Boats: Solo Transatlantic.* Clinton Corners, NY: J. de Graff, 1982.

McKie, Ronald Cecil Hamlyn. *The Heroes.* New York: Harcourt, 1960.

Peterson, H. C. *Instruction in Kayak Building.* Roskilde, Denmark: Greenland Provincial Museum and Viking Ship Museum, 1982.

____. *Skinboats of Greenland.* Roskilde, Denmark: National Museum of Denmark, Museum of Greenland and Viking Ship Museum, 1986.

Phillips, Cecil Ernest Lucas. *Cockleshell Heroes.* London: Heinemann, 1957.

Robertson, Dougal. *Sea Survival.* New York: Praeger, 1975.

____. *Survive the Savage Sea.* London: Elek, 1973.

Rogers, Joel. *The Hidden Coast: Kayak Exploration from Alaska to Mexico.* Anchorage, AK: Alaska Northwest Books, 1991.

Seidman, David. *The Essential Sea Kayaker: A Complete Course the Open-Water Paddler.* Camden,

ME: International Marine Publishing, 1992. An excellent beginner's manual—well illustrated.

United States, U.S. Naval Observatory. *Nautical Almanac.* Washington, DC: G.P.O., annual.

Washburne, Randel. *The Coastal Kayaker: Kayak Camping on the Alaska and B.C. Coast.* Seattle: Pacific Search Press, 1983. Solid information from an experienced West Coast paddler.

____. *Kayak Trips in Puget Sound and the San Juan Islands.* Seattle: Pacific Search Press, 1986.

Watts, Alan. *Weather Forecasting Ashore and Afloat.* London: Adlard Coles, 1968.

____. *Wind Pilot.* Lymington, England: Nautical Publishing, 1975.

Wilkerson, James, ed. *Hypothermia, Frostbite and Other Cold Injuries: Prevention, Recognition and Prehospital Treatment.* Seattle: The Mountaineers, 1986.

____. *Medicine for Mountaineering and Other Wilderness Activities,* 4th ed. Seattle: The Mountaineers, 1992.

Webre, Anne Wortham, and Janet Zeller. *Canoeing and Kayaking for Persons with Physical Disabilities.* Newington, VA: American Canoe Association, 1990. Essential reading for anyone working with paddlers who have disabilities.

Zimmerly, David W. *Hooper Bay Kayak Construction.* Ottawa: National Museums of Canada, 1979. [Illustrated monograph, 118 pp.]

____. *Qajac: Kayaks of Siberia and Alaska.* Juneau, AK: Division of State Museums, 1986.

PERIODICALS

Sea Kayaker, 1670 Duranleau Street, Vancouver, BC, Canada v6H 3s4; 7001 Seaview Avenue, NW , Suite 135, Seattle, WA, U.S.A 98107 (bimonthly).

Small Boat Journal, P.O. Box 400, Route 9 West, Bennington, VT, U.S.A.   05201 (bimonthly with occasional coverage of sea kayaking subjects).

Canoe, P.O. Box 3146, Kirkland, WA, U.S.A. 98083 (bimonthly with frequent coverage of sea kayaking subjects).

Paddler Magazine, 4061 Oceanside Boulevard, Suite M, Oceanside, CA, U.S.A. 92056. A bimonthly magazine with regular sea kayaking articles from prominent paddlers.

INDEX